"Only Bryonn Bain could bring together an incredible roster of activists, hip hop artists, organizers, and public intellectuals in one compelling book, *Rebel Speak*. Bryonn is a revolutionary and one of the greatest scholar-activists of our time. From the streets to the suites, he shows us what resistance and rebellion should look like and be like in this time of uncertainty. This work will make you want to become an activist if you're not one already."

—Rosa Alicia Clemente, Associate Producer, Academy Award–winning film *Judas and the Black Messiah*

"Through his work in the trenches as an artist, activist, and academic, Bryonn Bain has carved out a space over the past two decades as one of the most important voices of the twenty-first century. He exemplifies the power of the word as arguably the most effective weapon for social change and equality, and he wields it with a spirited conviction that moves everyone who hears his call."

—Lolita Files, best-selling author of *Child of God* and CEO of Griot Initiative

"*Rebel Speak* is not just a book. It is not just Bryonn having the courage to speak truth to power, or just walking, talking, and living while Black. This is love in all its forms telling Law and Order they can't exist without Justice. Justice can't exist without Mercy. Mercy without Understanding. And Understanding teaches us to forgive each other while still being held accountable. *Rebel Speak* is time itself, capturing generations of people who against all odds dared to believe and triumphed!"

—Nanon Williams, Death Row Survivor and Activist, Ramsey Unit Prison, Rosharon, Texas

"Bringing together critical race theory, oral history, and the prison reform/abolition movement, these dialogues allow the reader to hear the multiplicity of voices that have been at the forefront of this work. . . . Anyone who is familiar with the genre and the theoretical foundations used will be duly impressed."

—Miguel Martinez-Saenz, President, St. Francis College

"The beauty of Bryonn's engaging oral history is that these figures are able to emerge and claim the fullness of their space, their ideas, and their social contributions. His is the kind of textured writing that we need, the kind of writing that stays with you."

—Eddie Bruce-Jones, Professor of Law and Deputy Dean, University of London, Birkbeck School of Law

"Bryonn's distinctive combination of artistic presence and intellectual gravitas comes across quite clearly. This book stands out as a unique document that manages to communicate a vision integrating scholarship with activism and art."

—Thomas Jeffrey Miley, University of Cambridge

"This powerful book combines the perspectives of elder activists like Harry Belafonte and Dolores Huerta with the perspectives of younger ones to address issues of mass incarceration and racial violence by the police in new and profoundly important ways."

—Pedro Noguera, Professor of Sociology and Dean, USC Rossier School of Education

"The world needs to see how Bryonn carries the tradition of joining art and activism as an instrument for justice at a time when the prison system has our communities in crisis."

—Harry Belafonte, Artist and Activist

"A legend in the making!"

—DJ Kool Herc, The Father of Hip Hop

Named in remembrance of

the onetime *Antioch Review* editor

and longtime Bay Area resident,

the Lawrence Grauman, Jr. Fund

supports books that address

a wide range of human rights,

free speech, and social justice issues.

The publisher and the University of California Press Foundation gratefully acknowledge the generous support of the Lawrence Grauman, Jr. Fund.

Rebel Speak

A JUSTICE MOVEMENT MIXTAPE

Bryonn Rolly Bain

UNIVERSITY OF CALIFORNIA PRESS

University of California Press
Oakland, California

Frontispiece design by MM-Graphics.com.
Chapter-opener illustrations by Blaze Bautista.

Library of Congress Cataloging-in-Publication Data

Names: Bain, Bryonn, author.
Title: Rebel speak: a justice movement mixtape / Bryonn Rolly Bain.
Other titles: California series in hip hop studies; 2.
Description: Oakland, California : University of California Press, [2022] |
    Series: Hip hop studies; 2 | Includes bibliographical references and
    index.
Identifiers: LCCN 2021045187 (print) | LCCN 2021045188 (ebook) |
    ISBN 9780520388437 (hardback) | ISBN 9780520388451 (ebook)
Subjects: LCSH: Social justice—United States. | Imprisonment—United
    States. | Racism—United States. | Dissenters—United States—
    Interviews. | Political activists—United States—Interviews.
Classification: LCC HM671 .B33 2022 (print) | LCC HM671 (ebook) |
    DDC 303.3/72—dc23/eng/20211006
LC record available at https://lccn.loc.gov/2021045187
LC ebook record available at https://lccn.loc.gov/2021045188

31 30 29 28 27 26 25 24 23 22
10 9 8 7 6 5 4 3 2 1

In honor of
Veronica Mohamed Bain
My very first rebel teacher
The greatest mother of all time

Contents

FOREWORD

ANGELA Y. DAVIS

Foreword

Angela Y. Davis

Rebel Speak is an awesome collection of conversations that Bryonn Bain conducted with those who represent a wide spectrum of people's movements that demand revolutionary change. All are rebels in their own way, even considering the surprising inclusion of a character one would not necessarily expect to encounter in this company. But this book is what Bryonn calls a literary mixtape—a justice movement mixtape. And a requirement of the genre itself is the frequent inclusion of outliers and dissonances. In the hip hop mixtape, the choice of songs is based not only on individual rhythms, melodies, harmonies, and spoken meanings but also, and perhaps even more so, on the way they resonate with every other piece in the assemblage; echoes of each of these conversations are to be discovered in the others. This compilation of calls and responses— revealing the blues groundwork of hip hop (and, indeed, virtually all Black music forms)—pays homage to those who have kept our foundations strong while also spotlighting those who have created new rallying calls and demands for abolition and, ultimately, freedom

I first met Bryonn Bain at an event organized for Beyond the Bars, an annual conference cochaired by Kathy Boudin and Cheryl Wilkins at Columbia University. When Bryonn performed excerpts from his *Lyrics from Lockdown*, originally produced by Harry Belafonte and his daughter Gina Belafonte, I was impressed not so much by the story of his own arrest and wrongful incarceration during the period when he was a student at Harvard Law School, but by his implicit critique of the exceptionalism that so often characterizes such accounts. Audiences might be justifiably horrified that police mistakenly targeted the "innocent" and "prominent" Black man but remain persuaded that others who had not succeeded in distinguishing themselves as Bryonn has actually deserve the iron glove of the police. In that performance, he summoned the voices of those who have also been relegated to the ranks of the criminalized, transforming his individual predicament into a collective condition that manifestly demands an abolitionist response. *Rebel Speak* is another such *tour de force*, introducing to us the ideas, old and new, of movement leaders, young and seasoned, emphasizing throughout that music, spoken word, and other art forms are vital dimensions of our struggle for freedom.

Prologue

CRIMINAL MINDED: THE HIP HOP ROOTS OF
THE CRITICAL RACE REBELLION

What do you mean when you say I'm rebellious?
. . . I don't accept everything that you're telling us?
What are you selling us? The Creator dwell in us
I sit in your unknown class while you're failing us
I failed your class cause I ain't with your reasoning
You're trying make me you by seasoning up my mind

—KRS-One, "You Must Learn"

Moving the crowd on a microphone long before most of the world even knew what time it was, the blastmaster griot of the South Bronx broke through screens in millions of homes around the world when he dropped this critical history lesson in 1989 on his classic album *Ghetto Music: The Blueprint of Hip Hop*.

Five years after MTV aired its first music video by a rap group (Run DMC's "Rock Box"), the video for "You Must Learn" opened a cappella with a rebel teacher lecturing a class filled with the black and brown faces of students at the edge of their seats. Defiantly rejecting countless colorless Eurocentric remixes of the Bible, KRS-One's critical race analysis in verse declares, "Genesis. Chapter Eleven, Verse Ten—The genealogy of Shem. Shem was a Black man in Africa. . . ." The culturally responsive insight that follows drops in rhyme: "If you repeat this fact they can't laugh at ya!"

Moments later, a white principal and two police officers barge in yelling "Get out!" as they remove the teacher from the classroom, shut the map of Africa hanging in the class, and throw KRS-One out on the street. The inspiring lesson for the day is ripped away by state agents censoring the Peoples' history. I had no clue how much this was preparing me for the way my own work would be censored more than twenty years later. The cops' aggressive show of force foreshadows how the NYPD would pile into our New York public schools throughout the decades that followed—with loaded weapons as well as metal detectors and minimal (if any) training in de-escalation. They also lacked training in conflict resolution, child psychology, youth development, social work, or mediation practices. On the other hand, they came to our campuses with plenty of firearms training and varying degrees of experience unloading weapons into black bodies.

When the "Teacha" (another one of KRS-One's apropos monikers) picks himself up off the ground—dismissed, but not discouraged—he rises and makes his way to the top of a hill, like Moses climbing an urban Mount Sinai. With a tribe of black Israelites gathered around him, two stone tablets ascend and morph into the turntables that DJ D-Nice spins as if their grooves carry commandments sent by the Most High to his children as they exodus captivity. But in this Old Testament sample, America is the Egypt of scripture. Rather than a place of bondage, the Egypt of ancient times—or Kemet, as it was called long before the Persians, Greeks, and African civilizations. Though invisible in the standard twentieth-century New York public school curriculum, Africa and its diasporas continue to make global contributions for too long overlooked, marginalized, or whitewashed by colonial education systems designed to subdue us by those who, as the Teacha raps, "believed whites were superior."[1]

These critical rhymes fed me a taste of ideas I would devour a decade later as a law student in pages written by critical race studies pioneers and visionary legal scholars. Whether they knew it or not, in my mind, their groundbreaking challenges to the status quo were always remixing these classic hip hop critiques. In my own legal education, teachers who rebelled against the racial status quo were the exception, rather than the rule. I often felt as if "WHITES ONLY" signs were still hanging at places like Harvard Law School, where I saw colonizers' descendants desperately holding on to the spoils of race and culture wars past. Whether in the classroom or the courtroom, the refrain was the same one I heard KRS-

One speak: "Learn what we teach! Hear what we say!" But flipping the negative into positive is in the DNA of the hip hop culture that nurtured the rebel spirit born in me during my youth (i.e., "bad" not meaning *bad* but *good!*).

Before BDP's video ends, that classroom full of students hears a critical lesson uplifting the contributions of oppressed people in a space where they are accustomed to our erasure. After they watch their teacher expelled for exposing their untold stories, the abuse of power they witness transforms each student into a teacher. Lyrics flow from their mouths: dropping knowledge, affirming their value and humanity, centering the marginalized histories, cultures, and wisdom they bring to this highly political space called "school." This is where my earliest critical studies of race, class, gender, police, prisons, empire, and resistance began. And so, it is where this book begins.

1. ROOTS AND CULTURE

Origin Story

In 1987, before I was a teenager, I learned "Knowledge Reigns Supreme Over Nearly Everyone" (aka KRS-One). The birth of the *boom bap* was the big bang for Black and Brown youth coming up in New York City.[2] Quiet as it's kept, hip hop pioneer KRS-One was born in the county of Kings— Brooklyn. Much like many of the more than half-million people of Caribbean descent there today, my family emigrated to Brooklyn from the Caribbean in the 1960s. Following my mother and her sister—who came to New York on nurses' visas—my father won his way to Harlem in 1969 when, on the island of Trinidad, he was crowned Carnival king of the musical genre that was his life's sound track: calypso. Calypso, I learned much later in the epic poems of Homer, was the namesake of a sea nymph who conceals danger as her songs lure Odysseus to her mythic isle. My father's calypso was the music that Africans, enslaved on the island of his birth, used to conceal messages of uprising and escape with alluring melody and lyricism.

Turning this art of concealment on its head, KRS—born Lawrence Krishna Parker (aka Kris)—was one of the first scholars to reveal for me certain fundamental truths about the country both of our parents had emigrated to in the decade before I was born. And even after he left his native Brooklyn to head up north to the South Bronx, where he cofounded the legendary Boogie Down Productions crew, in my mind he forever carried with him a certain Kings County swagger shining through so many others from the West Indian American streets of my childhood. From Bethann Hardison to Big Daddy Kane and Biggie Smalls, Shirley Chisholm to DJ Spinderella and Spike Lee, Lena Horne and Michael Jordan to JAY-Z, the black Krishna who blew up in the BX was among that cadre of personas who made an indelible mark on the life of the boys and girls in the hood his lyrics began lifting up as we came of age in the 1980s.

For me, the crowning achievement of Boogie Down Productions was not just its fusion of thought-provoking vocals over thumping beats and bass lines that slap you out your seat and into next week.[3] All of that mattered, but it wasn't the main event that had me pressing rewind. What made me play back that *Criminal Minded* tape over and over was its mix of street knowledge, the celebration of intellect, and our limitless human potential. Like nobody I had ever heard on a record before, this brother was calling himself a teacher, a scholar, a philosopher, and a poet. At one point, he even went so far as to say he is all of these—even more than he is an MC.[4] Lyrical blasphemy to today's hip hop purist, but—in spite of his unapologetic embrace of vegetarianism—KRS had no fear of slaying sacred cows. Long before Whole Foods took damn near a whole paycheck to eat organic or to try "going" vegan. Before skinny jeans and waves of global hip hop ushered in any niche celebrating the virtues of the *Black Nerd*. Before the exaltation of Black Thought to keep late-night talk shows and newspapers relevant to the masses.[5] Back in the day, when both the boomers and the Grammys doubted if rap was even music and claimed it would be no more than just another passing fad. Before I watched in awe as my cousins transformed into the Fu-Schnickens crew in Flatbush, Brooklyn, and toured with Digital Underground (RIP Shock G) and a backup dancer few folks knew named Tupac Shakur. Way back then, as a backpacker devouring books and mixtapes, stringing together verses in rhyme books and poetry journals of my own, BDP was my refuge.

Frequently, and often with controversy, other lyricists would rise in the Empire State and around the nation announcing their self-proclaimed status as the "King of New York." They all reminded me of the Caribbean roots of that tradition in which my father was crowned "Calypso King" in San Fernando, Trinidad. But for BDP's Kris, whose poetry I was introduced to by my rebellious younger brother by the same name (known since his schoolyard fight club years as "K"), being king was never a prize worth chasing. As KRS put it on wax, "Kings lose crowns, but teachers stay intelligent." By boldly renaming himself after hip hop's fifth element, he celebrated his love of knowledge and did the same for others in his tribe on the same quest: "DJ Scott La Rock has a college degree/Blastmaster KRS writes poetry!"[6]

On other tracks, he declares himself a poet for the People, a bard for brothers and sisters in the streets, a teacher for the masses: "I'll get a pen, a pencil, a marker/Mainly what I write is for the average New Yorker." Yet he bucked trends and stereotypes for Black youth, declaring his commitment to eating veg long before it was in vogue: "no goat or turkey or hamburger—'cause to me that's suicide: self-murder!"[7] In 1991, three years after that record dropped, I stopped eating meat. And I wasn't alone: from Rakim's pescatarianism (I, too, missed fish—which *was* my "favorite dish"!)[8] to embracing vegetarianism like Wu-Tang's RZA, who shared the pain I felt at family BBQs where I caught side-eye whenever I passed up those chicken wings, ribs, and even my mother's incomparable curry goat— until she began making meatless masalas just for my rebel diet and me.[9]

These were the early influences that sparked my love of language and education. Long before I knew anything about the mandate of African temples to "Know Thyself"[10] or Socrates's version of this declaration, gleaned from Egyptian masters who taught him their sacrosanct "mysteries" and that sage wisdom he followed and spread until his execution: "The unexamined life is not worth living."[11] It was BDP that urged me toward a life of critical inquiry. By having the audacity to rename himself "Knowledge," KRS challenged me to see the life of the mind as urgent and deserving of dedication, development, evolution, and as much excellence as the nurturing of the body and soul. It was transformative for the teenage version of myself to have someone who looked like my uncles, my cousins—who looked like me—declare himself not only a poet, but a scholar for folks so often forgotten. A rebel voice for those who mattered to us most.

A decade later, I felt like the proverbial fish out of water as a student at Harvard Law School—until I met Lani Guinier. Professor Guinier arrived the same year I did, as the very first black woman to be tenured at HLS. After generations of struggle, led by movement visionaries like Derek Bell, Lani introduced me to a body of scholarly inquiry now known more widely as *critical race studies*. Hip hop had already become my Calypso and lured me in with the urgency of the outlawed Black intellect—like the one I saw in the music video for "You Must Learn" and heard on the iconic *Criminal Minded* album. BDP planted in my mind the idea that there was a path for me in this life of investigation and self-examination. I was urged to interrogate assumptions, push back on misrepresentative narratives, challenge misleading ideas accepted as truth, and speak out against injustice. Critical race studies expanded my vision and understanding of this calling.[12] And it made possible this work—*Rebel Speak: A Justice Movement Mixtape.*

2. CRITICAL RACE

Justice Movement Theory in Practice

One of the leading scholars in the nation on critical race studies (CRS), Laura Gómez, describes the movement as shaped by at least three influential critiques it offers to help us understand and challenge the hidden agendas within the United States' legal system:[13]

1. The law has been used to *perpetuate white supremacy* in the US and globally.[14]
2. The law's *adherence to "neutrality"* masks its oppressive power and its potential as a liberating tool.[15]
3. Racism is endemic in the law—not an aberration.

This final perspective rejects the "bad apples" theory offered to explain systemic injustice. Instead, it suggests that racial violence is but a symptom of a deeper sickness. Racism is a pandemic that for too long has spread an American way of death. If critical race studies is not *the* antidote to white supremacy, it is a key ingredient in the vaccine we need for recognizing its widespread trauma and harm and to begin healing ourselves.

Some of the oldest depictions of justice trace back to the ancient African concept of "Ma'at" (2700 BCE). As the Egyptian goddess of justice, truth, harmony, and balance, Ma'at is portrayed as a woman with wings and an ostrich feather on her head, which she uses to weigh the soul of the deceased on the scale of justice.[16] Nearly 5,000 years later—and over 10,000 miles away—that scale is replicated today in courtrooms throughout the United States, just as it is around the world. Despite the global influence of this iconography, the colonial era that birthed the American empire traded the concepts of "harmony and balance" linked to the goddess in exchange for a punitive paradigm—one that conflates justice with domination. Similarly, the logic of the Hammurabi Code of Babylon (1754 BCE) was significant in reducing justice to punishment in the systems that colonizers erected to legitimize the brutality of Indigenous genocide and African slavery.[17]

As a student of this nation's first school of law, I was introduced to "Justice" at one of the world's most influential legal institutions—only to later discover a less-worthy being dressed in her clothes. "Retribution" wears her blindfold and insists on pushing an eye for an eye—even after countless kings and teachers have recognized how this view leaves everybody blind. "Deterrence" dons Justice's gown and brandishes her sword, claiming that acts as harsh as severing limbs and life are the way to teach the poor and hungry not to steal ripe fruit or sell euphoric flowers. "Rehabilitation" holds a scale to the sky, ironically celebrating the return home of those never fortunate enough to be *habilitated* before they were taken captive and forced to endure unspeakable violence and trauma.

On the other hand, I have seen glimpses of Justice and recognized her unmistakable connection to more humane ancient and Indigenous practices. "Restorative Justice" calls on those it gathers together to examine the harm done by crime, as well as its impact on those harmed and those responsible for harming others. "Transformative Justice" builds on this vision of restoring balance and goes even further by calling into question broader social, historical, and institutional forces that create not only "victims," but the inhumane conditions that give rise to so-called "perpetrators"—who are themselves victims or "survivors" of systemic and structural injustice. Finally, the design created by an organization comprised of formerly incarcerated visionaries in my own community: "Human Justice." It began by challenging "Criminal Justice" with the understanding that if you begin with "Criminal," you are unlikely to ever get to "Justice." On the contrary, *human* justice begins with *human* rights, but sees that framework alone as necessary, but insufficient. Protecting the dignity of every human being is critical, but justice requires that we go further by creating conditions to support developing the full potential of each person. The Center for NuLeadership on Human Justice and Healing in central Brooklyn teaches the equation for this:

$$\text{Human Rights} + \text{Human Development} = \text{Human Justice}$$

In a nation forged by genocide and slavery, the daily carnage of Black and Brown women, men, girls, boys, transgender, and gender-nonconforming folks reminds us: racial violence enacted with the support of the legal system is not an exceptional part of American history.[18] It is the rule of law. Unearthing these elements is at the heart of how critical race studies inspires, provides guidance for, and opens up the uncommon dialogues on justice in this book. My goal here is to center critical perspectives that are systematically criminalized and dehumanized. Sampling a range of methods for critical inquiry, deepened by CRS as a tool for decriminalization and advocacy, I make the case for one of the most urgent demands of our time: *mass decarceration.* This is a critical step toward the abolitionist struggle for freedom. I view mass decarceration not as piecemeal reform, but as a pathway toward *decolonization.* (This project will not attempt to unpack why decarceration *is* decolonization; that is for another work to follow.) The law has been used as an historical and contemporary force for discrimination against marginalized communities and has aggressively criminalized, caged, and regularly treated us as undeserving of basic dignity and human rights. I envision a future in which the systems we create—far more than those we have inherited—are guided by movements built on our shared *humanity.* The dehumanizing systems that surround us will endure until we collectively demand they be undone and work together to dismantle them.[19]

Critical Race Theory

The theoretical framework undergirding critical race theory (CRT) has recently come under fire at the highest levels of power. Countless students of color regard it as a *life jacket* in the white supremacist sea so many of us find ourselves nearly drowning in during school. Anti-Black misrepresentations, however, portray it as a *straitjacket* on white free speech. Critics of CRT are more troubled by how it challenges white privilege, white entitlement, and white power. Without explaining what it is, even a former US president argued it is somehow "un-American" and poses a threat to the nation's sacred traditions.[20] This, in fact, may be on point if the traditions in question include legal doctrines rooted in colonial-era white supremacy. Adverse possession, for example, is a foundational property-law doctrine created to justify stealing Native land. Occupy it long enough, so the logic of the legal argument goes, and the law of the land declares you its rightful owner. Recognizing imperial legal traditions are not limited to the law; critical race theory and its studies also inspire educators to call out the racist propaganda used to indoctrinate children. Public schools continue celebrations of Columbus Day and Thanksgiving—despite the genocide these holocaust markers remix as holidays and replay for millions every year. And if you don't know, now you know.[21]

The conservative attempt to ban critical race theory from schools begs the question, Why are they so threatened by it? Why is it so dangerous? Simply because it causes us to question every system they want to conserve: Capitalism. Racism. Patriarchy. Policing. Prisons. Empire. Colonization. Conquest. Exploitation. The injustice perpetuated by those in power are the subject of CRT's scathing critique. CRT urges us to interrogate the assumptions that systems of oppression require. It puts a bull's-eye on the back of Injustice. Beginning with the legal system and branching out to education and all of the other systems of power it shapes, CRT calls out the socially constructed origin and reality of race, class, gender, sexual and national identities, immigration, incarceration, (dis)ability and religion. It reveals that just as each of these is *constructed,* they can also be *deconstructed.* These systems are most dangerous when we regard them as natural or innate and fail to recognize they are, in fact, man-made.

Challenging the naturalness and innateness of social constructs is at the root of what it means to be "critical." The etymology of the word *critical* begins in medicine and invokes a crisis in a condition of extreme danger. Before the mid-1500s, it was related to the crisis of disease. This medical sentiment is one echoed even as recently as in Albert Einstein's lecture at the first institution in the United States to award college degrees to Black students, Lincoln University. The Nobel Prize–winning scientist declared racism "a disease of white people." This was a departure from views he expressed as a younger man but ultimately outgrew, as his bond with artist/activist Paul Robeson evolved over the years.[22] The impact of those in our circle (cipher) cannot be overstated.[23]

Centering System-Impacted Voices

In a survey conducted by the Anti-Recidivism Coalition (ARC) of more than 250 formerly incarcerated members, participants were asked to list their top three priorities on the day they were released from prison. The second and third picks were housing and employment. What was the number-one choice selected? Mentors. Having someone who has been in your shoes and walked your path, or one close to it, was the formerly incarcerated members' leading concern—above food, clothes, shelter, and even a way to make a living. Without question, mentors have made an immeasurable impact on my life, continue to guide me—and certainly helped make the creation of this work possible.

I was blessed to have visionary prison activist Eddie Ellis take me under his wing for more than a decade. Not only did Ellis survive more than twenty-five years in prison for a crime he did not commit, during his time incarcerated at the Attica prison, he witnessed the 1971 uprising against inhumane conditions that forever changed the national conversation regarding prison education, reform, and abolition. Eddie led a movement of Attica survivors who were relocated to New York State's Greenhaven Prison. Their organizing and research have informed my work for more than twenty years. His demand that we divest from the prison industrial complex, and both invest in and center the voices of those incarcerated, inspired me to organize artists, activists, and educators in the Blackout Arts Collective to bring political education and the arts to prisons in twenty-five states, as well as internationally from Uganda to the United Kingdom. Ellis led the groundbreaking research study quantifying the impact of the prison crisis on our communities and created prison "think tanks" that have influenced countless initiatives, including the Graterford Prison Think Tank—which lifers in Pennsylvania launched before working with Temple University to develop their own college program known today as Inside Out. It was only after meeting with the lifers there that I discovered these efforts were modeled after the Greenhaven Prison Think Tank that Eddie organized.

That same think tank that Eddie led, documented in the *New York Times* during the 1990s, gathered the research revealing that more than 75 percent of those in New York State prisons were being extracted by the New York Police Department from the same seven neighborhoods—primarily Black and Brown communities (not unlike Africans kidnapped from villages and dragged onto ships before being forced across the Atlantic) that were wrestling with poverty, overcrowded and underfunded schools, and an impending invasion of real estate developers. In the decades that followed, these developers would come in droves to flip properties, effectively push out those in need of affordable housing, and make way for waves of gentrifiers reversing the white flight of generations past. The Greenhaven study led by incarcerated researchers was the foundation for "big data" projects like New York and Illinois's Million Dollar Blocks and Los Angeles's Million Dollar Hoods—quantifying the cost of mass incarceration to Black and Brown working communities in cities across the country.[24]

The impact of Eddie Ellis's efforts, as much as those of other life-changing mentors like Lani Guinier and Harry Belafonte, profoundly shaped my analysis and work. I saw his influence with my organizing and political education with the Prison Moratorium Project in the 1990s and continuing to the most recent incarnation of Eddie's peers' organizing the annual Beyond the Bars conference in Harlem, Community Capacity Development in Queens, and the Center for NuLeadership on Human Justice and Healing in Brooklyn. Inspired by the life and work of formerly incarcerated mentors like Eddie, Dr. Divine Pryor, Susan Burton, and countless others, these initiatives and this work itself build on the insights of hundreds of system-impacted activists, advocates, and professionals in every field from law and the arts to politics and medicine.

3. SANKOFA METHODOLOGY

Oral Histories and Futures

While grounded in the lived experiences that have shaped our lives, the dialogues in this book are guided by what we imagine ourselves becoming. One cost of this approach is that we delve into the past less than we might if we were not also envisioning possibilities for the future. On the other hand, the benefit I hope we achieve is that both perspectives together more effectively illuminate the urgency of the present moment. This strategy— *going back to move forward*—is embodied by the West African symbol for Sankofa: the bird reaching to grab the egg on its back before moving forward. Revolutionaries maintain that, of all our studies, history is best qualified to reward our research and urged us to remember: a tree without roots cannot grow.[25] At the same time, we are reminded by James Baldwin of that timeless scripture cautioning us against ignoring where we are headed: "Where there is no vision, the people perish" (Proverbs 29:18).[26] Through this Sankofa-inspired methodology, this project works to engage our histories and transformative visions for the future—bringing both imperatives together in these critical dialogues.

I am one of five children born to a family in which each of us has been either incarcerated or institutionalized at one point in our lives—from days to half a decade at a time. Growing up with these circumstances, I learned at an early age that when someone is locked up, their family is also incarcerated. We are all traumatized and, in our own way, imprisoned as well. This particular experience of family trauma is not adequately documented: from overpriced collect calls on prison phones[27] to communication through letters opened and read by strangers who screen prison mail, from unsustainably long family drives to bring babies to barbed-wired buildings amid plantation fields, to the repeated physical searches of visitors—often denied entry whenever clearance documents are "misplaced" or clothes deemed "inappropriate," from lengthy gaps in communication to "no-show" visits before being oddly relieved to learn your loved one was suffering alone in solitary during a lockdown but is still (at least for now) among the living.[28] These experiences are often sidelined in discourse on the impact of incarceration.

Not this time. The chapters that follow were significantly influenced by the vision and efforts of the Narratives of Freedom (NOF) Collective. Developed in Los Angeles correctional facilities in 2017, in collaboration with both incarcerated and university students on the outside, we launched NOF as a participatory multimedia initiative to examine the impact of incarceration on our families.[29] We build on the arts-based research methods so effective in transforming carceral spaces and our experiences within them. NOF continues to be inspired by the work of formerly incarcerated scholars, including Columbia University restorative justice practitioner Kathy Boudin, former Black Panther and Academy Award nominee Jamal Joseph, the Prison Theatre Project founded by Sabra Williams with Tim Robbins at the Actors' Gang Theater, and the Sankofa.org arts and activism organization founded by Gina and Harry Belafonte.[30] Our oral-history collective role-plays use a range of theater techniques to investigate and dramatize concepts such as informed consent and unethical research practices. Several of the chapters in this book were inspired by this work and would not be possible without the tenacity and diligent efforts of researchers who honed their skills in prison workshops designed to build community with the incarcerated and formerly incarcerated youth, women, and men we joined to reflect critically on these issues and experiences.

The oral narratives in the pages ahead meet at the intersection of prisons, police, gender, class, and race. We critically engage not only individual action but also the institutional policies and practices they create and maintain, as well as the impact of ideological narratives and movements. These dialogues document lived experiences—of a slave society that has become a prison nation—through annotated interviews with rebel voices and visionaries working to challenge the status quo. My collaborators call for a reimagining of justice.[31] Working together to create a dynamic and dialectal record of the impact of racialized policing, hyperincarceration, and other dimensions of racial capitalism and the prison complex, they offer invaluable insight for movements, the public at large, and legislatures to develop and implement strategies for mass decarceration.[32] Without centering the voices of those most severely impacted by systems of injustice, there can be no legitimate pursuit of the long-overdue and yet unachieved promise of American democracy.[33]

4. WHY DIALOGUE?

Call and Response

Arguably one of the most influential oral history projects of the twentieth century, *The Autobiography of Malcolm X* was written *as told to* Alex Haley. A Navy veteran who held vast differences of opinion and principle with X, Haley began these legendary interviews still viewing Malcolm as an excessively militant "Black Muslim."[34] When their dialogues began, Haley would not have predicted that their impact would transcend the decades ahead—opening minds and inspiring movements around the world (even influencing the second studio album from BDP, which features KRS-One emulating Malcolm by holding a gun as he looks out the window).[35]

Despite the universe of differences between Malcolm X and Alex Haley, through regularly scheduled interviews in Haley's studio in New York City's Greenwich Village, a magical transformation took place. The dialectic—the give and take, the push and pull—between these two organic intellectuals with extraordinary life experience and unabashedly fundamental disagreements gave rise to a synthesis that continues to spark consciousness and awaken millions of minds the world over. Perhaps it is that project's origin as a work of *orature* between these icons of Black storytelling that must be recognized for its enduring resonance, undeniable relevance, and resounding power. Within the conversations that shaped his autobiography, Malcolm references Socrates—but not to further exalt the teachings recorded by his most renowned student, Plato.[36] On the contrary, X invokes the so-called "father of western philosophy" to expose concealed knowledge about the forgotten teachers Socrates met on his travels through Asia and Africa. Malcolm reminds us that the Greeks, like others before them, learned from those who preceded their emergence on the world stage. In the case of Athens' towering intellectual, the rebel teacher ultimately forced to drink hemlock was most despised after returning from years of study and mentorship at the feet of black and brown master teachers. The foreign ideas and dialogic methods he brought home questioned those in power so critically that he was criminally charged with "corrupting the youth" and executed.[37]

On the heels of this history, X and Haley engaged in a dialectic exchange reminiscent of the dialogues Plato recorded of his own teacher that have been enshrined in legal education and academia writ large as the Socratic method.[38] That methodology was an unforgettable, and often undesirable, part of my own formal legal education. However, its roots in the pre-European, ante-colonial traditions—such as "The Negative Confessions" recorded in the ancient *Papyrus of Ani*—have been all but ignored by most historical, philosophical, literary, and legal accounts.[39] So let us set the record straight. Dialogue—as a critical method of inquiry, investigation, documentation, and dissemination of ideas, information, and knowledge—began with the world's oldest Indigenous and original pre-European civilizations: the Africans whose sacred practices, rites, and rituals include *call and response,* alternating as sacred stories and scripture read aloud by a griot and gathered villagers, reincarnated as preacher and congregation, then as the DJ and MC getting a crowd to shout affirmations celebrating survival. Can I get an "Amen?" Somebody say "Hallelujah!" When I say "Hip," somebody say "Hop!" The call is a catalyst for the dialogue to bring us shared understanding. The response is a critical reminder of our oneness. Our collectivity. Our common struggle. Our shared humanity.

While I am the central "caller" in this text, I am not the only one. I am joined in this capacity by invaluable colleagues in several of these dialogues: Alicia Virani, director of the Criminal Justice Program at UCLA School of Law, a longtime advocate for policies that reduce racial disparities in the educational and juvenile justice systems. Rosa M. Rios (aka Rosie), who directed UCLA's Prison Education Program with me, is the daughter of liberation theologists and started community advocacy work at just eleven years old. And Jingqiu Guan, the lead research associate for this manuscript, whose scholarly and artistic work examines the aesthetics and politics of postsocialist China. With their invaluable support, in the pages ahead I share opportunities I have had to build with eye-opening "responders." In the spirit of Boogie Down Productions' third studio album,[40] my *blueprint* for this mixtape's *tracks*—as I consider each of the ten chapters that follow—is listed below as a guide for what fills the pages to come.

5. TRACK SUMMARIES

Sharing the insight of two of the most visionary activists of our time, Track #1 kicks off this journey with "The Blueprint: The Radical Solidarity of Dolores Huerta and Harry Belafonte," examining their battle-tested perspectives on solidarity and drawing critical lessons from two of the world's leading justice movement veterans. Both argue for the dire need to build multiracial solidarity and demand radical change to challenge white supremacist, capitalist patriarchy. Their voices are both prophetic and resonant, given the recent rise of an unapologetically white nationalist, capitalist patriarch to the nation's presidency.

Track #2, "Panther Rising," brings readers to a conversation with Albert Woodfox, a founder of the first Black Panther Party chapter in an American prison. Now a freed political prisoner after forty-four years in solitary confinement, Mr. Woodfox reflects on his experience of institutional racism, inhumanity, and a lifelong struggle for justice—from challenging the rape of young men in the largest prison in the US to advocating the worldwide abolition of solitary since his release.

In Track #3, "21st Century Harriet Tubman: A Dialogue with Susan Burton," we delve into the life and work of one of the leading civil and human rights activists in the country. Ms. Burton's grassroots community advocacy is anchored in the belief that there are no throwaway people; everyone's life matters. Ms. Burton recounts her personal journey to prison, later founding A New Way of Life Reentry Project in South Central LA, and shares the challenges women face after coming home from prison and the often-ignored impact of the war on drugs and aggressive policing on women and children—like the LA police killing of her son, who was only five years old.

Cross-fading lessons learned from my mentor and visionary legal scholar Lani Guinier into a discussion moderated with rebel activists in Los Angeles, Track #4, "Critical Justice: Mass Incarceration, Mental Health, and Trauma," shares the perspectives of justice movement leaders Melina Abdullah, Shaka Senghor, Topeka Sam, and Joe Aguilar. These luminaries of my generation discuss their work and experiences of the detrimental impact incarceration has on youth and families. Their journeys to healing take us from police and prison trauma—from mental health challenges in prison and others women face behind bars—to healing strategies individuals and organizations pursue to effectively address these issues.

In Track #5, "Beyond the Bars," Jennifer Claypool and Wendy Staggs reveal their experience of returning home after surviving sentences at the California Institute for Women, the state's oldest functioning female prison—a facility with suicide rates eight times the national average. Both inspiring artists, students, mothers, and recently released women, Claypool and Staggs speak candidly about their physical and emotional trauma before prison, how they survived trauma in prison, how education and the arts during their time inside served their process of healing and rebuilding self-worth, and how they continue to cultivate self-love, self-care, and acceptance in their life after lockdown.

Track #6, "Fear of a Black Movement," builds with the artist, activist, author, and cofounder of the legendary hip hop music crew Public Enemy. An early inspiration for my own art and activism, Chuck D pulls no punches as he discusses how his upbringing shaped his commitment to justice and why he connects art with activism, the power of education, culture, as well as what people across disciplines and fields must do to end the systemic and structural oppression of institutional racism.

Combining a day of extraordinary actions linking a juvenile correctional facility and the most-applied-to college campus in the country, Track #7, "Live from Juvi" features two *artivists*—radical feminist MC Maya Jupiter and award-winning musician Aloe Blacc.[41] As part of the Connecting Art and Law for Liberation (CALL) Festival in Los Angeles, this dialogue explores how solidarity across disciplines, communities, universities, and those who are incarcerated can help create change in more informed and inclusive ways.

Track #8, "Trap Classics: Who's Capitalizing on Cannabis and Incarceration?" takes us on an investigative journey weaving interviews offering diverse and conflicting points of view. From a formerly incarcerated cannabis entrepreneur to a Compton preacher adamantly opposing the legalization of marijuana, from the vice president of the MedMen cannabis retail empire to a prison survivor and reentry advocate, we examine who is capitalizing most on decriminalization and the drug war incarcerations that have devastated communities nationwide.

The inner workings of one of the most infamous prisons in the world are exposed in Track #9, "Sing Sing Blues," from the perspective of the warden of Sing Sing, Michael Capra. A former NYPD street cop, Capra reflects on how his role evolved from kicking in doors during police raids to serving as a maximum-security prison's "top cop" and shouldering the responsibility of mediating corrections officers charged with abusing their power. Known as an uncharacteristically enthusiastic proponent of art and education, Capra speaks to the tough decisions he faces and the delicate balance he must maintain.

The final track, #10, "Homecoming," records a heartfelt conversation between my brother and me weeks after his return from federal prison in the spring of 2020 following a five-year bid. In this dialogue, my brother, Cheyenne, takes us through detailed accounts of his life inside several different types of correctional facilities, and the impact of incarceration on personal and family life, as well as how he is working through his own trauma. This dialogue reveals the injustices that prison staff witness and participate in, and highlights strategies that support post-prison reintegration into our communities.

Drawing on the roots of my critical consciousness—in hip hop culture and its pioneers—I imagine this book, in form and content, as a spoken-word concert, a record of ideas informed and inspired by the unforgettable lyrical tracks, music videos, and concerts that moved me as I was coming of age, including those featuring artists like Sonia Sanchez, Amiri Baraka, Gil Scott-Heron, the Last Poets, Sweet Honey in the Rock, Kool Herc, Public Enemy, Rakim, Queen Latifah, Poor Righteous Teachers, and BDP. This *literary* concert brings together rebel voices in a cipher I am honored to lead—as an "MC"—orchestrating this gathering. These ten tracks feature more than a dozen of the most extraordinary movement rebels I have been blessed to learn from in my lifetime. For my generation, that makes this more than just another record. When voices that call us into the best of our humanity are *in concert*, our call and response is greater than the sum of its parts. And so this is a mixtape. A dialogue-centered mixtape.

In more ways than one, KRS and BDP's influential album *Criminal Minded* helped to inspire this record. Not the least of these is the tradition both build on: subverting the criminalization of Black intellect by flipping the language used to attack our rebellion against the status quo. We come from a long line of rebels fighting against systemic injustice—from ancestors who faced off with slave traders on slave ships to those unbowed by those plantation slave catchers rebranded as paramilitary street cops. In the nation of my birth, it was a crime for folks who look like me to live and walk freely, to read and write openly, to stand and speak out in the face of savage acts against our humanity. So it is no surprise that each branch of the US government shares roots with the same lynching trees in a toxic orchard that continues to strangle breath from our bodies every day in America. Those so-called bad apples are no exception to the rule. In fact, they are *the rule* of law.

.   .   .   .   .

I recognize that exposing injustice has never been without its challenges. In 2013 I was sitting on the stoop of my family's house in Crown Heights, Brooklyn, when I opened a letter and learned that my book was banned in Texas prisons. At first I wondered what I did wrong. The closer I looked into why the Texas Department of Criminal Justice (TDCJ) refused to allow my writings to be read by the more than 150,000 people in the Lone Star state's prisons, I had a change of heart. I began to think that maybe I did something right. I suspected the ban was because the book included stories of US political prisoners like former Black Panthers Jalil Muntaqim, Mumia Abu-Jamal, and other rebels to systemic injustice who inspire me. At the same time, I was aware it might be because of the abuse and torture detailed in a dialogue with Nanon Williams—who is approaching thirty years in a Texas prison for a crime he did not commit.

Thrown on Death Row at seventeen years old, Nanon to this day has not read the account I wrote documenting the violence he has witnessed and suffered within Texas's prisons. Rather than confess its contempt for our exposure of the inhumane treatment Nanon and countless others endure, TDCJ blamed its censorship on the transcript of my *60 Minutes* interview. That interview, seen by more than twenty million people, ended with Mike Wallace asking me, "You ever wish you were white?" Somehow I had the presence of mind to recall a verse I'd just heard from a fellow Nuyorican poet: "I wish I were white—so I could know what it was like—

to want to be Black!" I was surprised it made the final cut of the episode, but even more surprised that publishing the transcript of that exchange would be grounds for censorship.

Adolph Hitler's autobiographical manifesto *Mein Kampf* is readily available in Texas prisons.[42] Yet TDCJ has banned more than ten thousand books, including Alice Walker's Pulitzer Prize–winning classic *The Color Purple*. TDCJ banned my book, *The Ugly Side of Beautiful: Rethinking Race and Prisons in America*, on the grounds that "it contains material that a reasonable person would construe as written solely for the purpose of communicating information designed to achieve the breakdown of prisons through offender disruption such as strikes or riots." Specifically, the "racial content" was characterized as constituting "objectionable material" deserving of this ban." Nothing in the text of that CBS *60 Minutes* episode was enough to spark a prison race "riot," as TDCJ suggested. The form letter they sent me was the only riot.

After reading TDCJ's poor attempt to justify its infringement of our First Amendment rights, I appealed the decision. In my appeal, I explained the book was widely read in colleges and prisons throughout the country for more than a decade and the claim that it was written "solely for the purpose of communicating information designed to achieve the breakdown of prisons" was not only unreasonable but false, given that it was written to recount my own and others' experiences encouraging critical conversations on systemic racism in the justice system. I concluded by arguing that "denying those imprisoned of their First Amendment right to read, write, distribute, dialogue, and debate books like *The Ugly Side of Beautiful*—which speak to and shed light on their experience from a range of perspectives—is unconstitutional and an impractical approach to the penological objective of rehabilitation. Censorship of this kind cuts those incarcerated off from the outside world, denies essential opportunities to deepen literacy and delve into the realities of the world awaiting most, and diminishes their ability to prepare for transitioning into life after prison." Unsurprisingly, my appeal fell on deaf ears.

Just this past year, the Thurgood Marshall Civil Rights Center has launched a campaign on this issue.[43] In its forthcoming report, the center cites how the ACLU of Texas—in conjunction with other civil liberties organizations—filed a brief in support of a similar case of prison censorship with the human rights publication *Prison Legal News*.[44] The ACLU offers even greater context for the censorship of those exposing what happens in US prisons: "Censorship of these books is a transparent attempt to suppress speech that is critical of the government—specifically, books concerning prison conditions, the mistreatment of prisoners, and/or the system of mass incarceration in this country."[45] Unfortunately, the ACLU's compelling arguments also went unheard, and the Fifth Circuit Court of Appeals affirmed the lower court's decision to allow TDCJ to maintain its ban.[46] These decisions to censor marginalized voices demonstrate how courts and state agents invested in the status quo so often serve as ineffective checks on prison conditions or as tools to remedy injustice. For me, they are also a reminder of the prescient way BDP dramatized censorship of critical race studies in their 1989 music video for "You Must Learn."

Should we be shocked when those who conserve the symbols and structures of the white supremacist Confederacy that fought to maintain chattel slavery censor cries for justice? Are you surprised when they condemn our rebellion against subjugation as "criminal"? If demanding justice is a crime, then what choice do we have? Will you willingly submit to a system designed to destroy anyone who looks, thinks, or moves like you if another option is available? If the nation's most sacred legal documents were written to enshrine in the law that we are no more than three-fifths of a human being, we can never stop demanding that our full humanity be respected— even if it means we are regarded as outlaws. If it is a crime to think critically about how to break the shackles of slavery's afterlife, to rise up and free our backs from under the boots of colonization and empire, to fight back until we snap the whips of slave catchers and the knees of overseers using deadly force to crush our necks, then go ahead—call us all criminal-minded.

Black studies pioneer and poet Sonia Sanchez once told me the first time she heard Malcolm X speak, it was as if sunlight came shining through the blinds in the morning: once it wakes you up, you can close the blinds and close your eyes, but you can't go back to sleep. For millions like me, the rebel spirit—the call and response and community-building resilience of hip hop—is what woke us up and got us all to be *critical* minded. What follows is my own record: mixing together more than a dozen rebels who inspire me by how they are willing to defy the status quo of systemic injustice, stand for freedom when it is unpopular and potentially life-threatening, and speak truth to—and with—power in support of movements demanding justice now.

LINER NOTES

1. Chancellor Williams, *The Destruction of Black Civilization* (Chicago: Third World Press, 1987).

2. *Boom bap* is a style of hip hop innovated in New York City during the mid-1980s to the early 1990s. "Boom Bap Music Description," accessed August 20, 2021, www.discogs.com/style/boom+bap.

3. Hip hop crew Boogie Down Productions was formed in 1987 by KRS-One, D-Nice, and DJ Scott La Rock.

4. KRS rhymes: "So, you're a philosopher? Yes, I think very deeply ... *I'm a teacher and Scott is a scholar ...* "

5. Hip hop artist Black Thought (born Tariq Trotter) of the legendary Roots crew, states, "Throughout history, it's been young people and creatives and intellectuals and philosophers and—just the visionaries—who understand the power in uniting," in Matt Dellinger, "A Civil War Political Movement Reawakens—Complete with Capes," *New York Times*, September 15, 2020, www.nytimes.com/2020/09/15/style/wide-awakes-civil-war-activists.html.

6. From the song "Criminal Minded," on the album of the same name, by KRS-One, produced by Boogie Down Productions.

7. From the song "My Philosophy" on the album *By All Means Necessary*, by KRS-One, produced by Boogie Down Productions.

8. Lyric by pioneering hip hop artist Rakim, from his 1987 single "Paid in Full," the title track of his record with DJ and producer Eric B.

9. Considered the leader of the Wu-Tang Clan, a hip hop crew formed on New York City's Staten Island in 1992, the RZA (born Robert Fitzgerald Diggs) is a musician, rapper, actor, filmmaker, record producer, and author.

10. Marcus Garvey's speech "Man Know Thyself" states, "For Man to know himself is to feel that for him there is no human master"; his Pan-African teachings spawned an unprecedented global mass movement for Black liberation. Marcus Garvey, *The Philosophy and Opinions of Marcus Garvey*, New Marcus Garvey Library No. 9 (Wellesley, MA: Majority Press, 1986); first published in two volumes in 1923 and 1925, this collection quickly became a celebrated apologia for the leader of the largest Pan-African mass movement of all time.

11. Plato, "Apology 38a," in *Plato in Twelve Volumes*, vol. 1, translated by Harold North Fowler, introduction by W. R. M. Lamb (Cambridge, MA: Harvard University Press; London: William Heinemann, 1966).

12. Erwin Chemerinsky, David L. Faigman, Kevin Johnson, Jennifer Mnookin, and L. Song Richardson, "Joint Statement," UCLA Law, September 11, 2020, https://law.ucla.edu/news/joint-statement-deans-university-california-law-schools-about-value-critical-race-theory-0.

13. Laura E. Gómez, *Inventing Latinos: A New Story of American Racism* (New York: New Press, 2020), and "Looking for Race in All the Wrong Places," *Law and Society Review* 46, no. 2 (June 2012): 221–45. See also "What Critical Race Studies Teaches Us about Racism, Resistance, and Policing," webinar, July 7, 2020, moderated by UCLA law professor and CRS cofounder Laura E. Gómez, featuring CRS faculty members E. Tendayi Achiume, Devon W. Carbado, and Cheryl I. Harris, https://law.ucla.edu/events/what-critical-race-studies-teaches-us-about-racism-resistance-policing. The Trump administration attacked CRS as an "un-American agenda": see Cheryl Harris, "What Is Critical Race Theory and Why Is Trump Afraid of It?" *The Nation*, September 17, 2020, www.thenation.com/article/politics/trump-critical-race-theory.

14. 163 U.S. 537 (1857). Several lawsuits over the ownership of lands by Native American tribes have called attention to the injustice of the appropriation of tribal lands by federal and state governments. *Adverse possession* is justified for usurping properties of Native Americans. See C. Fisher, "Adverse Possession in Context," *American Research Journal of History and Culture* 1, no. 1 (2015): 35–41. These are just a few examples of the US Supreme Court's white supremacist complicity.

15. See E. W. Sabella, "Take Back the Land," *Natural Hazards Observer* 40, no. 2 (2015), https://hazards.colorado.edu/article/take-back-the-land-a-grassroots-movement.

16. Joshua J. Mark, "Ma'at," *World History Encyclopedia*, last modified September 15, 2016, www.worldhistory.org/Ma'at.

17. John R. Sampey, "The Code of Hammurabi and the Laws of Moses II," Baptist Review and Expositor 1, no. 2 (1904): 233–43, https://doi.org/10.1177/003463730400100207; Kathryn E. Slanski, "The Law of Hammurabi and Its Audience," *Yale Journal of Law and the Humanities* 24, no. 1 (2012): 97–110.

18. Mariame Kaba, "Yes, We Mean Literally Abolish the Police: Because Reform Won't Happen," *New York Times*, June 12, 2020, www.nytimes.com/2020/06/12/opinion/sunday/floyd-abolish-defund-police.html.

19. Connal Parsley, "Is Law an Art?" *Law and the Humanities* blog, December 22, 2014, Kent Law School, University of Kent, https://blogs.kent.ac.uk/lawandthehumanities/2014/12/22/is-law-an-art-2; David Howarth, "Is Law a Humanity (or Is It more like Engineering)?," *Arts and Humanities in Higher Education* 3, no. 1 (2004): 9–28, https://journals.sagepub.com/doi/abs/10.1177/1474022204039642.

20. Victor Ray, "Trump Calls Critical Race Theory 'Un-American.' Let's Review," *Washington Post*, October 2, 2020, www.washingtonpost.com/nation/2020/10/02/critical-race-theory-101.

21. Belen Fernandez, "Thanksgiving: The Annual Genocide Whitewash," *Al-Jazeera*, November 23, 2017, www.aljazeera.com/opinions/2017/11/23/thanksgiving-the-annual-genocide-whitewash.

22. Ken Gewertz, "Albert Einstein, Civil Rights Activist," *Harvard Gazette*, April 12, 2007, https://news.harvard.edu/gazette/story/2007/04/albert-einstein-civil-rights-activist.

23. Since the 1970s, *cipher* has been a hip hop term for a group of artists "battling" or sharing either rhymes or dance moves as they stand in a circle. It is also an ancient term for "zero" in the numeric system the Moors brought from Africa and Asia to Europe when they introduced the Arabic number system. Thus, the dual significance of the "circle" for people of color in creative, competitive, constructive, or confrontational spaces. For further insight into the term, see Johanna Mayer, "The Origin of the Word Zero," *Science Friday*, July 17, 2018, www.sciencefriday.com/articles/the-origin-of-the-word-zero/; Murray Bourne, "Math of the Moors," *Interactive Mathematics*, February 7, 2007, www.intmath.com/blog/mathematics/math-of-the-moors-535.

24. Diane Orson, "'Million-Dollar Blocks' Map Incarceration Costs," National Public Radio, October 2, 2012, www.npr.org/2012/10/02/162149431/million-dollar-blocks-map-incarcerations-costs; Ralph J. Bunche Center for African American Studies, "Million Dollar Hoods," University of California, Los Angeles, accessed August 20, 2021, https://milliondollarhoods.pre.ss.ucla.edu.

25. Malcolm X, "Message to the Grassroots," November 10, 1963, Detroit, MI, in *Malcolm X Speaks: Selected Speeches and Statements* (New York: Grove/Atlantic, 1994).

26. James Baldwin, "A Talk to Teachers," Saint Paul Public Schools, October 16, 1963, www.spps.org/cms/lib010/MN01910242/Centricity/Domain/125/baldwin_atalktoteachers_1_2.pdf.

27. P. Wagner and A. Jones, "State of Phone Justice: Local Jails, State Prisons, and Private Phone Providers," Prison Policy Initiative, February 2, 2019, https://finesandfeesjusticecenter.org/articles/state-of-phone-justice-local-jails-state-prisons-and-private-phone-providers.

28. "Solitary Confinement Should Be Banned in Most Cases, UN Expert Says," UN News, October 18, 2011, https://news.un.org/en/story/2011/10/392012-solitary-confinement-should-be-banned-most-cases-un-expert-says; "United States: Prolonged Solitary Confinement Amounts to Psychological Torture, Says UN Expert," UN Human Rights Office of the High Commissioner, February 28, 2020, www.ohchr.org/EN/NewsEvents/Pages/DisplayNews.aspx?LangID=E&NewsID=25633.

29. In fall 2017, I helped launch the oral history research project Narratives of Freedom Collective at UCLA. Working with the Center for Oral History Research at UCLA, participants develop, research, and share their own narratives, using the

arts to document stories of system-impacted youth and women to expose collateral effects of incarceration on families.

30. Kathy Boudin, "Teaching and Practice: Participation Literacy Education behind Bars: AIDS Opens the Door," *Harvard Education Review* 63, no. 2 (Summer 1993): 207–32; Jamal Joseph, *Panther Baby: A Life of Rebellion and Reinvention* (Chapel Hill, NC: Algonquin, 2012); Susanne Rostock, *Sing Your Song*, film, January 21, 2011, Sundance Film Festival—a documentary that recounts Harry Belafonte's life and legacy, not only as a groundbreaking artist, but as an influential activist in the civil rights movement, www.nytimes.com /2012/01/13/movies/sing-your-song-documentary-about-harry-belafonte-review.html.

31. A rebel is a anyone who "resists authority, control, or convention" and "challenges authority," one who "presumes to be the defiant equal . . . of his king," according to the *Oxford English Dictionary*, "rebellious" (Latin: *rebellis* for "insurgent"), accessed August 2021, www.lexico.com/definition/rebel.

32. Kenton Card, "Geographies of Racial Capitalism," featuring Ruth Wilson Gilmore, 2019, https://antipodeonline.org/geographies-of-racial-capitalism.

33. C. L. R James writes that "as long as black people are denied freedom, humanity, and a decent standard of living, they will continue to revolt" in *A History of Pan-African Revolt* (Oakland, CA: PM Press, 2012).

34. Malcolm X, Alex Haley, and M. S. Handler, "Black Muslims," in *The Autobiography of Malcolm X: As Told to Alex Haley* (New York: Ballantine Books, 1973), 240–70.

35. Malcolm X's speech inspired BDP's second album, *By All Means Necessary*, released in 1988.

36. Malcolm X, Haley, and Handler, *Autobiography of Malcolm X*.

37. In front of a jury of 500 in 399 BCE, Socrates was accused of "refusing to recognize the gods" recognized by the state, of "introducing new divinities" after his travels to Africa and Asia, and of "corrupting the youth," then convicted of moral corruption and impiety against the Greek religion and sentenced to death. E. E. Garvin, "Plato: The Apology of Socrates," accessed August 20, 2021, https:// sites.ualberta.ca/~egarvin/assets/plato-apology.pdf.

38. Mariatte Denman, ed., "Socratic Method: What It Is and How to Use It in the Classroom," *Speaking of Teaching* 13, no. 1 (Fall 2003), newsletter of the Center for Teaching and Learning, Stanford University, https://tomprof.stanford .edu/posting/810.

39. Joshua J. Mark, "The Negative Confession," *World History Encyclopedia*, last modified April 27, 2017, https://www.worldhistory.org/The_Negative_ Confession.

40. *Ghetto Music: The Blueprint of Hip Hop* is Boogie Down Productions' third album, released in 1989.

41. *Artivism* bridges art and activism and focuses on how art in its multiple forms can embrace political intention—or how political action can become creative, poetic, sensorial, stir social change—and calls for new forms of artistic and political action. According to Ricardo Dominguez, artivism blurs "the lines between protest and art." Harrison Lee, "The Professor Who Fought Border Patrol with Poetry," *University of California, San Diego Guardian*, March 15, 2017, https://ucsdguardian.org/2017/03/15/the-professor-who-fought-border-patrol-with-poetry.

42. Lauren McGaughy, "Why Do Texas Prisons Ban Certain Books?," *Dallas Morning News*, November 27, 2017, www.dallasnews.com/news/crime/2017/11/27/why-do-texas-prisons-ban-certain-books-such-as-freakonomics-but-not-hitler-s-mein-kampf.

43. The Thurgood Marshall Civil Rights Center at Howard University School of Law examined the prison censorship policies in all fifty states by consulting publicly available materials located on department of corrections' websites, in court filings, and in secondary news sources. The center contacted nonprofit organizations that provide books to incarcerated individuals—both formerly and currently incarcerated individuals—to ascertain how incarcerated individuals access books. The center also submitted public information requests to all fifty states and the District of Columbia requesting a list of all banned books. Their report of state-specific policies will be published in spring 2022. The book-banning policies in several states are the subject of ongoing litigation and may change as a result of a court order or settlement. The Thurgood Marshall Civil Rights Center fuels social change by fostering collaboration between law, policy, scholarship, and grassroots organizing. See https://thurgoodmarshallcenter.howard.edu, accessed August 26, 2021.

44. "Prison Legal News v. Bezotte, Livingston County Jail Censorship Complaint," *Prison Legal News*, August 9, 2011, www.prisonlegalnews.org/legal-action-map/MI/prison-legal-news-v-bezotte-livingston-county-jail-censorship-complaint-2011.

45. Dotty Griffith, "ACLU of Texas Urges Reversal of Prison Censorship Decision," ACLU, May 31, 2011, www.aclutx.org/en/press-releases/aclu-texas-urges-reversal-prison-censorship-decision.

46. Prison Legal News v. Livingston, 683 *Federal Reporter* 3d 201, 218 (5th Circuit 2012).

TRACK #1
THE BLUEPRINT

DOLORES + HARRY

#1 The Blueprint

THE RADICAL SOLIDARITY OF DOLORES HUERTA AND HARRY BELAFONTE

> Too often it is assumed that change comes from above.
> Those of us who have been working against structural state
> violence, against over-incarceration, against police racism,
> know that these institutions do not budge—unless we push
> with greater and greater force and with ever-larger num-
> bers of people. It is movements that lead to change.
>
> —Angela Y. Davis, "Transcending the Punishment
>   Paradigm," 2017

The policing, caging, and public slaughter of black and brown bodies in the US continue to provide the world with coliseum-style American carnage through the lens of a cell-phone camera. The racial dimension of this pervasive violence is inescapable. As illuminated by the words of one poet: probable cause is probably 'cause you're not Caucasian. The daily news coverage of these public executions is focused overwhelmingly on the murder of young men and boys of color. Yet for centuries these acts of terror have also been directed against Black and Brown women no less deserving of our urgent attention and campaigns calling for justice. These women, often overlooked in efforts to call out state violence, have never ceased demanding this nation live up to its democratic promise. That promise made by a motley crew of self-described "revolutionaries"—who the British intended to hang for treason if their counterinsurgency prevailed back in 1783.

The irony of a once-insurgent American regime adopting the tactics of its predecessor is undeniable. In 1892 Ida B. Wells-Barnett documented

the public lynching of a Negro every thirty-six hours.[1] In 2013 the
Malcolm X Grassroots Movement reported the extrajudicial killing of a
Black person in the US by law enforcement and security officials every
twenty-eight hours.[2] Despite the lack of any national database document-
ing killings by police officers, in 2015 legal scholars at UCLA's Critical
Race Studies conference estimated these numbers exceeded 1,000 police
killings for the previous year. With the latest totals reaching as high as
three murders in a single day, who are the majority of those slain? Black
and Brown women, children, and men.[3] Is the system broken? Did the
American justice system fail Breonna Taylor? George Floyd? Daunte
Wright? Ma'Khia Bryant? Adam Toledo? Sandra Bland? Trayvon Martin?
Rekia Boyd? Tamir Rice? Ayana Jones? Eric Garner? Oscar Grant?
Eleanor Bumpers? And this list could continue and fill every page of this
book without being complete.[4] Or did it work exactly as it was designed to
and protect white life, liberty, property, and privilege—at the expense of
our dark bodies, descended from captives, taken by brute force, and
regarded ever since as subhuman? The US Supreme Court has since its
inception consistently allowed one's complexion to serve as "probable
cause" to search, seize, arrest, incarcerate, and end the lives of those who
are, as that poet reminds us, "not Caucasian."[5]

With more than a century of movement building between them in the
justice system, Dolores Huerta and Harry Belafonte have spent their lives
fighting. They are battle-tested activists who are now calling on the generations following them to "look where (we) haven't looked" and embrace more
radical visions of change. In the summer of 2013, just three months after
Huerta's eighty-third birthday, I sat with her, in awe of her work as one of
the most influential activists in American history.[6] Born in New Mexico and
raised in Stockton, California, Huerta began her life of leadership and
organizing as a student activist in 1955. By 1962 she was organizing with
César Chávez. Although his contributions have unfairly overshadowed hers
by some accounts, they worked together as equal partners to found the
United Farm Workers.[7] In 1965 she spearheaded and organized a national
boycott during the Delano grape strike, leading to the organization of a
worldwide boycott that forced growers to agree to some of the country's first
farmworker contracts.[8] By 1970 this groundbreaking work resulted in the
California grape industry signing a three-year collective bargaining agree-

ment with the UFW.[9] After decades of sacrifice, Huerta was awarded the Presidential Medal of Freedom in honor of her impact as a labor leader and activist.[10] A proud mother of eleven, she courageously faced Teamsters on picket lines and survived being beaten nearly to death by the San Francisco police.[11] Huerta was the originator of the iconic movement call "Sí se puede!," a motivational call and response chant that was famously sampled and remixed by President Barack Obama for his historic campaign as "Yes we can!"[12] Few possess the vast experience and immeasurable insight of a life as committed to justice as that of Dolores Huerta.[13]

Among the "organic intellectuals" who has held a seat alongside Huerta as a long-standing colleague is a Harlem-born artist, activist, and son of immigrants from Jamaica.[14] On the verge of turning ninety years old when I met with both of them, Harry Belafonte continues to serve as a force behind liberation movements, including the fight to end mass incarceration in the United States. His lifelong commitment began at twenty-six years old when he was asked by an even younger Martin Luther King Jr. for assistance in organizing the civil rights movement. One of the world's leading Black actors of his era, Belafonte was also the first singer in the world to sell more than one million records—with his 1956 *Calypso* album and its unforgettable workers' anthem and lyric "Day-O." Belafonte leveraged his worldwide notoriety to activate influential artists including Marlon Brando, Sammy Davis Jr., and Tony Bennett to rally support for groundbreaking civil rights legislation. Years later, he brought Miriam Makeba from South Africa to the world stage while urging divestment to end apartheid and joined forces with Quincy Jones to launch a global campaign for African famine relief with the all-star collaborative song and music video "We Are the World." Not nearly as well publicized was Belafonte's response to Dr. King's call for resources when the assassination of three activists left the civil rights movement on the verge of bankruptcy.[15] With a mettle tested during his World War II military service, "Mr. B," as the next generation of artists and activists that he mentors affectionately call him, once even recruited his friend and chief competitor Sidney Poitier to help him deliver a suitcase full of cash to southern organizers facing death threats from the Ku Klux Klan.[16]

Both veteran activists, Huerta and Belafonte remind us that organizers of movement coalitions have a choice: to see ourselves as working to repair and sustain broken systems, or to envision and fight for a fundamental transformation of structures that maintain the intersecting oppressions of marginalized communities. Rather than resurrecting the dead language of diversity politics, they challenge those historically oppressed and increasingly marginalized to reclaim and reimagine *solidarity* by forging relationships and building community through creative means. Witnessing the formation of today's movements, fueled by the arts, culture, new media, and technology, Huerta and Belafonte speak as visionary activists and lifelong rebels urging us to continue imagining new strategies. Challenging empty appeals to philanthropy that merely provide marketing tools for foundations and other institutions advocating *reform,* they push us to imagine and demand *radical change* that uproots white supremacist, capitalist, and patriarchal systems and institutions. As two of the world's most respected movement activists fighting for human rights and social justice, Dolores Huerta and Harry Belafonte have inspired millions around the world to critical reflection and direct action.[17] In the wake of the rise of Donald Trump to the American presidency, and amid a deadly pandemic for which the complete dereliction of his duties will be regarded by future generations as genocidal, it is all the more critical that this dialogue with Dolores Huerta and Harry Belafonte shares their unmatched perspective on multiracial solidarity and movement building in the twenty-first century. After this inspiring conversation with them, I was able to more fully grasp their call for a radical vision of justice and to understand how the work of movement builders requires critical examination by advocates, academics, activists, students, and scholars who understand, as Angela Davis reminds us, "It is movements that lead to change."[18]

Global uprisings are sounding the alarm in response to police killings, anti-immigrant violence, mass deportations, state violence veiled as "law and order," reinvestment in the racialized mass incarceration of the prison industrial complex, and growing white supremacist retaliation to #BlackLivesMatter, the Dreamers, the Dream Defenders, and the Water Protectors of Standing Rock. Huerta and Belafonte bring to this moment what only those who bear witness to the challenges and triumphs of movements spanning more than half a century have to offer. The historic conversation that follows calls on social justice movement builders to embrace radical solidarity between not only Black and Brown communities, but between all communities marginalized, oppressed, or under attack: from women, immigrants, Muslims, and LGBTQ folks to those currently or formerly incarcerated. Huerta and Belafonte critique strategies dependent on the moderate support of philanthropy or the reformative measures backed by leadership within the nonprofit industrial complex.[19] As we witnessed a conservative neofascist regime rise to the highest office in the land, Dolores Huerta's and Harry Belafonte's unparalleled movement building experience spanning more than six decades, like their ever-evolving vision of transformative change and social justice, is needed now more than ever.

A DIALOGUE WITH DOLORES HUERTA AND HARRY BELAFONTE

BRYONN BAIN: The Cuban poet and revolutionary José Martí said, "To be genuine is to go to the roots; and to go to the roots is to be radical." It is my great pleasure and honor to be here today to *go to the roots* and to sit with two of the tallest trees in our forest.

So I want to start off by talking first and foremost about the power of the moment that we are in right now. A lot of the conversation today is focused on civil rights and the kinds of changes happening in the civil rights context. What do you think are the power and challenges of this current moment?

DOLORES HUERTA: Well, I really believe that we have a very extraordinary and a very great opportunity right now. Because what has happened with the Trayvon Martin case . . . as told in the movie *Fruitvale Station*—about the young man in Oakland killed by a transit policeman . . .

BRYONN: Oscar Grant.

MS. HUERTA: . . . shown all over the country. Great reviews. So I think we got right now for this particular moment; we do have the attention of the nation that is now focusing, for I don't know how long, but it's focusing on the fact that we have so many of our young Black men, and I want to also say Latinos, that are being killed by law enforcement. So I think that we have this moment right now that we can build on. And, as you said, the New Jim Crow, but also the new lynching, you might say, of the young African American men and young Latinos.

HARRY BELAFONTE: I agree with Ms. Huerta. Let me first of all express my appreciation to the Ford Foundation for pulling this gathering together. And to you, Bryonn, for your art and for the work that you do. And of course, the extreme pleasure and joy to once again be sitting with Dolores Huerta. We've been on the trail for a long time and I got to know her in the best of worlds, along with César Chávez and the development of farmworkers in California, and the immense contributions that they made to the civil rights movement. And here we are some fifty years later, looking at the plantation and trying to assess what has the harvest really been or has there been a harvest. And this gathering gives us a chance to give a very swift overview of what we think on many of the issues that are unique to our time. I say unique not because the struggle is essentially any different. It's always the same rules, the same masters, the same themes, the same economics. Goals are set and people pursue them, much to the destruction of fellow beings, often in the name of a democracy, living freely and living to the best of our ambitions as a species.

What makes this unique is because there is Barack Obama. He is a bit different than what've had before. He gave us cause for hope, cause for opportunity and possibilities, and we, I think, endowed that moment with more than the moment was willing to yield. I don't think Barack Obama sees his governance in the way in which we would like him to see it. And I think the one essential ingredient missing through Obama's machine of a thought is that he has suffocated radical thinking. But he sits in harmony with many other forces that have power and possibilities that have also resisted radical thinking, resisted giving radical thought an opportunity to express itself openly and freely and to be discussed among honorable thinkers, as to what we can extract from one another and change the paradigm, change the environment that we find ourselves in.

I think philanthropy is a big part of the problem. I think what it does, and all the contribution made by remarkable young men and women who fill that culture and that space, still misses the mark because what we do not hear in America, what we do not find funded, what we do not find being given the platform to reveal itself is what really other change thinkers are up to. What can the real change makers expect and whether they have to go once we fail to give them the resources, to give them the empowerment that they need.

I'm fascinated at the little titles we get: "post-racial" period. I don't know who makes these things up. And I spend a lot of time trying to apply it to something that I am familiar with and I find that I always fall short. There is no "post-racial" period in America. America has always been in a racial period, from the very beginning, from its inception. When the European conquerors landed here, they found people of color. And they found people of color that they did not embrace and did not give love, and they did not give opportunity to them. But they took the opportunity for their own fulfillment and their own mandate. And they crucified people in the pursuit of that sense of new history, and when they overran that population and genocided that culture, they went and got people from Africa. I cannot remember a time when America had an issue without being deeply rooted in race.

Race was not the only driving factor; it was mostly economic. Of course, we all know this. And in that economic context, we made racial definitions. Issues that face us are not just exclusively identified in race. It's also caught up in a lot of the class issues. And class is where we have great distance in any debate and dialogue. Even the titles of most of the philanthropies, Ford and Rockefeller and Kellogg, come from institutions that have had a great history of economic manipulation and oppression and rule-making that has not been always to the best interest of the human species. But in their names we now have philanthropy. And whether or not you draw a line between what we are permitted to say to them in the field of battle, we are now given the opportunity to say through their generosity and their benevolence, as we are constantly hunting for our way.

BRYONN: I would like to hear from both of you on that particular point, that contradiction. We talked earlier about this idea that "the revolution will not be funded"—some of the challenges that come with organizing community work, grassroots work, and linking with foundations. As we sit here in this space, I think that it's an important conversation for us to have. When we look at the movement today, what is the state of the

movement? Particularly with voting rights . . . and continued voter suppression around the country. Because of all these challenges . . . are we
fighting some of the same fights? Or are we in some ways moving back-
ward because of the challenges we're seeing and the contradictions we're
facing?

MS. HUERTA: Well, the thing is, you cannot have movement without
organization. When we talk about the civil rights movement and when
we talk about the Montgomery bus boycott, that didn't happen sponta-
neously. That was planned years in advance, before it ever happened.
And in the farmworkers movement, the farmworkers just didn't go on a
strike. There were a lot of organizations; César and I organized for three
years before that strike. I met with farmworkers at their homes to make
them understand that they have power and that they can make changes
and that nobody would make those changes for them, that they had to
make those changes, right?

And we were able to organize farmworkers and pass a lot of laws to
help farmworkers in California. By the way, lots of those laws are not in
New York State. Forty years later, you don't have those same laws to protect farmworkers here that we have in California. But that took a lot of
base building, empowering people. Oftentimes what happens with the
philanthropy or foundation [is that] they'll fund a program, but you
need to build a base first before you fund the program. They will not do
that. And when the program is gone, everything is gone.

And that's what I think the foundations need to do. They need to fund
organizing, just basic organizing, civic engagement so people can vote, so
people can understand why they have to vote, why they have to stay on
top of their legislators once they get elected. And this is a very basic step.
I remember back in the '70s, Sargent Shriver actually funded community
organizations all over the country from the government. This helped
build the civil rights movement, and this is what we need.

You know, we can make Texas a progressive state in a year, or two
years, really. You can do it. But we need people on the ground that would
go out there and organize those folks out there and let them know that
they have power and that they have to vote. And if we don't do that, you
know, I'm going to quote [Venezuelan] President Hugo Chavez on this
one. He said when he took over . . . "This is going to be an electoral revo-

lution." And this is what we need in the United States of America. We need an electoral revolution. Because so much of the racism that we have is institutionalized. I mean it's in the law enforcement.

BRYONN: What role does education—and *mis*education—play in this?

MS. HUERTA: We haven't even talked about education. My organization is working with the foundations right now. We are fighting on expulsions and suspensions of African American kids and Latino kids. And it's like the crib-to-prison pipeline. As Marian Wright Edelman has said many, many times. Kids are suspended and are truant and they go into the criminal justice system. This is very institutionalized, what's happening with our young people of color.

And this is where we have to start. We can address those issues there on the institutionalized side by taking power in terms of people that we elect to office. And then of course the other issue that we've talked about: how do we get Americans to understand that racism still exists in our everyday lives? When we talk about the immigrant rights issues, nobody talks about NAFTA. Why did all these eleven million people all of a sudden show up in the United States? Because of our free trade agreements, right? Allowing American corporations to go to Mexico and Central America and take over their economy.

Mexico now imports more corn from the US, then it goes to Mexico where corn is originally from. All of those millions of corn farmers: they can't compete with agribusiness in the US. So now they're here in the US because they're not going to starve. So we got to start looking at the big issues that really create the problems. A lot of this is strictly political. They don't want these eleven million people to become citizens because they're not going to like the way they're going to vote, right?

I mean the same thing with voter suppression. They're trying to make sure that African Americans and Latinos and young people don't vote for the same reason. They're attacking women for the same issues. Let's keep everybody distracted on women's wombs and the right to choose because we don't want people to look at the economic issues. What's happening over here when you got the one percent that got all of the money of the United States of America? We talk about the gay rights movements . . . the marriage equality movement. Why has this movement been so successful? Because they've been out there organizing. Why have the Dreamers been successful? Because they have been out there organizing.

BRYONN: Ms. Huerta, you mentioned the placement of our elected officials into office using the vote. At the same time, we also have a history of elected officials not acting in a way that is accountable to the communities who put them in positions of power. The simple answer for that is organize and get them out of office. Mr. B, what are your thoughts on how the progress you fought for, over the last half century, now has folks actively organizing on the other side to peel that back?

MR. BELAFONTE: The question is very complicated. And there is no way to answer that will sufficiently explain. We can't fully explore the concept as we would like in these forums. More often we really get a chance to zero in on conclusions and ideas and thoughts. And I would recommend that we get off the sound bite culture and find a way in which we sit down and seriously talk at length about the things that bedevil us. But within the space that I'm given, more often than not, at this time in my life, I spend most of it among the young, and I spend most of it among the young who are in prison, and I spend most of that time among the young who are not only in prison but who are in the pipeline to prison. In the communities and [with] children and with remarkable people like Marian Wright Edelman and Connie Rice from California who are out there trying to stir it up.

And what I think I find myself doing more—not I think, but what I know I find myself doing more—is encouraging young people to be more rebellious, to be more angry, to be more aggressive and making those who are comfortable with our oppression uncomfortable. King once said that our greatest mission with our movement is to take those who are indifferent to our calls and to make them feel responsible to our goals and our choices. And he did that.

One of the reasons that was able to mature into the kind of movement we have was because we had these disparate voices, different voices, willingly merged with a vibrant energy about their cause. The American Indian Movement, AIM, and what they did out of a group at Wounded Knee. All of these movements had one thing in common: they had great radical thinkers at the forefront. And we have muted that seriously. And

I go around America, North and South, and say, Where are the radical thinkers? Let's have dinner. Let's just have an exchange on this to see if we even exist. And if we exist, what can we do to feel them or to fully give them the platform to say things the nation needs to hear.

When I grew up in the civil rights movement, I was an elder at twenty-six. I was an elder at twenty-eight really. I met Dr. King when I was twenty-four, but all the people around me, all the people in the movement—John Lewis, Julian Bond, Diane Nash, go on and on and on—were in their twenties or younger. Julian Bond was eighteen years old, Jesse Jackson was twenty. John Lewis was nineteen. I looked at all these young men and these young women, and the one thing that bonded us together was that we had radical spirit, and nothing stood in our way. We didn't need a press conference to state what our issues were; we were the issue and the press was required to come 'cause that's where the news was. [*applause*]

When I say to young people, I say you got to seize the moment, you got to make it inconvenient for those who find convenience in our oppression. And I think to a great degree philanthropy falls in that same cultural zone. We do great work, and let me not have anybody here feel dismissed or put upon because the goodness that you bring to the table is not being recognized. It's not about that; it's about the application of that goodness. . . . How radical is your commitment to hear voices that can really make change?

Any economy that requires cheap markets for that economy to thrive is already fully flawed. It tells you the story; that's what America thrives on. And the greatest hurdle for us is our loss of moral vision. We have no moral barometer. We surrendered to greed. We surrendered to our hedonist joys. We destroyed the civil rights movement and look at the great harvest of achievements; we had all the young men and women of our communities run off to the feasts of Wall Street and big business and opportunity.

And in that distraction, they left the field fallow. And our young people grew up in the midst of that. I'm amazed by how many young people I've talked who I've made great assumptions that they knew exactly what their history was, they knew exactly what went on. And how they opted not to deal with that information. But that is not true, they didn't have

that option. There was a calculated effort to redesign the way in which
people thought and what the news media tells them, the headlines we
put, the talent shows we put on, the talk shows, all of it is headed toward
a vast barren field of greed and indulgences.

I don't know how else to put it. I think the only thing that can change
that is to make getting to work, for a lot of people that work at Wall
Street, a little more inconvenient. The movement made a social upheaval
and you couldn't go anywhere without bumping into us, and what happened is that we have become a shadow of need, rather than a vision of
power, forcing you to look or forcing others to look at what we need to do.

And the world has given us an opportunity, because it's not just about
America. And the last half of the twentieth century when I went off to
the Second World War, filled with the joy of democracy and defeating
white supremacy and getting rid of Deutschland . . . and beating the fascist on the battlefield, being led to this sense of a new future. When the
victory was achieved, we came back and we found the very things we
were fighting for were the possessions of the "free world."

The "free world" was very busy with its colonizing of Africa, with its
oppression, with its racism and its laws in America. And we came back;
we had no choice: either yield to the status quo and go on with business
as usual, or rebel, because that's what a lot of us who came out of WWII
chose to do. And parallel to our thinking, here was also parallel to the
thinking of the people on the continent of Africa who are also experiencing oppression and racial violence. And in Asia, hence Vietnam and
Cambodia; there's great global upheaval around these class issues, and
we are upon a time where we are forced to change. Good change.

I get too carried away. [*laughter*] But we were given the opportunities
to look very carefully at the world we were shaping. But the more they
threw money at our leaders, the more we gave them electoral power, the
more we gave them Black Caucuses and Progressive Caucuses, they'd go
sit in these tiny rooms and dance to their own melody. They completely
lost sight of what's going on down below in the communities. And I had
a gathering not too long ago where I brought all the Progressive
Caucuses, Black Caucuses. . . . It was adult leadership. The voice. And we
sat in the room talking about child incarceration, about the fact that our
children were being put through this prison system. This new slavery.

And this little girl I just saw from St. Petersburg, Florida—five years old, in the classroom, being thrown across the desk and handcuffed by three white police officers. And to look into that five-year-old child's face and to see the horror. What bothered me was not just the image and the morality of all of that, but it was how this could be going on at such a furious pace. And to be so cleverly manipulated into our social fabric that the police have worked into our classrooms to settle questions that have to do with the fact that we have abandoned our responsibility to our children, to our learning process, and to throw all that into the hands of elected officials we have anointed with the responsibilities and solutions.

So we got into this discussion. We haven't even come to page one until that radical thinking and giving this an opportunity. I was not too sure I wanted to come here because, you know, I'm here begging these people all the time . . . writing proposals and recommending to others what proposals to write. But I am tired of begging. I'm tired of saying the same things. I'm tired of giving proposals, being sent back to read new criteria. You meet up in your boardrooms, telling the street how to shape our language so it will appeal to you, for your meager generosity. [*applause*] At some point, some way, somebody has to find out where are you relevant and why are you irrelevant . . . talk about where do we find radical thought.

I think lot of young men, and a great number of young women, are emerging. People in the community would say, Where are the young? The young have always been there. They have a voice. They have geniuses. They are better than SNCC [Student Nonviolent Coordinating Committee], better than CORE [Congress of Racial Equality], better than SCLC [Southern Christian Leadership Conference] in our heyday. But they haven't been heard because there has been an option by the poli-elite to make sure those voices are never heard. They should be heard, and we play into that. We give them all the approvals that they need to think that they are doing good—and they're not.

BRYONN: I want to throw in a concrete example . . . Ms. Huerta, your son, Ricky Chavez, who is an artist, who is an MC, who is a hip hop artist. The kind of content that he talks about in his work—and we've talked about this, everything from pollutants to misogyny—these are not topics

that are embraced by the corporate mainstream machine cranking out a
lot of our culture to us and to the country at large. So I want to think
about the next generation of leadership and link that to how you see arts
and culture. Arts and culture obviously have been a part of every significant social movement going back as far as we can remember. What do
you see as the role of young leaders using arts and culture to advance
social movement in the next generation?

I know, Mr. Belafonte, you mentioned Jamie Foxx, you've been in conversation with him. And you and JAY-Z have beef now, I hear, about
"social responsibility." . . . [*laughter*]

Ms. Huerta, what have been Ricky's challenges in getting his message
out, given the way that the structures work to get our culture deployed
around the country and around the world?

MS. HUERTA: Well, he really couldn't because he wouldn't do gangster
rap, and he really can't get out to the major public. And I think that's one
of the problems that we have: so much of the music for young people is
around gangster rap. Of course, everybody embraces it, but the positive
messages don't get out. Earlier, we were talking also just about messag-
ing. How do we get to the hearts and the minds of the community that
needs to hear it? We know hip hop—young people pick it up, but the old
people can't even understand the words, right? So you know I think
that's a big challenge that we have: how do we get these messages out to
that community over there? Besides, being able to go and sit down with
them and explain to them all of these things we've been hearing about
today. The statistics and what happens to young Black people and Brown
people when they get accosted by the police, you know, and how do we
get those messages out to them so that they can understand what is
going on. I think we have a little, you know, an empty space in there that
needs to be filled.

And the things that Harry's talking about too. You know, I do a lot of
lectures all over the country and sometimes when I talk to people, talking about the economics of the US, which I think is a big part, maybe
one of the reasons that they want to put many people in prison is because
they don't have jobs. . . . They don't have jobs for everybody so if you
keep a couple million people in prison, then you don't have to provide

jobs for them. And again, that's one of the questions about the economy we don't really bring up, when we look at other countries. You know, places like Cuba for instance—which is a small socialist country—and they're able to provide free education for everybody in that country, right? And free medical care to everybody in that country. And I think these are the questions that in the US people don't even think about.

And another issue, talking about radical thinking, is that we are the only developed country in the world that does not own our natural resources. We don't even tax them, right? We don't even tax oil companies that should be taxed. General Electric doesn't pay tax, et cetera. In fact, we subsidize a lot of our energy companies, and yet we don't have money for education, you know, not even for K–12. Tuition rates have gone up so high. All of these young people are being incarcerated. Then they can't go to school afterward. They have not even been in school. These are like the big major questions that I think as long as they are attacking undocumented people and attacking women's right to choose, then people don't really focus on the big issues, which are issues of the one percent and the issues of, okay, what kind of country do we have? We don't really have enough money to educate our own population? We haven't even talked about the homelessness, right? That issue hasn't come up. What is the proportion of African Americans in terms of the homeless population? It's got to be huge! You know because we can see this visibly through all of our streets in the United States of America. And so these are the really hard issues that we're sort of skirting around, and people kind of turn their backs on and don't even think about them.

BRYONN: So what is the disconnect between the conversation we're having around this sort of civil rights strategy that you, for the last half century, have been promoting through organizing, through work, through using art and culture? Between the civil rights generation and sort of the hip hop generation, which is sort of caught up in this greed that you talk about, caught up in this sort of consumerism you're talking about, but at same times has activists who are doing work, organizers doing work, but haven't been able to rise to the level that they certainly should be able to—given their potential and the level of commitment of some of these folks who are out here doing the work, in the prison, in the public schools, in the communities?

MR. BELAFONTE: From the point of view of culture, I think that the hip hop movement and its infancy, in its birthing, was really rooted in radical thought. It's really rooted in young people, caught up in violence, in pain and anguish and depravation, and rather than use the traditional courses to resolve feelings and emotions, they got into this place of poetry and art and finding other ways in which to express themselves and to shape course. And in that moment, we had the greatest revelation of America's future from a cultural perspective. They spoke to issues that were political, that were racial, that were gendered, as well as generationally important.

And the more they did this under their own aegis, under their own titles, under their own momentum, the more they demonstrated the willingness by a large segment of the American population to be attracted to that voice and what it was saying. When Wall Street heard the jingle, then the merchants stepped in and began to adorn this culture with all the distractions that ultimately took the culture over. And instead of speaking to issues that were important and passionate among people who are suffering, they began to turn their attention to this rather destructive set of instructions being given in the verse being sung.

So one day we walk up to the nobility of change, watching our politicians as the vocal discourse would have us hear it and then all of a sudden, we woke up and instead of hearing that, we're hearing "bitches," "hoes" and "niggas" and all the other things that have filled up our airwaves. We gave into it, we paid for it, we adorned it, we gave it a platform, we gave it an opportunity to celebrate itself in huge festivals under the banner of First Amendment right to speech, right to a point of view. Under the guise of all these rights, we continue to crush humanity. I say, well, let's stop that moment and reexamine where we've been in a cultural perspective.

The NAACP Legal Defense Fund calculated it and offered me an award. And when I was invited to come participate in this award ceremony, I understood what I was. I was a centerpiece. I was another hook for the evening to get guests and entertain and delight while they spoke to their regal selves. And I got people to continue to support the NAACP Legal Defense Fund. This was the first time that this particular award was celebrated in a cultural space. The Image Awards, and that's usually about art and about theater and movies.

And I walked in and watched everybody dressed to the nines, ready for the high moment and looking for the after party. I walked in with my moment and just said I didn't mean to piss on your parade, but I don't get it. All this power in this room, and all this money, all this celebrity, all this opportunity to hum eight bars and make a difference, and you all are just giving it away and sitting here and behaving as victims. Somehow behave as people who are on the right trajectory here for change. But it's all about nothing, and you have betrayed the cause, you've betrayed the People. The rest of America is discussing guns, about the rights of citizens to own one, while nobody, especially the victims, discusses the racial carnage in the wake of what's going on with guns. And I said to them in that space, "Where is your voice?"

What are you doing in speaking to the blood that flows in the streets of America in the name of the right to own a gun? Where is Black America? Where is the Black Caucus? Where is our legislative power? Where are those who sit at the head of the big corporation, whether it's American Express or Time Warner and all these big Black folks sitting at the top of the heap? Where is the noise? It ain't in our block, but we need to hear that. So when I go out and talk to these guys I say, "Do me a favor, let's talk about using your platform to put a light on. What would happen when you put a light on farmworkers? The needy of America?" When we made a great cultural renaissance and emerged and we could sing the songs of Pete Seeger. The world was ready for us.

BRYONN: Right?

MR. BELAFONTE: Let's take it back. Culture—you own this. Why are you giving it to Wall Street and giving it to the top ten manipulators?

BRYONN: It's gonna be a plantation again.

MR. BELAFONTE: We are a plantation. I said, "Let's get off the plantation." And all of a sudden, much to my amazement, up comes Jamie Foxx. He's my new best friend in there. [*laughter*] Then Kerry Washington. Then up comes Chuck D, and then up comes Mos Def and everybody, and sixty of us are living in New York and we began. And they go, "Okay, Mr. Belafonte, what's the agenda?" I say, "I'll tell you the truth,

Man, the agenda for us is to find the agenda. Because there's been a million agendas out here. Most of them are startlingly well anointed, well
displayed, but you all have missed that. So let's get back to the table. Find
how we reconnect. Not reconnect to just your past history, but how do
you reconnect to struggle? You have left struggle, and your voice is
needed."

And as a consequence, I think the young men and women gave us
twenty songs, twenty stories of the most brutalized of the children, some
committed suicide, some are waiting for their terms to become adults so
they can be tried in an adult culture. And I said, "Let's talk about that,
let's think about that, let's talk about the kids." So these rappers are each
taking the songwriting to the story of that song. I mean, I have twenty of
them. We are looking around the country and saying, "Where are the
most powerful centers? Where are the most powerful stadiums? Use
your collective celebrity power, and let's give several nights. Let's reward
Barrios Unidos. Let's reward those farmers. Let's reward Marian Wright
Edelman. Let's find our own funding source through the powerful voices
of artists."

And I must say I'm very much encouraged by these artists who
stepped to the table. What are we missing? We're missing the capacity to
develop the content, to develop the songs, to develop the poetry, to
develop the plays. And now we're turning for the first time to philan-
thropic America to say, "Can you give us a hand?" All we want is a start-
up. We'll take care of the rest.

Because once we open the gates to the audience of the world, because
this thing is hooked up not just through Black and white and poverty
that we see in America. It's hooked up to Wall Street. It's hooked up to
Tunisia. It's hooked up to Egypt. It's hooked up to what's going on in
Syria. It's hooked up to [a] bunch of people in South Africa. This new
group, looking at what's happening with the termination of life that's in
the offering in the next few days.[20] For Nelson Mandela, there is a chaos
waiting to emerge in that society where young people are desperately
asking for ideas and thoughts, because the claw box on the wall have left
us without fingernails. And when you listen to these voices and you see
the culture and what artists are saying to one another, when we go on

down to Brazil and talk to the Brazilian artists. Chuck, Mos Def, right now in Sao Paulo. . . . We're pollinating. We're getting there.

We don't get CNN. We don't get big-time hit shows. We're talking through our own design. I think that will fully erupt to be some kind of demonstration. I'm hoping it does. That stops the traffic. I say, now slow down the [Interstate] 405 in California. Let's stop the subways in New York just for a day. And let's do this. And one of our greatest parts of our campaign is to root younger people into deeper understanding in the fundamental power of nonviolence. This is not no loose talk. This is no church stuff. Nonviolence as a powerful weapon, as resistance to oppression, it is undefeatable.

That, King proved time and time again. . . . Down in South Africa, where people are going to be in a huge explosion between white and Black on race. Nonviolence through Mandela's manipulations, and that of the ANC, brought people to a healing table to say, "Let us talk about coming together as one." Nonviolence everywhere has been applied and reflected itself successfully. And we have turned our backs on all of that here, and we have relegated it to something in the past. These young people think Dr. King somehow has to do with the pharaohs. [*laughter*]

MS. HUERTA: I think that I've said before that we have an opportune moment right now. With everything that we learned here today, with what Harry Belafonte just said right now, we can duplicate this in every community. Because the stories of people that are being incarcerated, expelled, harassed by the police, immigrants that are being deported, families that are being split by deportation, this is in every community.

And I think that with the people that are here right now, like we started off with a song—"This Little Light of Mine"—right? I think this little light that we've gotten from this conference today that we can take it out there. And make sure that it gets out to all these communities and by organizing people, then we can bring these stories to the larger community. Because once people hear these individual stories, then that is again what touches our minds and touches our hearts, right?

So we can get them on board, so we can start really attacking the issues of racism. And not be afraid to talk about and say what it is you know. I always like to say when I talk to everybody, "Remember, we all

came from Africa, right? And we're all Africans, okay?" We can say that
to the KKK, the White Citizens Council, "Get over it, you're Africans, all
right. [*applause*] Get over it."

BRYONN: Some of us have cultural amnesia.

MS. HUERTA: You have to just go out there and do the work, do the
organizing. That's all it takes. It's all of us getting out there and doing the
work. And it's not a US issue, as Harry said; it's a global issue, right?
Starts here, but it goes throughout the world.

BRYONN: I want to open it up to questions, and as we position ourselves
for that, I have to agree that I think using the arts, the culture, hip hop,
theater, spoken word, film, all these media, I think these are among the
most powerful and potentially revolutionary tools, as much as they have
been co-opted by the mainstream—they're some of the most powerful
tools to bridge the gaps between generations, between other groups,
Black, Latino, Asian, Native, white working class, the arts is one of the
powerful tools that has not been fully explored, so I'm glad to hear it's on
the radar.

AUDIENCE QUESTION #1: You mentioned, Mr. Belafonte, that human
rights exploitation is one of the undercurrent racial issues in the US and
elsewhere. I just wondered, in the civil rights movement and more
broadly, how corporate influence over government needs to be addressed
and whether that needs different strategies going forward? How do we
factor in private sector impact on human rights organizing from a local
level to the national level?

MS. HUERTA: In terms of the private sector, I mean first of all a lot of
the prisons are privatized, okay? That's one of the reasons you have such
an increasing number of people being incarcerated because people are
making money off of the bodies of young men, basically. In terms of the
private sector in the United States, I really don't think that they have
stepped up. You have, for instance, every time I go to a Latino event . . .
National Organization de la Raza, any of these organizations, you have
all of the big corporations that are putting money in there, the Walmarts,
the Chevrons and et cetera, but these are the same people that are giving
money to make sure that the labor unions could not survive in the

United States of America. So they give a little bit of token money over here, but right in there with the one percent to contribute to the oppression of our country.

In my organization, we won't take Walmart money; I'm sorry—we don't want your money, okay? [*applause*] And I think that the private sector has not stepped up. And I think a major part of the problem would include the major corporations, and you include the banking system. They're creating the problems that we have in the United States of America. And I think they need to be held accountable also. And how do we hold them accountable? Well, way back in the day, when I was with the United Farm Workers, we had these things called boycotts, right? And guess what? They work. They work! And I think at some point in time we got to start looking at those people there, they're not paying their taxes, as I said before, they're not contributing. They're actually a part of the problem that we have in the United States of America.

MR. BELAFONTE: There, I think, lies the point. The private sector isn't some social monolith, waiting to just spread its joy to the universe, out of deep spirituality or religious fervor. It does because it's necessary to keep the plantation triangle. It's necessary to give a job here, give a little image there, give a little taste here, while we mount the profit machine. And I think that one of the ways to let the private sector pay attention is to let it know that it's on the file. To let it know that it cannot continue to reap its rewards and its humongous profit over the bodies of those who are languishing in the streets. We've got to hold their feet to the coals. And in the talks we've been having, this is just not directed at that sector or just at the wealthy.

One of my biggest challenges and my biggest fights is with the church. And when I speak at the Union Theological Seminary or other forums . . . to bishops from Brooklyn, I say, "You know the church is morally bankrupt. You all have become part of the oligarchy, you become part of the rule, you have become part of the game and part of the charade. You're not preaching in that pulpit every Sunday or every Saturday, at the synagogue or whatever your choices are. You're not hearing dialogue and passionate speeches about the human suffering and how to alleviate it. You're deferring all this passion, this need, to some altar of abstract thought and abstract words so some God will step in and give us the way."

Well, maybe God will do that. God is a very peculiar creature. How God chooses to mete out what they say he metes out has eluded me for a long time. This doesn't mean I don't believe in Christ. . . . Let's forget the myth and just hang with the science of religion. . . . The church has suffocated so much and the voice of those who need to be liberated.

Dr. King said at the end of his life that "I'm afraid that with all of the struggle we've seen, we're integrating into a burning house." And I said, "If you as a leader had that vision after all this strife and struggle, if you think we're integrating into a burning house, then what would you have us do? What would you have us do in the face of that? . . . After everything we have mobilized? What are we gonna have to be?" And he looked at me and just said, "Well, we're just gonna have to become firemen!" [*laughter*]

BRYONN: We have time for one more question, and I have to say a word about sacrifice. In one of the earlier panels, Bryan Stevenson mentioned the bus boycott. Folks had to walk three miles to get to work and three miles after ten or twelve hours of work to get back home. So it requires us being willing to make some sacrifice. If Starbucks is using prison labor now to make their products, are you willing to turn back your lattes? Are you willing not to support Victoria's Secret because they are now using prison labor to pay folks ten to fifteen cents an hour? . . . Not allowing folks who are incarcerated the right to unionize? We participate in our own oppression. So if we are gonna hold folks accountable, we have to figure out a way to make our actions in alignment with what we are suggesting other folks do.

AUDIENCE QUESTION #2: Ms. Huerta, please invite those you see in the Latino community to build those bridges, because you impacted me as a little girl growing up on the south side of Chicago. You did and Dr. Martin Luther King did.

MS. HUERTA: Actually, I have been with Harry at these conferences that he's talking about. We were all together in Atlanta. We had a big conference, and Native American women were there and many other of the Latino and Asian leaders were also at that conference. And I think that was kind of the beginning of giving people a little nudge about things that needed to be done.

You know, for my eightieth birthday, I had Danny Glover there and Ed Begley from the environmental movement, Carlos Santana, Zack de la Rocha, all these great people. And this is the idea of weaving movements together, and I think that we've gotta come together. If we don't come together, we're not gonna make it, okay? Because it's all the same struggle, and we are in different silos, but every community can bring everybody together. And if we all come together, we are a majority, right? And then we can win.

But we got to come together, and we got to take that direct and nonviolent action that Harry was talking about and we can make it happen, but we just gotta get out there and make a commitment. I know it's hard. I mean, back in the day, in the civil rights movement, you know rents were what? Forty dollars a month. Now they're what? A thousand dollars a month maybe. Gasoline was, what, seventeen cents a gallon? Now it's four or five dollars a gallon. And I think this is purposeful too, because it is very hard for people without money to travel and to do this organizing work. But we do have the social media, right? That we didn't have back in the '60s. You got the cell phones and you got the internet. You got the Twitter. You got the Facebook. So in my ways, the Dreamers, by the way, use this very successfully. I mean, can you imagine these young undocumented people got the president to sign an order saying you're not gonna get deported, right? And you can go to school. And how did they do that? They do that on social media. So we have tools now that we didn't have before. So we have no excuses . . .

We heard what the issues are. We heard what the problems are. We just got to get out there and start working. Let's do something else together. That means "yes we can!" As you know, Obama used that and when I met Obama he said, "I stole your slogan." I actually was the author of "sí se puede." But we gotta do it all together in an organized way so let's say, "Yes we can! Sí se puede!" In Spanish, okay? And we do it in an organized way . . .

MR. BELAFONTE: I'd like to make one last observation in response to the coming together of the tribes and the cultures. I very early on understood the importance of that phenomenon, coming together of tribes to look at our common interests and understand our common struggle and make united friends in dealing with it. It was at the time of [Hurricane] Katrina that the elders were brought together in Atlanta, where Ms. Huerta was, and everybody was there: Cornel West, Charlie Rangel, the Black Caucus, Barbara Lee, and on and on. And out of that, after the two days of the retreat, I really understood that I was dealing with the wrong audience. They were mighty forces. Powerful forces that have carved out empires for themselves and positions for themselves and goals for themselves. All of which were honorable.

But all of which somehow found their paths away from the community, away from the deeper resonance of what was going on. They became so preoccupied with organization, with bureaucracies, and with title and writing proposals and things. And I realized that when I talked to them about digging deeper, I was looking for the moral image, part of which was a strategy I learned from Dr. King. Politics without morality is tyranny. And if you have a political objective, one of the things you have to ask yourself is, What are the moral consequences of what you are doing? What are you betraying and what are you supporting? And if your moral purpose is with great clarity, let that be part of the centerpiece.

Because one thing America suffers is its illusion of morality. It thinks of itself in relation to the greater calls of human existence, when in fact it is the great violator of the calls of human existence. You got to hold that mirror before the audience all the time. So I looked at my peers and my group with love and affection and I got to talk to another. It's going to take longer, be a little more difficult, but it's got to get to the nitty-gritty. We got to get to the grassroots, so we went to Alabama, because that place goes back and was part of the great charge during the civil rights movement. Got them farmers in them overalls, sucking hay string still.

And I said to the farmer, "Give us space . . . kids are coming, from gangs in LA, from the Bloods and the Crips and all over the country. And we need to have a retreat for a few days." They housed us. We didn't get it through philanthropy. We had to go. We had to thank the workers for what they gave to us, and we had an incredible three days with these young people, who started off with the premise that, although they were in gangs or shot one another, browns and blacks, they really knew nothing about each other.

Let's start from square one. You live three blocks away from each other, and you murder each other, and you never even sung each other's song or been to one another's birthday party or visited the playgrounds in which your children play. And this group coming together began to talk and it was mostly black. And then as we went around the room and discussed and we said, "You know we gotta get out of this rule, we got to get out of this pocket." And we got the Latino community in northern California to give us [a] complete Latin environment . . . from Tracy . . . Nane Alejandrez . . . from Barrios Unidos and all of these players show up, and there were these thugs from the Bloods and the Crips.

They were glad to hear these browns, all standing there, tall and tough and tattooed. Yet they were talking to each other about their common experience. Never had such an exchange before. Then they struck a peace treaty. Then they, as a group, met and when Black people heard what the Latinos had to say, and the Latinos, all from the same space, and they heard that for the first time. And they made another decision. There's more to this than just us. So they got the Native American community to organize a huge Indigenous people gathering. And the Latinos and the Blacks visited the reservation and they had to go through some strange rituals, sit in a circle, look at the peace pipe, the sweat lodge, listen to all that stuff, and Black people are like, "What the hell? They did that? You getting us to do this Indian shit?"

But before it was over, they understood a new dimension to the spirituality. A new dimension to suffering. Here were the original people. Here is what they live through, and genocide. I remember the white group. The people from the mining community. I listened to what the white incarcerated youth had to say. And what they found out at the end of that year traveling to these communities and having these retreats— and some of it, I must say, was Ford Foundation money and Kellogg here . . . and we got enough gas to get us to the station for the big trip—but what happened was that they founded a loose body of people called the Gathering, which is, in part, founded in the midst of the Wall Street rebellion.

In these places people say, "What do they want?" Well, they don't want a damn thing more than we wanted when we were in their space, and they're doing it just as well if not even better than when we did it. You're asking, "What do they want?" You know what they want, and you don't wanna give it to them because it means that you're gonna have to sacrifice something.

You'd rather deal with the absence of information than deal with the power of truth. And you play this place. What do they want? You know what they want! They want what we wanted: They want freedom! They want the right to express themselves! They want the right to have education! They'd like to have stability economically for the rest of their lives! Trying to work off the debts of the guys on Wall Street who hold them in suffocation. That's what they want. Although they don't use the classic socialist Marxist ways from the days when the great organizers came from the Communist Party. Great organizers that came from socialist thinking. . . . It wasn't just Lenin sitting there. A lot of people didn't even know him. They were talking stuff that had to do with thinking of class issues and the like. All of this, in this space, stimulated these young people . . .

All the young women and the people in the past two years of touring this country, I am amazed at the harvest we have in intellectual thought, and passion is searching for materials, searching for something to belong to, honest search in struggle for change. I think we always talk to ourselves, to just take a deeper look at what we really are doing here. A lot of time and energy and good thinkers are caught up in this space.

My mother used to say something to me when I was a kid, and this is the last of it. I would lose a sock somewhere, I couldn't find the damn sock in the drawer, and I would get on the bed and move all the junk and go look under the couch and the cushion, and in a few minutes I would go back to the same drawer, same under the bed, and she would watch me. And after a few minutes she said, "Harry, let me ask you something. You keep looking in the same place for the sock? Is that what you're looking for?" "Yeah, Mom, I'm looking for it." "Has it ever occurred to you that since you can't find it where you're looking, it may be where you're not looking?" [*laughter*]

I use that little simple folk—this little casual moment, with this incredible undereducated immigrant woman domestic worker, and she said, "It's where you're not looking." All of my life has been spent wrapped around that metaphor. I've always looked where I haven't looked before. Because if I'm looking where I'm looking all the time, if I can't find the thing, it's got to be somewhere else. Let me stop paying homage to these gods. Let me stop meeting their criteria. Let me stop doing their dance and do the dance I know I got to do.

So if I go down to you and you hear me talking about Bush as the greatest terrorist in the world, it's not that I'm looking for a platform to run my mouth. I'm looking to grab your attention, and I grabbed it—albeit with some fallout, but at least I got some moment to talk about what Bush was really doing here with this war. What's Barack Obama done really with rights? . . . With homeland security? What is he doing with secret police? Where are we caught up in this bullshit politeness to not be able to say, "Yo, brother, you're crossing the line! Got to hold you to it! We like all the rest of the stuff you do. We love your Harvard. We love that you're married to Michelle. We love you're part African. Yeah, but come on. Let's shake the tree!"

You can't continue on this ruptured path and have us anoint you. My presence here validates you and if you want a validation, you got to pay off the price. We need to get back and stop looking where you're looking and start looking at us in places you can't find us and listen to what we have to say and listen to these young men and women carefully, not through your filter but through your honest open willingness to let their voices resonate in your cranium. Maybe you'll find a catchphrase or two to put you on another path.

When Dr. King called me, I was at the height of my game. He said, "I need you!" I said, "It's great to hear that, Doctor. I'm coming to New York." . . . I said, "May I come to hear your speech and then we can talk afterward?" and he said yeah. And so I got to see him make his speech at the Baptist Church, and when he got through . . . I knew I was forever committed to this, this cause that he represented, because he put it right on the money. He told the church, "You're morally bankrupt. You've turned on the gifts of spirituality and what we could be doing."

Birmingham jail. You can go back to all of these places. I carry in my computer all of Dr. King's speeches, and I will type them any moment on the plane, on a train, in a hotel room at night after we watched the late show, whatever we do. I type it to hear Dr. King again. Not because I am familiar with the speech, but I am reminded of the time I grew up and I hear his voice and I find its relevance to today. And although I miss him, I have not lost him. And that application is constant. It's a ritual, and I think that all of us need to get away from the distractions that have taken our eyes off the spiritual. The world is waiting to hear from us.

LINER NOTES

Track #1 is revised and excerpted from "Rad Talk: The Radical Solidarity of Dolores Huerta and Harry Belafonte," *National Black Law Journal* 26, no. 1 (Spring 2017), https://escholarship.org/uc/item/6xv6m274; annotated, revised, and published here courtesy of the Ford Foundation, the original source of the work, per its Creative Commons Attribution 4.0 International license, www.fordfoundation.org/terms-and-conditions-of-use/. Legal research assistance provided by Ian Stringham.

Epigraph: Angela Y. Davis, "Transcending the Punishment Paraditm," keynote address at Beyond the Bars conference, March 5, 2017, Columbia University and University of California, Los Angeles, https://blogs.cuit.columbia.edu/cji/beyond-the-bars-3/beyondthebarsconference/beyond-bars-2017/; via Skype at https://livestream.com/CenterforJusticeatCU/BTB2016FridayKickOff.

1. Ida B. Wells-Barnett, *The Red Record* (1895), Gutenberg.org, accessed June 22, 2017, www.gutenberg.org/files/14977/14977-h/14977-h.htm.

2. Malcolm X Grassroots Movement, "Operation Ghetto Storm: 2012," *Annual Report on the Extrajudicial Killing of 313 Black People by Police, Security Guards and Vigilantes* 15 (2012). Malcolm X Grassroots Movement is a community-based organization in New York City, website accessed June 6, 2017, https://mxgm.org.

3. "Race and Resistance: Against Police Violence," eighth annual Critical Race Studies Symposium, Los Angeles, October 16–17, 2015.

4. These names represent just of few of the Black women, men, and children who have been murdered by law enforcement and security officials: "943 people have been shot and killed by the police in the past year," Fatal Force: Police Shootings Database, *Washington Post*, updated August 16, 2021, www.washingtonpost.com/graphics/investigations/police-shootings-database/.

5. "Articulating precisely what 'reasonable suspicion' and 'probable cause' mean is not possible." They are not a technical "set of legal rules." Ornelas v. United States, 517 *US Reports* 690, 695 (1996).

6. "Courting Change: Looking Back to Move Forward," a Ford Foundation symposium, New York City, July 17, 2013.

7. Richard A. Garcia, "Dolores Huerta: Woman, Organizer, and Symbol," *California History* 72 (1993): 57, 65.

8. Margaret Rose, "Traditional and Nontraditional Patterns of Female Activism in the United Farm Workers of America," *Frontiers: A Journal of Women Studies* 11 (1990): 26.

9. Inga Kim, "The 1965–1970 Delano Grape Strike and Boycott," United Farm Workers, accessed June 22, 2017, http://ufw.org/1965-1970-Delano-grape-strike-boycott.

10. Matt Compton, "President Obama Awards the Medal of Freedom," White House, May 29, 2012, https://obamawhitehouse.archives.gov/blog/2012/05/29/president-Obama-awards-medal-freedom.

11. Dan Morian, "Police Batons Blamed as UFW Official Is Badly Hurt During Bush S.F. Protest," *Los Angeles Times*, September 16, 1988, http://articles.latimes.com/1988-09-16/news/mn-2389_1_police-chief.

12. Katie Mettler, "Obama's 'Yes We Can' Almost Didn't Happen. You Can Thank Michelle for Saving It," *Washington Post*, January 11, 2017, www.washingtonpost.com/news/morning-mix/wp/2017/01/11/obamas-yes-we-can-thank-michelle-for-that/?utm_term=.a39e53521354.

13. "Dolores: Documentary of Labor and Feminist Icon Dolores Huerta," *PBS Presents*, March 27, 2018.

14. "Gramsci believed that Black Americans were absorbers of American culture as opposed to specific contributors to the overall cultural development of the United States. Due to their intellectual capacity, Gramsci believed that these '[Organic] Intellectuals' should return to Africa and, in turn, teach Africans." Regina Bernard-Carreño, *Nuyorganics: Organic Intellectualism, the Search for Racial Identity, and Nuyorican Thought* (Los Angeles: Peter Lang, 2010), 19.

15. *Sing Your Song*, S2BN Films, 2011.

16. Harry Belafonte and Michael Shnayerson, *My Song: A Memoir of Art, Race, and Defiance* (New York: Penguin Random House, 2012), 4–10.

17. For further analysis of the trajectory of relevant global standards established by human rights law, see Samuel Moyn, *The Last Utopia: Human Rights in History* (Cambridge, MA: Harvard University Press, 2012), 179.

18. From Davis's keynote address at the Beyond the Bars conference at Columbia University Center for Justice, New York, March 4, 2021, https://test3-blogs.cuit.columbia.edu/cji/beyond-the-bars-3/beyondthebarsconference/beyond-the-bars-conference-2016.

19. For an introduction to the concept of the nonprofit industrial complex, see Incite! Women of Color Against Violence, *The Revolution Will Not Be Funded: Beyond the Nonprofit Industrial Complex* (Durham, NC: Duke University Press, 2007).

20. An article that includes comments from members of the LGBT advocacy community in South Africa states that "women regularly are burying women who have lost their lives in homophobic assaults and fighting an incredibly difficult

campaign to try to get authorities to take the threat of hate crimes seriously. They are burying still more whose lives are cut short by HIV. At the same time, though, many of those HIV-related deaths seem to result from the stigma that remains unconfronted within their own community." Kaiser Family Foundation, "KFF Daily Global Health Policy Report," July 17, 2013, www.kff.org/daily-news /July-17-2013.

TRACK #2
PANTHER RISING

A. WOODFOX/ANGOLA 3

#2 Panther Rising

HOW ALBERT WOODFOX SURVIVED FOUR DECADES IN SOLITARY

Nobody in the world, nobody in history, has ever gotten
their freedom by appealing to the moral sense of the people
who were oppressing them . . .

—Assata Shakur

2020. As I write this, the world is witnessing protesters facing off police
officers in cities around the US. Uprisings have erupted and could not be
stopped by paramilitary forces and the National Guard. Fearlessly facing
soldiers armed and ready to use deadly force on communities challenging
state violence, thousands are flooding the streets of US cities and 350
countries worldwide. These global explosions are in response to the latest
extralegal executions of unarmed Black men and women by police in the
US. The unjustifiable murders of George Floyd and Breonna Taylor follow
what James Baldwin called America's "bloody catalogue" of killings.[1]
Police kill more than 1,000 people every year in the US. Black people are
three times more likely to be killed by police than whites are.[2] With public
executions by law enforcement reportedly taking the lives of people who
look like Breonna and me every twenty-eight hours, one thing is as clear
as ever: the reforms proposed to combat police violence and systemic racism in law enforcement have failed to turn the tide of violence born of
white supremacy and racial capitalism in this colonial settler nation.[3]

The justified rage of this transformative moment has refocused the
vision of liberation movements and relit the fuse of global solidarity. It
calls for the structural change of systems that have for centuries stolen life

from black and brown bodies. As community activists call for the defunding and, yes, even the abolition of the police, radical demands are reaching more diverse national and global audiences than ever. Yet it is not enough to challenge the impact of state violence as simply a problem with policing. The policies and practices maintaining prisons warrant the same scrutiny. After all, that is the destination to which police bring those of us who survive encounters with them on our own streets. One of the oldest prison monitoring organizations in the world, the more than 170-year-old Correctional Association of New York, maintains, "Prisons are part of a continuum of state violence."[4] As such, they include the actions of the men who murdered Floyd and Taylor and the countless women and men who die behind bars every year—where cameras never expose the inhumanity and injustice, the state violence and abuse they endure every day.[5]

THE ALBERT WOODFOX STORY

As punishment for starting the first prison chapter of the Black Panther Party for Self-Defense, Albert Woodfox was thrown into solitary confinement for forty years. A member of the Angola 3, Woodfox was reportedly confined in isolation longer than anyone in American history. Since his 2016 release, he travels the world sharing the story of his survival and advocating for the abolition of solitary in all prisons. I had the good fortune of meeting with Mr. Woodfox in both 2018 and 2019. In each of our conversations, I was grateful for the opportunity to sit and build with the Black Panther Party prison chapter founder, this freed political prisoner, and one of the Black radical tradition's most resilient living freedom fighters.

His National Book Award–winning and Pulitzer Prize finalist memoir, *Solitary,* is the unforgettable life story of a man who served more than four decades in a six-foot-by-nine-foot cell, twenty-three hours a day, at the notorious Angola state prison in Louisiana—the site of four former slave plantations. Woodfox was forced to survive there in what has been described as the nation's most inhumane cages. That survival is in itself a feat of extraordinary endurance against the violence and deprivation he faced daily. That he was able to emerge from his odyssey in America's criminal punishment system is a triumph of the human spirit that makes his story a clarion call. Although it would be just one step toward the broader goal of abolishing mass incarceration, his testimony of nearly four and a half decades of torture urges us to call for an immediate end to the inhumanity of solitary worldwide.[6]

Raised in New Orleans, Albert Woodfox was inspired while behind bars in his twenties to join the Black Panther Party because of its social commitment and community-minded code of living.[7] On April 17, 1972, while serving a fifty-year sentence for armed robbery, a white prison guard was killed. Albert and another member of the Panthers were accused of the crime and thrown into solitary by the warden. The trial, without a shred of evidence against them, resulted in life sentences and decades in solitary confinement. After Woodfox spent years without an effective lawyer, it took sixteen more years and several appeals before he was released in February 2016—on his sixty-ninth birthday. In spite of the seemingly insurmountable odds he has overcome, the fire in his belly, for speaking truth to power and demanding justice for those subjected to state violence, has not waned one bit.

·   ·   ·   ·   ·

BRYONN BAIN: I want to just start off by asking, What was your vision when you decided that you had to share your incredible story with the world? And how did that evolve into *Solitary?*

ALBERT WOODFOX: You know, while I was still in prison, I wanted to write a book. Emotionally and intellectually, I never gave up hope that I would be free. So this was always in the back of my mind. Going through all this, I had all these experiences, all this hard stuff. And so in the event ancestors call you home, you need a way to still reach out to the people and tell them the harm that's going on in their name. . . . Prison officials are quick to say "in the name of the people," when the people actually have no idea what's going on, what their taxpayers' money is being used for, the brutality, the racism, the sex slave markets, the administrative corruption. You know, these are the type of things that we are actively harmed by and I had to organize against in the prison. And the remarkable thing about that kind of point is that [the Black Panthers] were one of the few, that is the only, political organization I know of that saw better of men and women even though they were in prison and reached out a hand and said, "Be a part of us. We think you have something to offer to the struggle."

BRYONN: You talk about the importance of your mother, and that resonated with me powerfully. How has her passing while you were incarcerated impacted you?

MR. WOODFOX: I grew into her wisdom and the strength and her sense of love, devotion, character, and sacrifice. You know, these were the things that my mom didn't see or sit down and talk about, but these are the examples she gave to me. I took care of my brothers and my sister. You know? And so it was a sad thing, and it was so difficult.

BRYONN: What was most difficult for you in writing this?

MR. WOODFOX: I had about twenty years of notes! Opinions and views on day-to-day things that I was going through and other men were going through. I was able to sneak them out of prison. . . . A woman named Leslie George helped me. And the reason for that is, she was a journalist and executive producer for *Democracy Now!*[8] My goodness, she was the first interview I was allowed to do in thirtysomething years.

And she became an artist supporter. . . . So she knew a lot about what we were going through. So when I decide to write the book, to actually sit down and write, I'm like, "Let's not be stupid. Right? You're going to need some help with this." She was able to ask the questions that I wouldn't ask myself. She was able to force me to confront issues . . . I probably never would have dealt with on my own. You know? Like losing my mind, my mom, and being denied the right to say good-bye.

You know, in African families it's a tradition to see that final good-bye. But I was denied that. (. . . same thing with my sister. I lost her in 2002. Both had cancer.) And so you have to live with that burden. . . . even though in my mind I knew it wasn't my fault. I knew that there were evil forces that prevented me, but in my heart and soul, somehow I felt as though I had, you know, let my mom down or I let my sister down. So I carried that burden, you know? And after, when I was released, I went from prison cell to graveyard, and it was so crazy because there was a two-hour delay. So by the time we got to the graveyard, the graveyard was closed. I waited twenty years to say good-bye. So I wasn't gonna let this stop me! I got out of the car and started climbing. My sister said, "Oh, no, no, no, no. . . . I ain't trying to do that!" So they talked me to getting back in the car. . . . My sister's name is Viola.

So we went to where she was buried, and her husband, who was a childhood friend . . . I was able to see it. Then the next day, I think we bought every flower in the supermarket. We went in . . . and I was able to finally get that burden off of me and signify—tell her how much I loved her. You know, I am happy to see that. Before I lost her, she knew the kind of man I had become and was very proud of what I did.

BRYONN: You show her a lot of love in your writing. I want to ask you a bit about family and the epigraph. Your poem "Echoes" is a powerful piece that begins the book.[9] Then throughout you go back to her. There's a point where you go through some of the words of wisdom she gave you.

MR. WOODFOX: Right. And that's what inspired. You know, one day I was sitting out and I was real perplexed about a problem that was going on. There were these two guys, and one of the most despicable ways of fighting had developed in prison, where they were throwing human waste. You know, . . . brother George Jackson spoke about it. They put him on a tier with these Nazis, and they used to come and throw waste. Some idiot thought that was okay, and so I was trying to figure out a principled way of stopping this.

So I start thinking back . . . and I realized this had been a pattern with me for a very long time. I would always hear her. Some of the things she said. My relationship with my mother, who was my voice. And it was so strange because I became an avid, voracious reader. And for a while I thought about the great men and women I know I read about . . . the inspirational stuff, but as you get older and you develop, self-education leads to wisdom and experiences, and I realized this: my mom was the hero.

BRYONN: Can you talk about the lack of a consistent father figure early in your life? There are moments where you became a father figure for brothers inside. Even when you had this consciousness come to you while in New York, [imprisoned] in the tombs, and then when you came back to Louisiana. How do you make sense of that? Despite not having access to a father figure in your life, you were able to step up and provide that for so many brothers who needed to hear the message you were sharing with them?

MR. WOODFOX: You know, I always had strong male figures in my life. I had uncles. Unfortunately, because of the racial, economic, political, and social politics in America, opportunities for African Americans was very limited, but I have images of strong men. It was almost determined that because of the institutional, individual, and systemic aspects of racism in America that one out of every four African men would wind up in prison.[10] And, unfortunately, I was that one out of four.

BRYONN: Was your mother prepared to face those challenges on her own?

MR. WOODFOX: My mom was functionally illiterate. She could hardly read or write her name. . . . That dictated almost 90 percent of the lives of African Americans in this country, but she was one of the wisest women I ever knew in my life.[11] And I'm just so grateful that she was there for me at the times when she was most needed . . . some of the other brothers inside didn't have the privilege of literacy.

BRYONN: You talk about recognizing men in prison who took the same kinds of shortcuts that your mom used to get around—not being able to read and write.

MR. WOODFOX: Yeah, there was a guy I became real close with toward the end. They called him Goldie. His name was Charles. And I was able to detect in him, and in some of the other people who can't read or write, they have developed these little defense mechanisms so they can disguise it.[12] So I recognized that in Charles, and I felt as though we were close enough where I could talk with him. And so one day I just asked. I'm like, "You can't read or write. Can you?" And he kind of like dropped his eyes. I said, "Look, don't drop your eyes . . . look me in the eye!" You know? He looked up and I said, "If you want to read and write, I will teach you."

But I'm going to tell you something . . . one of my mom's echoes. She said, "Change is 100 percent design and 10 percent doing it." I said, "If you want to read and write, I will teach you, but I'm not going to run behind you. Know you're going to have to run to *me*!" And in six months' time, he was reading at a high school level. . . . I had the easy part. Change is probably the most difficult thing for human beings. The one thing we need to survive is the thing we fight the hardest. 'Cause change takes you into new territory. Unfamiliarity. And so we would rather suffer in the position we have than accept change or do something to change that position. But with Charles, there were times when I was like, "I shouldn't have said that!" At like three o'clock in the morning, sometimes he'd wake me up and he would ask me . . . "I can't get this word." And I never forget one day, we were talking and he looked at me and said, "You know something, man . . . you opened the world!" And that's profound. You know?

BRYONN: I hear in that story the spirit of the Black Panther Party. Each one, teach one. "Empowering each other" is your description of how you came to know the party. I definitely want to ask you about that because you started the first Black Panther Party [chapter]—in the largest prison in the country.[13] Six thousand people in Louisiana—known today as the Angola Penitentiary. How were you inspired to do that and how did you manage to make it work?

MR. WOODFOX: You adjust. You change. You make whatever adaptations you have to make based on the objective world that you're exposed to. And so, obviously, I couldn't use the same technique that the party used in society. Herman [Wallace] and Robert [King]—who's the other living member of the Angola 3, we had to develop techniques. Teach guys who had no concept of training or unity, who had been mistreated their whole life. Because of the policies of America, they didn't have strong male figures. Positive male figures. So we became that for a lot of them. In a sense, it was harder on me and Robert and Herman because we had to know when these guys came to us for an answer or a solution. We had to know, and the only way we had to get the wisdom or the knowledge was the library . . .

I was in New York in the Tombs,[14] and you had the Panther 21 event.[15] It happened, and the Panthers . . . they come on the [prison] tier. Normally in prison you're looking for a victim. You know, you either are a victim or you're victimized. But when these brothers come on a tier . . . the kids start talking about African unity and pride, and so I told them about the political system. . . . Now at this time, I was listening to what they were saying, but I wasn't hearing it.

An elder came and he had been locked up twenty-five years, and he came down and he was trying to get his freedom. And we started talking and I'm talking this smack, you know, and I'm still a knucklehead. And he says, "I have a book I want you to read." And he gave me a fictional piece of a book based on real life migration of African people from the South to the West, not East of the country, thinking they would find a better life. And the name of the book was *A Different Drummer*.[16] And the author, who I actually communicated with for a while, his name is William Melvin Kelly. It's a wonderful book. It's still in print, I think. And so that was the book.

That book taught me that one individual can make a difference. And all of a sudden, at the meetings that the Panthers was having, I started hearing. Not just listening to what they say, but I started *hearing* what they were saying and understanding. You know? The nature of capitalism and economics and racism. And then this light went off in my head. You know? I'm not a bad guy. Yeah, I was placed in a society that almost *forced* me to come to prison.[17] And that was the first step that's still ongoing and has me here tonight . . .

BRYONN: You talk about your experience in school early on. And it reminds me of the way, today, we are calling out the "school to prison pipeline," or "track," according to the grassroots organization Youth Justice Coalition—or even, in the words of Marian Wright Edelman and the Children's Defense Fund, the "cradle to prison pipeline."

MR. WOODFOX: So many of the things that happen in our public schools can push us out. It's not a dropout rate. It's a pushout rate! It is.

BRYONN: Can you talk about your early experiences of institutional racism? Things you experienced that pushed you in a direction that made prison inevitable?

MR. WOODFOX: Well, for one thing, I didn't even know that Black people had a history.[18] I didn't know that we contributed to the development of civilization worldwide. I didn't know about the great African civilization . . . literature, and in the history books, in civil rights books, and all this about Black people and the contributions . . . you know? So when the party inspired all this, it gave me that thirst for knowledge. They were used to who I am, where I come from, and what happened. Why my people seem to be so vilified. Not just in America, but around the world, you know? And so I started writing, reading . . . Malcolm X. Somewhere in my mind, I wanted my place in history. You know?

BRYONN: Here we are and it's so fitting. We're at the oldest Black bookstore in Los Angeles, named after the Egyptian civilizations that are the cradle of all civilization . . . so appropriate.[19] You also reference James Baldwin in your work as well. There's a passage where you're referencing Baldwin talking about how if a white man stands up and says, "Give me liberty or give me death!" it's celebrated, but if a Black man does that?

MR. WOODFOX: We're seen as a criminal. It brings me to thinking about the kind of assumptions that have been associated with blackness and the link to criminality that exists.[20] But I am also highly aware that we carry our assumptions too. Some of them. We internalize the oppression and we put it out to each other.[21] And then, in other ways it emerges, that we have to sort of think critically about. And you have a moment where you kind of check your own assumptions.

BRYONN: Brent Miller, the guard who was killed, you got wind that his widow might be interested in actually being an ally and a supporter of the Angola 3's freedom.[22] You want to say a bit about that situation?

MR. WOODFOX: She was a very young bride. I think she was about seventeen or so when they got married. For most of her adult life, she had been told all the lies and deception that the state of Louisiana had used to persecute Herman, Robert, and myself. And so we got some real good lawyers. And around, I think it was 2005 . . . she read about our case and she contacted us and we had an international support committee . . .[23]

She arrived with an attorney practicing in Sacramento . . . still a law student, you know. She contacted him and invited him to events and said, "I'd like to meet you, and Herman and Robert. Can you arrange that?" And so there was a process where you had to fill out a form and request for somebody to be put on your visit list . . . it normally takes about thirty days. Well, six months later, they still hadn't approved. So one of the correctional officers [a young woman who had just started working there and hadn't been corrupted by the system], she was assigned to where I was zoned. So when she came through, I asked her, "Why hasn't this been approved?" Later that day, I got a note from her saying I was approved.

And so the attorneys call the Department of Corrections and say, "If she's not on his list, and within two weeks' time, see you in court!" I think about three or four days after that, I got the paper approving her. So she became a very good friend as well for them. And I never forget that. Yeah, the first time she was approved to visit, we had one contact visit as a concession, but we could only get one once a month. So she came and, I'm a pretty confident guy, you know, but for this one time I'm like, "What in the hell am I doing? Don't talk with this woman!" You know?

In my mind, she was about six feet tall. And when they call me for the visit and I went down, I see just a little tiny woman sitting at the table, but there was something in her eyes. You know? And I walked over and I said, "Ms. Rogers?" and she stood up and hugged me. And you know, we started talking . . . about five minutes later, she was telling me dirty jokes. And from that point on, I'll never forget, she says, "I understand y'all having a problem raising money for attorneys." And I said, "We got men and women that make up the coalition. They didn't have to raise money—they could be doing a lot of other stuff."

And she said, "Well, that's not a problem. Who you want? Johnny Cochran?" I'm like, "No, no, no. Johnny Cochran is a good trial lawyer. We need some good appellate law. We need lawyers that know their way around the appeals process and the court." Right? And at the time, the lead attorney's name was George Kendall. He was a partner in a law firm in Newark called Holland and Knight. I see he since went to a bigger law firm, but they took on our civil case pro bono. We file a civil suit on our own about long-term cell confinement, but the state was running circles around the court. We were confined. We couldn't do research. A lot of the prison inmate council would sneak stuff to us, trying to help us out, but once this law firm came . . . we talked and I explained the case, and eventually we have them taking on the criminal case as well. And so George came to prison and talked with Herman and me and got to know how we feel about it. . . . Given the, the job they was doing with the civil case . . . I mean, they turned the whole thing upside down.[24] You know?

One story I like to talk about. . . . They [didn't want to] provide the attorneys with certain documents. . . . So they took them to this big warehouse where they keep all the legal documents to sit in there some-where. . . . They thought they was doing that. . . . So the next day [we] had twenty-five Cadillac Escalades at the front gate with lawyers, clerks . . . and they went back to that warehouse. And in a week's time, we had everything. The court documents and everything they didn't want the lawyers to have. So Robert, Herman, and I are now like, "This case is getting serious!" You know? Because we had spent so many years battling on our own. Right . . . you had to teach yourself the law, both civil and criminal. And you know, the court system, it's a different lan-guage. It's different way of thinking. A different philosophy.

You have to make that transition from survival mode to attack mode, but you have to attack in a certain way. So there were many nights I can remember, you know, where I would be sitting on the floor by myself and I would have like five or six law books spread out. And you know, this case would say one thing. Another case would say, "No, that case is wrong." I began to understand the language of the court, and we were able to shape an argument based on the Eighth Amendment's "cruel and unusual punishment" clause, and the Fourteenth Amendment's equal protection under the law.[25]

BRYONN: Can we talk about what "cruel and unusual" means just for a moment? There is a piece of this that speaks to your activism when you were in prison—challenging rape. And now, in challenging solitary con-finement. And that is really trying to hold folks accountable for this vio-lence that they either claim doesn't happen or nobody wants to be held accountable for.

You quote one of the brothers in Angola who seemed to be reading Kahlil Gibran at the time.[26] He has a line in his section on crime and punishment where he says, "A single leaf on the tree turns not yellow but with the silent knowledge of the whole tree."

MR. WOODFOX: Right. So this violence is happening and it's happening right under the noses of the prison staff administration hierarchy, but nobody's being held accountable until the Panthers step in and say, "It's not happening!"

BRYONN: Can we talk about the connection between that and the activism you're engaging now?

MR. WOODFOX: Well, I was transferred. A little back history. I was convicted of robbery and sentenced to fifty years. I escaped and made my way to Harlem.[27] So you come to understand that the violence and the corruption in prison, it exists because there is no oversight. So we are on protests and hunger strikes and just refusing to do certain things. Or not allowing them to handle us a certain way. Or call us certain names without a thing. And as a result of that, there was a lot of gassing and beating and putting us into the dungeon. And so we like, "Damn, man! These nightsticks hurt. You know, we got to find another way!" So there was a guy on the tier. His name was Arthur Mitchell, and he had a reputation as being one of the best jailhouse lawyers. As a matter of fact, they locked him up because he filed a suit challenging something that was going on in the prison. We like, "That's the brother. That's the brother!" But still, it was like my mom's saying, "Change is 100 percent design, 10 percent doing it!" Still was up to us . . . he could talk about the law, but the actual understanding of the court system and the language that's used and the philosophy, that was on us . . . had to internalize that within yourself. And so that's what we did know. Whatever challenge was presented to us, and whatever we had to do to meet that challenge head on and not be ashamed and look in the mirror the next day. That's what we did.

BRYONN: I was really moved by just how in the midst of all the corruption, like other Panthers . . . just the level of integrity you had in the face of all the racism and the abuse and the violence. We are in a moment right now here where we have fascist leadership, from Brazil to here in the United States, right?[28] You know, white supremacists running the government. Blatantly. Openly. White supremacists. But we also have these movements from the #MeToo movement, challenging a lot of toxic masculinity and patriarchy, to the #BlackLivesMatter movement, which is challenging white supremacy . . .[29]

MR. WOODFOX: Robert and I, we speak at a lot of universities . . . whoever is asking us to come . . . if they are the #BlackLivesMatter movement, we meet with the young leaders. . . . We try to do that and I think, my personal feeling is, that #BlackLivesMatter is the most promising movement and the #MeToo movement is very close.

BRYONN: I hear that. They could benefit from each other?

MR. WOODFOX: Yeah. Of course. That's important. That's the intergenerational connection and dialogue. We know when you strip it all away it's about change, right? And this is why in my book I talk about changing and transitioning. I became a firm believer in what's called materialism and dialectics . . .[30] [*cell phone alarm rings*] . . . so that's the material of your phone blowing you up right now. That might be the signal that we should take one more question and open it up.

BRYONN: That might be the sign. I just have one last question I have to pose to you. Around the issue of trauma. You know, I watched all the interviews with you—Amy Goodman, Juan González, everyone else— and everyone talks about how you survived forty-four years and ten months in prison and most of that time in a six-by-nine cell.

MR. WOODFOX: And it's actually not six-by-nine because you have the bed, the bunk, the toilet. Right? So only this narrow pathway. 'Cause you have a table and chair attached to one wall. You got two bunks attached to the other wall. So there's only that narrow pathway. And, you know, there's a movement. We're part of the movement to end solitary in prison.

BRYONN: And it's only growing. Even the United Nations finally came along and declared fifteen days or more in solitary to be torture.[31] Would you say it should be even less?

MR. WOODFOX: People ask me how I feel about it. Spend one day in your bedroom. Take anything you want in there with you. Or go out in your backyard and draw nine feet by six feet in diameter and stay in that area. Then you come back and tell me if you think fifteen days is fair.

BRYONN: Is it fair to say you're for abolition?

MR. WOODFOX: There are guys and women in prison who are antisocial or have other conditions that are going to be problems, right? But there's a difference between separation and solitary confinement.[32] Most of these people who have problems that they create can be solved by separation.

Solitary confinement is the most nonphysical cruel and "usual" punishment a human being can inflict upon another human being because it robs you of a sense of self.[33] It robs you of your identity and who you are if you allow it. And it takes away your dignity, your pride, your self-respect. You know, I've seen men, very strong men as far as the prison life, go insane. And men have cut their wrists and cut their throats and sliced their bellies open to try to get out of solitary confinement.

So there's no logical point. Other than to destroy a man, a woman, or a child. It has no other purpose. And so I always tell people who are like, "Well, they got people who pose a threat to others!" I say there's a difference between, as I said earlier, separation and solitary confinement. . . . You can remove an individual from a situation to another environment . . .

BRYONN: Despite all of that, you survived. Any questions from the audience?

AUDIENCE QUESTION #1: My question is, while you were in prison, why was most of it in solitary? Was it related to this chapter of the Black Panther party you started?

MR. WOODFOX: They'd put two men known to rape in a dungeon with the new young guys. We had a pretty good grapevine. So when we find out, Robert, Herman, and I checked into it. We would do something to get sent there. A part of my survival was our friendship. That developed with Herman and Robert. That went beyond being comrades. There was no doubt in my mind that either they were going to be in the dungeon already, or they would be in there and this would happen. . . . And about ten minutes later, Herman came and then Robert came and when we got in there, we see it and say, "We know why y'all in here. It ain't going to happen!" You know? "And if you mess with that child anywhere in this prison, you're not going to be able to live." And so a couple of hours later, they come and get him out.

BRYONN: What was it about the Panthers that shut down those known "rape artists" from attacking the "fresh fish," as you put it, when they first came to prison? You think it was the discipline of the Black Panther Party? The way the Panthers genuinely cared?

MR. WOODFOX: The thing that caused me to form the antirape squad was a young kid in the dormitory. I was living there and he had been raped. He was right across from me. And it was the first time in my life that I had seen a human being whose spirit had been broken. You know? And it's so difficult to come back from something like that. Which is why I have such tremendous respect for people who made that transition from being broken. And finding dignity, pride, and self-respect again, you know?

And so I started asking myself questions. "You're a Black Panther. You are a revolutionary. You're a humanitarian. How can you accept this?" So the next day, I went to Herman. And one of the ways we used to have meetings is we would go on the football field and throw the ball around. Like we were playing football. While we having political discussions. So we talked about the rape that was going on and these young men . . . and so we decided. I'll never forget. There was about ten of us who went down. And I'm not gonna lie; what we were doing was very dangerous. As a matter of fact, one of our chapter members lost his life trying to defend a young kid. We went where the buses come in, and when the kids got off, we just started talking like, "Remember the Black Panther Party. We here to protect those with needs. There are guys here who want to rape you. Who want to force you to a life of slavery." That was like pouring gas on fire, but they knew. A lot of security benefited financially from looking the other way. And so we did the honor challenge to the entire prison population. And that included security. There would no longer be the rape of young men and forced sexual slavery. And so for a while we pretty much stopped it. And then the Brent Miller thing happened. And they locked Herman up and a lot of the other brothers who had joined the Panther prison chapter. Young brother named Marvin . . . [with all] his dedication to the party, went to lie back down [to sleep] and, unfortunately, he lost his life.

BRYONN: I'm so grateful you bring this into the conversation. So often in the culture and the media, rape is talked about in a very gendered way—as if it happens only to women.[34] Not that it should be any less important in those conversations, but rape is rape. And Angela Davis talks about how more than 200,000 rapes are reported as happening in prisons every year. <u>And that's just what's reported.</u> We know there's so much more that's not recorded. So we need to begin to have a deeper conversation about it. And your book and your stories are helping to move that forward. So thank you. Any other questions?

AUDIENCE QUESTION #3: I just want to again say thank you because I feel like it's important that these conversations are being had or someone is talking about them as a former prisoner. I'm twenty years old and my dad was incarcerated for a really small crime. Bootleg DVDs and CDs. Anyway, I just see the aftereffects of him [being incarcerated] from 2007 to 2019 and how they still affect him today. And I just want to know, like, if you had any words encouraging you or any words of advice about life after prison? To help build that self-worth back in himself? To help him realize you have a duty still? Or you have some sort of job to do now that you have this information? You know? Based on the aftereffects of your own life? 'Cause as you said, "I went through this and now I have to speak about that." But where does that courage come from? How do you ignite that courage in someone that doesn't really understand it? 'Cause they're incarcerated and like "What do you mean?"

MR. WOODFOX: Prior to the Party, I always masked my fear. Every human being has to mask their own fear. And I remember the experiences. There's a group all of us founded with a good friend of mine who was an inmate-counseling angel named Norris Henderson, and he used to help us get by. You know, making copies and sneaking logbooks to us and stuff like that. So I remember they had a meeting every fourth Wednesday of the month. And we had this meeting and I saw this guy and he was withdrawn. I could sense there was so much he wanted to say, but he didn't know how to say it. So I went over and I asked him and he said, "I don't know what to say."

Well, the first thing you have to do is believe that you belong here. You have a right to be here as much as any man, woman, or child in this room, and that's what you have to take with you from this night. Wherever you at, you belong there, you know? And so we call it a Circle of Truth. And everyone talks about some event in their life. You know? I mean he stood up and he said, "My name is Clovis. I did fifty years . . . and I just got to talking with brother Woodfox and I belong here." And he talked about some of the things that he'd bottled up in him for so long. The one thing prison does is, it takes. It tries to take away your parts. You know?

I don't subscribe to any particular religious belief or practice, but I am a very spiritual man. I am able to connect with whatever I'm involved with to the point where I can feel it in my soul. I once read about Nelson Mandela—who was one of my great heroes. And he said something, not verbatim, but he said that if a cause is noble, you can carry the weight of the world. They was asking him about apartheid, and in the most brutal prison known to man at that time. And they wanted to know how he survived. So for your dad, you have to find his noble cause. You have to find a cause he's willing to sacrifice everything for. It's like finding yourself again . . . can't nobody give it. You can help him realize that something is missing, but it always comes down to you. You know? And if I represent anything, it's the strength of the human spirit and the willingness to sacrifice.

And the one thing I would like to say to everyone here is that prisoners don't come from another planet. They come from families. They started with a mother. They come from your mother's wound. And they are daddies and uncles and brothers and sisters and grandparents and aunties and uncles. You can't stop loving them because they are in prison . . . either you're a political prisoner [like King], or you're a political victim. We live in a society that thrives on class to sanction separation and racial hatred. Because these conditions exist don't mean that we have to give in to them.

One of the things I have found in my studies is that African Americans—we adapt. We take negatives and turn them into positives, right? And while that may have been good up to a certain point, especially during slavery, we have to move beyond that. We have to move beyond taking negatives and turning them into positives, and reject negatives and replace them with positive thoughts, positive acts, but it all, again, comes down to the individual. If you can't be honest with anyone else, be honest with yourself. If you're not willing to make whatever sacrifices necessary. If you're not willing to, you know?

Herman made the ultimate sacrifice. He died three days after he won his freedom. He had liver cancer and the prison people knew this.

Medical people knew this and they were telling him that he had an allergy. . . . One of the top geriatric doctors, who practices in San Francisco, came in and examined Herman because he had started losing weight. When they realized she was coming a couple of days before she was scheduled, they rushed him into the hospital and he got the diagnosis. And even after that, the medication that was prescribed was some kind of chemo pills.

Ten days without giving him his medication. One of the nurses, whose level of conscience had been raised, called our lawyer and said, "These people trying to kill Herman still! They haven't, but they're not give him his medication." And unfortunately, whatever damage may have been stopped in those ten days, it caused him to lose his life. So in essence, they more than harmed him because they couldn't break him. And so those are the types of things that still motivate me. Herman giving his life trying to protect a kid from harm. You know?

BRYONN: They did everything they could to break you.

MR. WOODFOX: And Robert—who got out after twenty-nine years—got out and there is not a continent on this planet he didn't go to and talk about our case. He made sure the world knew about the sacrifices that we had made and the fact that they could not break us after decades of solitary confinement.

BRYONN: To be in the belly of the beast, in the largest empire human history has ever known, with the most powerful military, more technology and surveillance on the globe than we have ever seen, to survive *that* is truly phenomenal. And as the man who survived solitary more than anyone we know of in history.[35] I have to ask you, What is your call to action?

MR. WOODFOX: Well, I intend to do what I'm doing. I consider myself to be a revolutionary. I'm a social activist. I love. My noble cause is humanity. I want to be able to better contribute to building a better human being. And then, in terms of a better society, my personal thing is that I have four very beautiful great-grandbabies.

BRYONN: How young are they?

MR. WOODFOX: Five to thirteen. I don't want them thirty years from now sitting before people such as yourself saying the same thing. You know? Talking about the same horrors. You know? So that's my personal motivation, and humanity is my philosophical reason for it. You know, I'll never forget, we took this trip to New York, we wanted to go and see the [Black Panther] chapter, [see] what was there. The building had a lot of people hanging around. And this young guy used the term *OG*—old gangster.[36] You know? You know, they knew who I was and the history. So that's my voice. When I hear that . . . when whatever torch is in our hand goes to the next person. I wanted to be in charge of dignity, pride, self-respect, nobility. So I don't want to hand them a torch with a small light. You know? I wanted the light to be so bright they have to cover their eyes until they take it in their hand. You know?

BRYONN: Thank you. I'm very grateful for this time with you. Thank you for all of your immeasurable struggle and unparalleled sacrifice.

MR. WOODFOX: Well, my pleasure. Thank you.

LINER NOTES

Track #2's interview took place at Eso Won Books, Leimert Park, Los Angeles, on May 2, 2019. Published courtesy of Albert Woodfox.

Epigraph: Attributed to a letter written by Assata Shakur, n.d., as described in "Patrice Cullors Shares the History of the Protest Chant Inspired by Assata Shakur," video produced by Dwayne Johnson, Dany Garcia, and Dream Hampton, YouTube, March 5, 2019, https://youtu.be/zmuaWInh8BQ.

1. James Baldwin, "The American Dream and the American Negro," *New York Times*, March 7, 1965, www.nytimes.com/images/blogs/papercuts/baldwin-and-buckley.pdf.

2. While no national publicly funded data system has accurately tracked the number of people who die during contact with police, these deaths are public health data and can be counted. Gabriel L. Schwartz and Jaquelyn L. Jahn found that "Black people were 3.23 times more likely to be killed compared to White people," and they estimated rates of fatal police violence for every metropolitan area in the country, as well as racial inequities in those rates, by analyzing the most recent complete data—from 2013 to 2017—from FatalEncounters.org, a citizen science initiative that tracks and verifies incidents of fatal police violence from media reports and public records. Gabriel L. Schwartz and Jaquelyn L. Jahn, "Mapping Fatal Police Violence across US Metropolitan Areas: Overall Rates and

Racial/Ethnic Inequities, 2013–2017," *PLOS ONE 15*, no. 6 (June 24, 2020), http://doi.org/10.1371/journal.pone.0229686.

3. Arlene Eisen, "Operation Ghetto Storm," Malcolm X Grassroots Committee, November 2014, www.operationghettostorm.org/uploads/1/9/1/1/19110795 /new_all_14_11_04.pdf.

4. Nicola Carr and Shadd Maruna, "Legitimacy through Neutrality: Probation and Conflict in Northern Ireland," *Howard Journal of Criminal Justice* 51, no. 5 (2012): 3.

5. The US cages an estimated 20,000–25,000 human beings in solitary confinement. Since 2015, the United Nation's "Mandela Rules" have offered a minimum standard defining solitary confinement as "the confinement of prisoners for twenty-two hours or more a day without meaningful human contact." Juan Méndez, Special Rapporteur on Torture, argues, "Segregation, isolation, separation, cellular, lockdown, Supermax, the hole, Secure Housing Unit . . . whatever the name, solitary confinement should be banned by States as a punishment or extortion technique." It is "contrary to rehabilitation, the aim of the penitentiary system." Méndez's perspective was adopted by the UN, which now agrees that over fifteen days should be "subject to an absolute prohibition." "Solitary Confinement Should be Banned in Most Cases, UN Expert says," *UN News*, October 18, 2011, https://news.un.org/en/story/2011/10/392012-solitary-confinement-should-be-banned-most-cases-un-expert-says.

6. Albert Woodfox, *Solitary: Unbroken by Four Decades in Solitary Confinement; My Story of Transformation and Hope* (New York: Grove Press, 2019).

7. Huey P. Newton and Bobby Seale put together the Ten-Point Program, which was released in *The Black Panther*, the Black Panther Party's weekly newspaper, on May 15, 1967. The Ten-Point Program is described in Joshua Bloom and Waldo E. Martin, *Black Against Empire* (Berkeley: University of California Press, 2013), 70–72.

8. *Democracy Now!* is a global independent daily radio news hour by award-winning journalist Amy Goodman and Juan González. Reporting includes breaking daily news headlines and in-depth interviews with people on the front lines of critical issues. The program is broadcast across the US and Canada as well as in countries around the world. See www.democracynow.org/about, accessed August 20, 2021.

9. Albert Woodfox, "Echoes," 1995, in *Solitary: Unbroken by Four Decades in Solitary Confinement; My Story of Transformation and Hope*, by Albert Woodfox (New York: Grove Press, 2019):

> Echoes of wisdom I often hear,
> a mother's strength softly in my ears.
> Echoes of womanhood shining so bright,
> echoes of a mother within darkest night.

Echoes of wisdoms on my mother's lips, too young
to understand it was in a gentle kiss.
Echoes of love and echoes of fear
arrogance of manhood wouldn't let me hear,
Echoes of heartache I still hold close
as I mourn the loss of my one true hero.
Echoes from a mother's womb,
heartbeats held so dear,
life begins with my first tears.
Echoes of footsteps taken in the past,
echoes of manhood standing in a looking glass.
Echoes of motherhood gentle and near,
echoes of a lost mother I will always hear.

10. Jerome G. Miller, "From Social Safety Net to Dragnet: African American Males in the Criminal Justice System," *Washington and Lee University Law Review* 51, no. 2 (1994): 479, https://scholarlycommons.law.wlu.edu/wlulr/vol51/iss2/6. Also, "About 1 in 3 black males, 1 in 6 Hispanic males, and 1 in 17 white males are expected to go to prison," according to T. P. Bonczar in *Prevalence of Imprisonment: 1974–2001*, Bureau of Justice Statistics Special Report, August 2003, www.bjs.gov/content/pub/pdf/piusp01.pdf.

11. Janet Duitsman Cornelius, *When I Can Read My Title Clear: Literacy, Slavery, and Religion in the Antebellum South* (Columbia: University of South Carolina Press, 1991).

12. Malcolm Gladwell, "David Boies: You Wouldn't Wish Dyslexia on Your Child. Or Would You?" in *David and Goliath: Underdogs, Misfits, and the Art of Battling Giants*, by Malcolm Gladwell, ch. 4 (New York: Little, Brown, 2013).

13. Robert King, Albert Woodfox, Juan González, Jamal Joseph, and Amy Goodman, "Surviving Members of Angola 3 on Black Panther Legacy; Need to Free Remaining Imprisoned Panthers," *Democracy Now!*, October 26, 2016, www.democracynow.org/2016/10/26/surviving_members_of_angola_3_on.

14. "The Tombs" is the colloquial term for the Manhattan Detention Complex at 125 White Street in lower Manhattan, www.prisonpro.com/content/manhattan-detention-complex.

15. "The Panther 21" refers to the twenty-one members of the Harlem chapter of the Black Panther Party who, on April 2, 1969, were charged with 156 counts of "conspiracy" to blow up subway and police stations, five department stores, six railroads, and the Bronx-based New York Botanical Garden, according to Workers.org, May 2016, www.workers.org/2016/05/25321.

16. W. M. Kelley, *A Different Drummer* (New York: Anchor Books, 2019).

17. "One in three young African American men will serve time in prison if current trends continue, and in some cities more than half of all young adult black men are currently under correctional control—in prison or jail, on probation or parole. Yet mass incarceration tends to be categorized as a criminal justice issue as

opposed to a racial justice or civil rights issue (or crises)." Michelle Alexander, *The New Jim Crow* (New York City: New Press, 2010), 9.

18. "A people without the knowledge of their past history, origin and culture is like a tree without roots." M. Garvey and T. Bookman, *Beyond Survival: How Judaism Can Thrive* . . . (Lanham, MD: Rowman and Littlefield, 2019), 36.

19. Eso Won Books, Leimert Park, Los Angeles, www.esowonbookstore.com.

20. "In the United States, race has always played a central role in constructing presumptions of criminality. After the abolition of slavery, former slave states passed new legislation revising the Slave Codes in order to regulate the behavior of free blacks in ways similar to those that had existed during slavery." Alexander, *New Jim Crow*, 28.

21. "The man who is not able to develop and use his mind is bound to be the slave of the other man who uses his mind." Frantz Fanon, *Black Skins, White Masks* (New York: Grove Press, 1967).

22. Andrew Cohen, "'I'll Believe It When I See It,'" the Marshall Project, February 22, 2016, www.themarshallproject.org/2016/02/21/i-ll-believe-it-when-i-see-it.

23. Billie Mizell, a young investigator, joined the case in 2015 while Robert King, Albert Woodfox, and Herman Wallace were still in solitary. She conducted a social history investigation, which is not typically done unless the defendant is facing execution. During Mizell's investigation, she also tracked down Brent Miller's widow, Leontine "Teenie" Rogers. Mizell said, "I expected Teenie would slam the door in my face, but she welcomed me in." Mizell found that many of Teenie's questions had gone unanswered. Juan Haines, "Billie Mizell's Calling with Insight Prison Project," *San Quentin News*, July 1, 2016, https://sanquentinnews .com/billie-mizells-calling-with-inside-prison-project.

24. George Kendall, a former staff attorney for the American Civil Liberties Union's Eleventh Circuit Capital Litigation Project who has worked closely with the Innocence Project and the NAACP on policy issues, took on the case pro bono in 2005 alongside Corrine Irish, Carine Williams, and Sam Spital. Woodfox, *Solitary*, 288, 330–31.

25. The Eighth Amendment was ratified on December 15, 1791, prohibiting the federal government from imposing excessive bail, excessive fines, or cruel and unusual punishments. Sharon Dolovich, "Cruelty, Prison Conditions, and the Eighth Amendment," *NYU Law Review* 84, no. 4 (2009), www.nyulawreview.org/issues /volume-84-number-4/cruelty-prison-conditions-and-the-eighth-amendment. The Fourteenth Amendment was ratified on July 9, 1868, granting citizenship to "all persons born or naturalized in the United States," including formerly enslaved Africans recently freed. M. K. Curtis, "Fourteenth Amendment: Recalling What the Court Forgot," *Drake Law Review* 56, no. 4 (2008), https://lawreviewdrake.files .wordpress.com/2015/06/irvol56-4_curtisfinal.pdf.

26. Kahlil Gibran (1883–1931), *The Prophet* (New York: Knopf, 1995), 24.

27. See Campbell Robertson, "For 45 Years in Prison, Louisiana Man Kept Calm . . . ," *New York Times*, February 20, 2016, www.nytimes.com/2016/02/21/us/for-45-years-in-prison-louisiana-man-kept-calm-and-held-fast-to-hope .html.

28. See Samuel Earle, "How White Supremacists around the World Are Being Connected," *New Statesman*, October 2019, www.newstatesman.com/science-tech/2019/10/how-white-supremacists-around-world-are-being-connected.

29. #MeToo began as part of an activist campaign led by Tarana Burke to support marginalized women of color who experience sexual assault. Elizabeth Adetiba, "Tarana Burke Says MeToo Isn't Just for White People," *The Nation*, November 17, 2017, www.thenation.com/article/archive/tarana-burke-says-metoo-isnt-just-for-white-people. "#BlackLivesMatter was founded in 2013 in response to the acquittal of Trayvon Martin's murderer and is now a global organization in the US, UK, and Canada whose mission is to eradicate white supremacy and build local power to intervene in violence inflicted on Black communities by the state and vigilantes." Alicia Garza, "A Herstory of the #BlackLivesMatter Movement," *Feminist Wire*, October 7, 2014, http://thefeministwire.com/2014 /10/blacklivesmatter-2.

30. To understand the *dialectic* of "African resistance to enslavement and exploitation . . . look outside the orbit of capitalism. Look at West and Central African culture. . . . Marx had not realized fully that the cargoes of laborers also contained African cultures, critical mixes . . . the actual terms of their humanity." C. Robinson, *Black Marxism* (Chapel Hill: University of North Carolina Press, 2005), xiv.

31. Human Rights First, "International Human Rights Law on Solitary Confinement, 2015," *Prison Legal News*, February 22, 2016, www.prisonlegalnews .org/news/publications/international-human-rights-law-solitary-confinement-hrf-2015; Elizabeth Vasiliades, "Solitary Confinement and International Human Rights: Why the US Prison System Fails Global Standards," *American University International Law Review* 21 (2005): 80.

32. To some extent, all incarcerated individuals are isolated and deprived. However, solitary confinement has "fundamental components that make it distinct from general incarceration." Tracy Hresko, "In the Cellars of the Hollow Men: Use of Solitary Confinement in US Prisons and Its Implications under International Laws against Torture," *Pace International Law Review* 18, no. 1 (2006): 1, https://digitalcommons.pace.edu/pilr/vol18/iss1/1.

33. "Medical studies on the effects of solitary confinement have overwhelmingly shown that it can cause severe psychological distress . . . extreme anxiety, hallucinations, violent fantasies, hypersensitivity to external stimuli, and an increased tendency to inflict self-harm." Hresko, "In the Cellars of the Hollow Men."

34. Lara Stemple and Ilan H. Meyer, "The Sexual Victimization of Men in America: New Data Challenge Old Assumptions," *American Journal of Public Health* 104, no. 6 (2014), http://doi.org/10.2105/AJPH.2014.301946.

35. Erwin James, "37 Years of Solitary Confinement: The Angola Three," *The Guardian*, March 9, 2010, www.theguardian.com/society/2010/mar/10/erwin-james-angola-three.

36. According to former South Central LA gang members, the term was first used in the 1970s by LA's Original Gangster Crips. Members used the OG abbreviation as a shorthand for the part of the gang they belongs to (e.g., Original Eastside Crips, or OG Eastside). As the Crips expanded in the 1970s and many new members came from other gangs, the term evolved into someone deeply devoted to their subset gang, and younger members of the gangs began to use it in reference to the elders. The term became so popular that even the Crips's rival gang, the Bloods, started using it. The term entered mainstream vernacular in the '80s and '90s through hip hop, notably Ice-T's "O.G. Original Gangster," which hit number seven on the Billboard charts in 1991. See also www.dictionary.com/e/slang/og.

21st Century Harriet Tubman

A DIALOGUE WITH SUSAN BURTON

Moses, rise up early in the morning and present yourself to
Pharaoh . . . say to him, "Thus says the Lord, 'Let my people
go, that they may serve me.'"

—Exodus 8:20

During the decade I taught at the world's largest penal colony, Rikers
Island caged nearly 15,000 people. When I came to California, LA's jails
held over 17,000.[1] The City of Angels is, in fact, the City of Incarceration.

I have worked in prisons for more than thirty years. In the late 1980s,
I began performing hip hop, spoken word, blues, and theater in prisons
back east in New York City where I was born. But it was only after I was
racially profiled and wrongfully jailed by the New York Police Department
that I saw the power of my work as an artist to be used for activism. I have
spent my career since working to build transformative learning communities by bridging those in prisons and institutions dedicated to the arts and
education. After more than a decade of facilitating and teaching programs
that link facilities like Sing Sing prison and Wallkill prison to institutions
like New York University, Columbia University, and Carnegie Hall, I was
invited to the University of California, Los Angeles, to develop a prison
education program linking the nation's leading public university to those
incarcerated in Los Angeles.[2]

While the carceral crisis in LA has led the United States' devastation
of Black, Brown, working, and marginalized communities, there are
also extraordinary leaders, as well as grassroots and community-based

organizations, here in abundance. From Youth Justice Coalition, Dignity and Power Now, the Anti-Recidivism Coalition, and InsideOUT Writers, Angelenos have long organized to fight for change in this city and have developed visionary strategies and programs to move the national conversation and policies in the *left* direction: toward the liberation of those of us who are system-impacted, formerly incarcerated, and/or surviving what some refer to as post-traumatic prison disorder.[3]

On an unforgettable Monday morning in 2018, I walked into a bustling office in South Central Los Angeles. A half dozen ethnically diverse women staffers were gathered around a table, trying to reconcile speaking requests from both near and far: That legendary church in Atlanta. Some classroom at Princeton. Somewhere across the pond in Portugal. At the head of the table, the woman at the center of this avalanche of invites— wearing a vibrant orange dashiki with black trim—listened to the discussion with gentle patience and a loving smile.

I stood at the entryway in anticipation of her embrace. A week earlier, we had just missed each other on separate visits to the largest federal detention center in the country, the Metropolitan Detention Center in Brooklyn, New York—a facility that would soon come under scrutiny by human rights activists and the New York City Council after a power outage left men inside without heat for four days amid a freezing polar vortex.[4] As soon as we locked eyes, she welcomed me with a heartfelt "Hello!" and a warm hug. I was hoping I would not be an intrusion on the more important business of a woman regarded around the world as one of the great freedom fighters of our time.[5]

Susan Burton is the founder of A New Way of Life Reentry Project (ANWOL). Since 1998, ANWOL has secured and provided housing, case management, pro bono legal services, advocacy, and leadership development for more than 1,000 women and children rebuilding their lives after prison.[6] While countless voices in the rising movements for racial and gender justice call for "changing the narrative" around mass incarceration, Ms. Burton and her organization are changing the narrator.[7] Through her advocacy, this formerly incarcerated Black woman has become a central voice in leading the conversation on mass incarceration. In her inspiring memoir, *Becoming Ms. Burton*, she shares her personal story of healing, redemption, and resilience. Her book has received overwhelming acclaim since its 2017 release.[8] In fact, Ms. Burton told me, her publisher's website crashed after the book received a shout-out from Michelle Alexander, legal scholar and author of *The New Jim Crow*, causing Burton's book release announcement to go viral.

This is the new normal for a People's heroine who has quickly become regarded as one of the nation's leading civil and human rights activists.[9] Without any hint of hyperbole, her name is being compared today to legendary women including Angela Davis, Ida B. Wells-Barnett, Sojourner Truth, and yes, even Harriet Tubman.[10]

.   .   .   .   .

BRYONN BAIN: Your book now has over 11,000 copies in print.[11] Congratulations!

SUSAN BURTON: Thank you.

BRYONN: I know it's been a long journey to get here. Can you tell us a bit about what inspired your journey toward *Becoming Ms. Burton?*

MS. BURTON: I was born in a housing project. My mother and father, through the conditions of the South, came to California looking for a better life for themselves and had six children. I was the only girl. I had five brothers. The household was full of stuff. There was laughter, there was fun, but there was also lots of trauma, violence, and childhood—different levels of abuse.

And I endured, and I endured, and I endured all types of abuse up until the time I lost my son. My son, KK. He was five years old. He was accidentally killed by an LAPD detective, and at that point I kind of fell off.[12] My body couldn't hold any more pain, disappointment, and especially the grief of losing a son, so I began to drink and that escalated to illegal drug use. It was during the time that our communities were saturated with cocaine that escalated to crack, and I succumbed to using it and was imprisoned for that.

For twenty years, I traveled in and out of incarceration because of a drug addiction—really because of medicating the pain, the loss, the grief, and the disappointment of life.[13] And in 1998 I found a place on the west side, in Santa Monica, that gave me treatment for my addiction and counseling for the grief and trauma and early childhood abuse, and I became stronger.[14]

And that led me to look at what happened in that west side of Santa Monica area—how people were not sent to prison for the things that we were sent to prison for in South LA. And I began to think that if women had a safe place to go, if they had a place, that if they would find safety and a welcoming community like I experienced in Santa Monica, then just perhaps they wouldn't go back to prison.

I saved my few little dollars from a minimum-wage job and got a house. And I would begin to greet women at the bus station as they got off the bus and welcome them back to the community and offer them a bed at my home, which I called A New Way of Life.

BRYONN: What was the reaction of women at the bus station when you first approached? Did they expect you to be there?

MS. BURTON: They did not expect me to be there. Some women were cautiously suspicious. Some women were glad to have a place to go and some women declined, so it was a mixture of responses to the offer of a safe place.[15]

BRYONN: What are the challenges women coming home from prison in South LA experience?

MS. BURTON: First of all, every woman that comes back to South LA gets off a bus at the downtown Greyhound bus station on Skid Row, and there are lots of predators waiting for women to step off that bus.[16] You're very vulnerable. You are a woman. We carry certain attributes. Period.

So, people are just so ill prepared to begin their lives without an ID, without a safe place to go. Women have so much around keeping the family together that they carry that burden of motherhood: getting back into the community to make a life, make a way and being vulnerable to relationships that might have been why they were incarcerated in the first place, hailing from the abuse of not only before incarceration but while incarcerated—beginning to understand how to make better choices, safer choices.[17] You know women are much different from men.

BRYONN: So, from the point at which you decided to purchase a home, meeting women coming home from prison, what were some of the major challenges you faced to get A New Way of Life from that point to where it is today?

MS. BURTON: Bryonn, I was so happy to be able to make my life count and be useful. I didn't realize the enormity of the challenges that I was taking on. It was so nice to see women and have that community of sisterhood in the household. I didn't really understand the enormity of the challenges I was facing because we were a community, we were all healing, we were all important to one another and so the outside prejudices and discriminatory practices didn't impact us to get in the way of our healing or our thoughts about what we meant to each other in that community.[18] But going outside of that community and trying to get a job or trying to get a woman's child back, there were serious problems.

And I began to understand that after you do your time, you continue to do time with the level of practices and policies and laws that are in place, and that led me to begin to do some advocacy and policy work to address the discriminatory policies and practices that all people who have been convicted of a crime face.[19]

BRYONN: You say in your book—specifically in the letter that you write to incarcerated men and women—you say there are no "throwaway people" and your life matters. That's a big part of the message you've shared all around the country and internationally—I hear you've been invited to speak from Princeton to Portugal. So when you met [A New Way of Life participant] Ingrid Archie, was that a part of your message? What was that meeting like? And how did that relationship begin?

MS. BURTON: So, I first met Ingrid Archie in 2007 and she was a bright-eyed, bubbly young woman and she had a little girl tagging along behind her, holding her hand. And they came into the home, and I would take her with me to meetings and we would share our story and we began to understand that sharing our story was an important part of getting the message across and our own personal power to voice. And she did well and she moved out and we always had this closeness and the bond and especially with her little daughter.

Unfortunately, in 2015, Ingrid had to return because she ran into a store while she left her daughter in the car—and she was rearrested for child endangerment even though the child was not hurt, and I often wonder: had Ingrid been in another part of town or if she had not been Black, would she have been given services—parenting classes, counseling— instead of three years in prison and labeled a "child endangerer"?[20]

BRYONN: The numbers I've seen show that 75 percent of the women involved with A New Way of Life don't return to prison?

MS. BURTON: For a third of the cost of incarceration, we can house a woman for a year and she's much more functional, she's much more able to provide for herself and her family, she becomes a tax-paying, contrib- uting member of our society.[21] We spend $75,000 a year to incarcerate a woman. And for $16,000, women can be here at A New Way of Life and return to her power—beyond her power—and to being a functional member of our society.[22]

BRYONN: The work you've been doing for decades now has such an impact that I've heard multiple people in completely different situations refer to you as the Harriet Tubman of our time—that says so much. But I know a part of why you're motivated by this work is because of the real lives that you're impacting rather than the glorious claim of that kind of connection. How do you feel when you come across women like Ingrid, other women, and see that because of the work you've been doing, their lives have been so transformed? How does that feel?

MS. BURTON: It feels so powerful to be a person in the midst of being a change agent—leading women to their purpose and leading women to their power and ultimately their freedom. You know, Ingrid is not a throwaway person and her children are not throwaway children, and by Ingrid finding that path, it also empowers her to become an efficient par- ent and lead her children in a way that they'll become great women. Her children are girls.[23] And her fifteen-year-old has an appointment to shadow [State] Senator Holly Mitchell. [Ingrid's] daughter aspires to be an elected official, and we're able to support that and Ingrid is able to facilitate that because of who she is and who she's becoming.[24]

BRYONN: Can we go deeper into the impact of the drug laws? We are living in a time with a lot of changes happening and a lot of challenges at

the federal level. You have this whole tension between the federal government refusing to get rid of prohibition of marijuana, of cannabis,
whereas half of the states in the union from California to Colorado and
so on have decided to decriminalize marijuana.[25] We are looking at it
specifically in the sense that—from Proposition 64[26] to this recent
California voter initiative [the Adult Use of Marijuana Act] last year
[2017]—the issue has come up quite a bit. What are your thoughts on
the impact of the war on drugs, specifically as it relates to women who
have been involved with A New Way of Life? To what extent have drug-
related crimes been a part of their journey?

MS. BURTON: We really are able to understand that we are living in a
country that's divided. There are the people who are liberal and want
equality and fairness, and then there are the people who are bigots and
racists and capitalists. And we're coming out of a time that our communities, urban communities, were under a hell of an attack through the
war on drugs and that those attacks, I believe, just devastated the women
in our communities and drove them in droves, by the thousands, into
prisons across this nation.[27] And now we're realizing what happened
and we're beginning to repair that damage that happened through the
war on drugs.

   While we're having a divided country, a lot of the women who come
into A New Way of Life have had drug convictions and nonviolent
crimes. But there are also the women who come into our communities
and come into our homes that have had crimes that they have been
tagged "violent."[28] I don't see either of those [kinds of] women being different in the way of being able to recover from whatever happened in
their past, and many times these women were defending themselves and
someone got hurt and they got labeled "violent."[29]

   But each one of them have healed and each one of them is capable of
being great members of our society, great parents[30] and contributing
members—and I think that this country, when it makes a distinction
between a person who's been convicted of a "nonviolent" versus a "violent" crime, I think they're making a big mistake because one instant
cannot label a person, one instant cannot label a person "deserving" or
"not deserving," because we really need to check that out and look at that
and understand what we're doing, making a distinction between the

"deserving" and the "undeserving."[31] Again, there are no throwaway people, and we're all able to recover from that instant or from that way of being.

BRYONN: Why do you think politicians—elected officials—are trying to make that distinction so much, in conversations and in how they frame some of the legislative proposals? What do you think is behind them in trying to label "nonviolent" drug-related offenses as something different from folks who have other kinds of offenses?

MS. BURTON: Politicians are not deep investors or risk takers. And right now, in this era of decarceration or mass incarceration—depending on how you look at it—it's safe to say, "Let's help the nonviolent ones." It's not safe to say, "Let's help everybody." You know, somebody always has to get thrown under the bus. And that's just not fair, nor is it the best, most effective approach when we look at cost and long sentences. I had a woman who came to A New Way of Life who had been incarcerated forty-seven years.[32] It doesn't take that to rehabilitate. Forty-seven years.

BRYONN: And you make the point about the cost—obviously the deep cost to our communities, to our families, there's the human cost of it. But it doesn't make sense, even in the logic of these bigoted capitalist folks, who actually are committing these resources you talked about, it is not an effective use of resources. If over 95 percent of the folks in prison are coming home, you'd rather invest in truly rehabilitating and educating, giving folks opportunities—not keeping folks in this system that has never worked for us. So, I'm curious to know if you think that using some of the resources, the taxes that are gonna be taken from the decriminalization of cannabis, toward community programs like legal aid, like drug treatment, addiction treatment, like community gardens and beautification of the community—if that's one effective step toward using those resources in a more responsible way?

MS. BURTON: Here we are in 2018, and on January 1, legalization of marijuana has taken place in California and there's a tax on there that will benefit the community. But I think back to all the people that languished in prisons and were criminalized for this marijuana that's legal now and the pain that we suffered on the back of marijuana being illegal.[33] So, we can't undo the past, but we can step into a future that will help our communities become whole, safer, and resourced.[34]

I think about how people capitalized on the incarceration of folks for marijuana, and now that it's legal we'll get some resources, but who is also capitalizing off the marijuana industry now? Is it the same people who provided services and capitalized off the incarceration of folks? So, I guess we'll take the tax dollars and resources and try to make the most of it in our communities—but these other questions really linger in my mind.

BRYONN: National Public Radio did a story a couple weeks ago about all these major corporations setting up to take advantage of legalization, and [NPR] spotlighted one sister in Oakland who had been in and out of prisons around multiple marijuana charges, and she was having a hard time just getting the license to be someone who could actually benefit from legalization. So as this contradiction happens, it seems like we should be concerned about who is going to make the most of it, who's actually going to benefit from what seems like progress—but we've seen it before.

MS. BURTON: We've seen it before.[35]

BRYONN: And the bait and switch is happening—so I think being cautiously optimistic is a way to approach it.

MS. BURTON: We'll take the tax dollars and try to do the most and the best that we can with them. But I have to interject and say, we know how to make our community safe—we know how to do that. Hopefully these tax dollars will resource us to do that.

BRYONN: The Department of Corrections and Rehabilitation in California—what can it do to effectively incentivize rehabilitation, to support rehabilitation?

MS. BURTON: Ah, the Department of Corrections! When I was imprisoned it was called "Department of Corrections"—then they put "Rehabilitation" on the end of that, but it never did go back and correct its core mission, which is to punish.[36] So, I believe we need to go back and look at that core mission and build out from there—you can't just tag a word on the back of a department and think that it's done. Its core mission is to punish, and it needs to go back there and begin from there to push out its function from its mission.

BRYONN: I know we can't wait for any department to do the work we need to do. That's why I am so honored to know you and to have the opportunity to share this time with you. Thank you.

MS. BURTON: Well, I am just one person . . . and I can't do this work alone. You are in the community and working in the prisons and on the campus too. So, I thank you.

·   ·   ·   ·   ·

As our conversation ended, Ms. Burton's day was just beginning—with a host of meetings and community events to come. While her hectic schedule highlights the transformative organizing underway to bring an end to mass incarceration, it also speaks volumes to an undeniable factor worth noting: Ms. Burton's unyielding commitment to advocating for women and families.

Ms. Burton is a true change agent and has the results to prove it. Seventy-five percent of all women residents of A New Way of Life do not return to prison for at least eighteen months.[37] The women go on to serve in their communities, find fulfilling work, and build meaningful relationships with their families and communities. In meetings with California legislators and at campus lectures, at community gatherings from Watts to Washington, DC, and around world, Susan Burton shares the same message: "There are no throwaway people; everyone's life matters." She believes her work is to lead women to their power, their purpose, and, ultimately, their freedom. And it is that steadfast leadership and commitment to others' liberation that continues to draw on comparisons to the legendary Harriet Tubman.

In an 1886 interview, Tubman declared, "There was one of two things I had a right to: liberty, or death. If I could not have one, I would have the other. . . . I should fight for my liberty as long as my strength lasted."[38] And today, more than 130 years later, Susan Burton carries the torch with the same fire and unyielding power as that legendary architect of the Underground Railroad who laid the foundation for the railroad Ms. Burton continues to forge today.

LINER NOTES

Track #3's interview took place on February 12, 2018, at A New Way of Life Reentry Project, South Central Los Angeles. It was originally published as "Twenty-First-Century Harriet Tubman: An Interview with Susan Burton," *Harvard BlackLetter Law Journal* 35 (Spring 2019): 27–38, and in the *Prison Service Journal*, UK.

1. Breeanna Hare and Lisa Rose, "Pop. 17,049: Welcome to America's Largest Jail," CNN, September 26, 2016, www.cnn.com/2016/09/22/us/lisa-ling-this-is-life-la-county-jail-by-the-numbers/index.html.

2. For ranking UCLA the number-one public national university in the United States, see "Top Public Schools: National Universities," *US News and World Report*, 2021, www.usnews.com/best-colleges/rankings/national-universities/top-public.

3. Shawanna Vaughn, "Post-Traumatic Prison Disorder," paper presented at a California State University PTPD conference, Bakersfield, May 5, 2019.

4. For an inspection of the Metropolitan Detention Center in Brooklyn, New York, by Judge Analisa Torres, see Transcript of Evidentiary Hearing at 165–89, United States v. Segura-Genao, No. J257 (Southern District NY February 5, 2019).

5. Michelle Alexander, "What I Learned from Susan Burton, a Modern-Day Harriet Tubman," *The Nation*, May 11, 2017, www.thenation.com/article/what-i-learned-from-susan-burton-a-modern-day harriet-tubman.

6. "What We Do," A New Way of Life Reentry Project, June 6, 2019, http://anewwayoflife.org/what-we-do.

7. For example, see Marian Wright Edelman, "Changing Our Racial Narrative," *Huffington Post*, December 6, 2017, www.huffpost.com/entry/changing-our-racial-narra_b_1135 4146.

8. Susan Burton and Cari Lynn, *Becoming Ms. Burton: From Prison to Recovery to Leading the Fight for Incarcerated Women* (New York: New Press, 2017).

9. Kathleen Toner, "'Magic Happened' after She Gave Ex-cons a Chance at New Lives," CNN, February 19, 2010, www.cnn.com/2010/CRIME/02/18/cnnheroes .burton.

10. Abolitionist critiques of marginal reforms support "nonreformative reform" led by Black women activists, such as Ruth Wilson Gilmore: "Overall, reforms have not significantly reduced incarceration numbers, and no recent reform legislation has even aspired to do so." Rachel Kushner, "Is Prison Necessary? Ruth Wilson Gilmore Might Change Your Mind," *New York Times Magazine*, April 17, 2019, www.nytimes .com/2019/04/17/magazine/prison-abolition-ruth-wilson-gilmore.html.

11. Liz Button, "*Becoming Ms. Burton* Publisher Encourages Booksellers to Join Prison Distribution Initiative," American Booksellers Association, January 30, 2018, www.bookweb.org/news/%E2%80%9Cbecoming-ms-burton%E2%80% 9D-publisher-encourages-booksellers-join-prison-distribution-initiative.

12. "Unarmed blacks are killed by the police at five times the rate of unarmed whites . . . one in three blacks killed by police were identified as unarmed." Burton and Lynn, *Becoming Ms. Burton*, 239. In 2015, police killed at least 102 unarmed Black people, nearly 2 weekly. Of these, only 10 deaths resulted in charges and only 2 saw convictions. One officer was sentenced to jail for one year but allowed to serve his time exclusively on weekends. Jon Swaine, Oliver Laughland, and Jamiles Lartey, "Black Americans Killed by Police Twice as Likely to Be Unarmed," *The Guardian*, June 1, 2015, www.theguardian.com/us-news/2015/jun/01 /black-americans-killed-by-police-analysis.

13. With 2.2 million people behind bars, the US imprisons more "than any other country in the world." Burton and Lynn, *Becoming Ms. Burton*, 2.

14. More than 60 percent of incarcerated women report being "sexually assaulted before the age of eighteen." Burton and Lynn, *Becoming Ms. Burton*, 41. "As many as 94 percent of incarcerated women were victims of physical or sexual abuse." Ibid., 93.

15. In large urban areas such as LA and San Francisco, up to "half of those on parole are homeless." Burton and Lynn, *Becoming Ms. Burton*, 117. "Nearly 80 percent of formerly incarcerated women are unable to afford housing after release. Like no other country, most US public housing authorities automatically deny eligibility to anyone with a criminal record." Ibid., 209.

16. Language matters. The Center for NuLeadership on Human Justice and Healing (formerly the Center for NuLeadership on Urban Solutions) and the University of California Underground Scholars Initiative are organizations committed to using more humanizing language. Many on Skid Row are housing-insecure and formerly or recently released from prison. We are in a constant dialogue about ways to reframe how we talk about system-impacted people and to acknowledge and communicate our diverse issues. The use of the word *predators* is an example of this discourse. See, for example, Eddie Ellis, "An Open Letter to Our Friends on the Question of Language," Center for NuLeadership on Urban Solutions, accessed June 6, 2019, https://cmjcenter.org/wp-content/uploads /2017/07/CNUS-AppropriateLanguage.pdf.

17. "The majority of incarcerated women are mothers of underage children. Over 40 percent of these mothers, report that, upon incarceration, they were the only parent in the household." Burton and Lynn, *Becoming Ms. Burton*, 53.

18. "Black women comprise 40 percent of street prostitutes, though 55 percent of women arrested for prostitution are black, and 85 percent of women incarcerated for prostitution are black. Two-thirds of those working as prostitutes disclosed having been sexually abused as children . . . over 90 percent said they never told anyone." Burton and Lynn, *Becoming Ms. Burton*, 39.

19. "Every year in L.A. County, 45,600 people are released on parole. A survey revealed that over 40 percent of L.A. employers would not hire a person with a criminal record." Burton and Lynn, *Becoming Ms. Burton*, 39. "In the US, one in

three adults has a criminal record—though black men are six times more likely than white men to be incarcerated. Over 60 percent of the formerly incarcerated will still be unemployed a year after release. Those who do find employment are typically in low-level jobs, earning 40 percent less pay than adults with no criminal background." Ibid., 174.

20. "The California Department of Corrections and Rehabilitation has one of the highest recidivism rates in the country, with nearly half of women with a felony conviction returning to prison—and a 61 percent recidivism rate overall. The majority of people returned to prison within the first year of release." Burton and Lynn, *Becoming Ms. Burton*, 196. "Black women represent 30 percent of all incarcerated women in the United States, although they represent less than 7 percent of the country's population." Ibid., 213.

21. Ms. Burton and ANWOL maintain that "every person has inherent value and holds the power of possibility within." A New Way of Life Reentry Project, accessed April 20, 2019, http://anewwayoflife.org. However, "tax-paying, contributing member of society" could imply a person's value is based on their financial contribution to a society, rather than being valuable unequivocally, whether or not they add value to the capitalist market. Ms. Burton's invaluable work is deserving of our utmost respsect, and her choice of words is included here as stated. It is also clear that Ms. Burton's critical role as a grassroots leader requires her to regularly respond to conservative, financially focused critics of decarceration. My vision for justice movement work aims to center the voice of those who are system-impacted and the work we must do in solidarity.

22. "Most states end the right to vote for anyone convicted of a felony until their sentence plus parole or probation end. Voting rights may be permanently revoked in ten states. . . . Only Maine and Vermont allow voting inside." Burton and Lynn, *Becoming Ms. Burton*, 227.

23. "Most women are behind bars for social or victimless crimes—while the real victims, which the flawed system perpetuates, are the children. Since 1991, the number of children under age eighteen with a mother in prison has more than doubled. Ten million children have or have had a parent in prison." Burton and Lynn, *Becoming Ms. Burton*, 161.

24. "How Ingrid Archie Is Empowering Formerly Incarcerated Women with A New Way of Life," *Kismet Magazine*, 2020, https://kismetmag.co/blog/how-ingrid-archie-is-empowering-formerly-incarcerated-women-with-a-new-way-of-life.

25. Recreational use of cannabis is legalized in eighteen states, the District of Columbia, the Northern Mariana Islands, and Guam; another thirteen states and the US Virgin Islands have decriminalized its use. Commercial distribution of cannabis has been legalized in all jurisdictions where possession has been legalized, except the District of Columbia. Michael Hartman, "Cannabis Overview," National Conference of State Legislatures, July 6, 2021, www.ncsl.org/research/civil-and-

criminal-justice/marijuana-overview.aspx. Medical use of cannabis is legal, with a doctor's recommendation, in thirty-six states, four US territories, and the District of Columbia. "State Medical Marijuana Laws," National Conference of State Legislatures, August 23, 2021, www.ncsl.org/research/health/state-medical-marijuana-laws.aspx.

26. On November 9, 2016, California Proposition 64 legalized personal use and cultivation of marijuana for adults twenty-one and older, reduced criminal penalties for specific marijuana-related offenses for adults and juveniles, and authorized resentencing or dismissal and sealing of prior eligible marijuana-related convictions. It includes provisions on regulation, licensing, and taxation of legalized use. "Proposition 64: The Adult Use of Marijuana Act," California Courts: The Judicial Branch of California, updated June 2021, www.courts.ca.gov /prop64.htm.

27. "The majority of offenses committed by women are nonviolent drug and property crimes, motivated by poverty and addiction. Most incarcerated women are under thirty years old, disproportionately low-income, black, and didn't complete high school. The probability of prison for white women is 1 in 118; for black women, 1 in 19." Burton and Lynn, *Becoming Ms. Burton*, 147.

28. "Ninety percent of women imprisoned for killing someone close to them were abused by that person." Burton and Lynn, *Becoming Ms. Burton*, 202.

29. As many "as 94 percent of incarcerated women were victims of physical or sexual abuse." Burton and Lynn, *Becoming Ms. Burton*, 93. "Being abused or neglected as a child increases the likelihood of arrest as a juvenile by nearly 60 percent, and the likelihood of adult violent crime by approximately 30 percent." Ibid., 111.

30. "More than 75 percent of incarcerated women had at least one child as a teenager." Burton and Lynn, *Becoming Ms. Burton*, 29.

31. "Sixty-five million Americans with a criminal record face a total of 45,000 collateral consequences that restrict everything from employment, professional licensing, child custody rights, housing, student aid, voting, and even the ability to visit an incarcerated loved one," and according to American Bar Association President William C. Hubbard, "These collateral consequences become a life sentence harsher than whatever sentence a court imposed." Burton and Lynn, *Becoming Ms. Burton*, 132.

32. "Women commit far fewer murders than men, but receive far longer sentences. A woman who kills a male partner receives, on average, a 15-year sentence . . . a man who kills a female partner typically receives 2–6." Burton and Lynn, *Becoming Ms. Burton*, 187.

33. Drug use and sales occur at similar rates across racial groups: "Substance Abuse and the American Woman," Pew Charitable Trusts and Bristol-Meyers Squibb Foundation, June 1996, https://citeseerx.ist.psu.edu/viewdoc/download? doi=10.1.1.196.5627&rep=rep1&type=pdf. However, Black and Latina women

are more likely to be incarcerated for drug crimes: Black women are "more than twice as likely as white women." Burton and Lynn, *Becoming Ms. Burton*, 100.

34. "Only around 15 percent of those serving time for a drug-related offense are given access to a drug treatment program with a trained professional." Burton and Lynn, *Becoming Ms. Burton*, 86.

35. Due to the crack epidemic and the "harsh, racially discriminatory policies of the Anti–Drug Abuse Act, one in three black men will see the inside of a jail cell." Burton and Lynn, *Becoming Ms. Burton*, 213.

36. For two decades, states with the toughest crime laws saw the largest spikes in prison population; California's three strikes law, "one of the harshest," sent people to prison for life for offenses such as "petty theft." Burton and Lynn, *Becoming Ms. Burton*, 81.

37. Toner, "'Magic Happened.'"

38. Sarah Hopkins Bradford originally published *Scenes in the Life of Harriet Tubman* (1869), which she revised at Tubman's request (who hoped its sales would raise enough funds for the building of a hospital for elderly and disabled Black people) as *Harriet, the Moses of Her People* (New York: G. R. Lockwood and Son, 1886; repub., Chapel Hill: A DocSouth Book, distributed for University of North Carolina at Chapel Hill Library, 2012), 41, accessed August 22, 2021, https://uncpress.org/book/9781469607818/harriet-the-moses-of-her-people.

TRACK #4
CRITICAL JUSTICE

LANI G. + GEN BLM

#4 Critical Justice

MASS INCARCERATION, MENTAL
HEALTH, AND TRAUMA

After decades of struggles shattering glass ceilings and breaking up old boys' networks, Lani Guinier became the first woman of color to serve as a tenured professor at Harvard Law School (HLS). As groundbreaking an achievement as that was, for me she became so much more. When I entered law school in 1998, the same year "LG" (as I would afffectionately call her years later) joined the faculty in Cambridge, Massachusetts, I never dreamed that twenty years later she would become not only my teacher and mentor but ultimately a longtime collaborator and dear friend. Never a fan of the static title *role model*, Lani believed nonetheless in the invaluable role of mentors. For all her visionary mentorship, she never hesitated to recognize that she too stood on the shoulders of the critical and rebellious visionaries who came before her.

Before meeting Lani, I met critical race studies pioneer and legal scholar Derek Bell[1] when he advised me to accept the offer of admission I received from the nation's oldest law school—over other enticing offers to half a dozen of the other leading schools in the country. This was noteworthy because he famously quit his job teaching there in protest because HLS failed to hire a woman of color to a tenured professorship in their 181-year history. That was before Lani. It was Bell's sacrifice, along with countless others supporting the movement to desegregate the faculty of the nation's oldest and most elite law school, that laid the foundation for Lani's last gig before her retirement—and to our very first meeting.

I got into her course Critical Perspectives on the Law: Gender, Class, and Race by the skin of my teeth. As the first person in my family to attend law school, I was out of the loop on the ins and outs of securing a spot in the most popular classes. I missed the deadline for the formal paperwork that students were supposed to submit to get into her seminar. None the wiser, I showed up anyway. The only guy in a class of twenty-six, I would also be pushing the class past its mandated cap. Lani asked me to leave the room, and after a rigorous debate, the other students voted to allow me into the class. I learned years later that the votes were divided along racial lines. All of the white students voted against me. All of the Black students voted to keep me in the class. Several Black women even offered to take turns remaining silent for entire class meetings—if it made the white women feel as if I would cost them too much of their coveted time with the world's top voting rights expert. As absurd as it was that such an offer had to be made, that vote, those visionary Black women, and the process Lani orchestrated changed my life forever.

While home in New York City one weekend in the middle of the term, I was racially profiled by the NYPD and unjustly jailed with my brother and my cousin. The following week, Professor Guinier asked the class to write a reflection essay on "an experience of injustice," which led me to write the story that was later a cover story published by the *Village Voice* called "Walking While Black," which went viral, setting a record by receiving more than 100,000 responses. It also landed me on *60 Minutes* telling my story to Emmy Award-winning journalist Mike Wallace to more than twenty million households. Lani's invaluable edits and notes on that piece undoubtedly contributed to its rhetorical and analytical nuances, broad resonance, and widespread impact. The story of that 1999 incident has been a defining experience in my personal and political development and in my professional work.

The following year, 1999, Lani asked me to return the favor (as if I could ever) by reviewing the unpublished manuscript of her soon-to-be-published book, *The Miner's Canary: Enlisting Race, Resisting Power, Transforming Democracy.* Written in collaboration with her longtime friend, colleague, Chicano legal scholar, and Yale Law School professor Gerald Torres,[2] even the *process* through which the book was created reflected the virtues of multiracial coalition-building and solidarity advocated and urged by the *product* itself. Guinier's and Torres's critical analysis of the *gross* investment in prisons by states like New York,[3] as compared to their shameful relative underinvestment in public schools, stands out two decades later as a tragedy we continue to relive like Groundhog Day even now. We shared this revealing information in prisons, at performances venues, in public schools, and at community spaces. It was evidence that the criminal justice system is not broken but is in fact in dire need of not only disruption but also of radical reimagining and rebuilding.

Guinier's allegorical use of the canary in the coal mine, as a frame for critical race, gender, and class analysis, had a lasting effect on me.[4] If the canary's fragile respiratory system suffered from toxins in the mine long before any human lungs began to experience negative effects, we should see the bird's vulnerability as a call to action for us all to do more than give it a little gas mask. Unlike political reforms that are mere "gas mask"—styled fixes that serve only to maintain oppressive, toxic systems, we need to completely change the air in the mine. By focusing on the needs of the most vulnerable, we have the capacity to build a healthier world in which we live and breathe humanely.[5] I understood the metaphorical "mine" as analogous to America and the toxic systems in it. It was obvious that among "the vulnerable"—the canaries—were women, people of color, the working class, the poor, the queer, and those incarcerated, formerly incarcerated, and system impacted. What I failed to see was that Lani was also speaking so prophetically about herself and others who ultimately struggle with mental health challenges.

Named after Alois Alzheimer (1864–1915), the German neurologist credited with identifying the disease, Alzheimer's is a progressive mental deterioration that often occurs in middle age or later in life, due to a general deterioration of the brain,[6] and is largely underdiagnosed and underreported. Studies show that mild cognitive impairment (MCI) may remain unrecognized in up to 80 percent of affected patients in primary care.[7] Given the devastating effects and lingering historical impact of medical exploitation on marginalized communities,[8] the reluctance of communities of color—especially Black folks in the United States—to engage mental health institutions that have never effectively met, or intended to meet, our needs, the challenges facing women of color wrestling with mental health ailments is exponentially compounded. For the population at large, there is already a "reluctance of patients and care partners to report signs or symptoms due to stigma" around the disease and a vastly disproportionate lack of diagnostic resources to which we generally have access.[9]

At Lani's retirement gathering on a February morning in an old Radcliffe building, her son Niko, with insight beyond any I had to offer, spoke to the village convening to honor his mother by saying, "This disease takes away the two things my mother's made her life with—her memory and her family."[10] Memory and family. And not a second passed after he spoke this truth before I thought, Those are two words anyone who spends anywhere from a day to a decade in a jail cell can't help but wrestle with for countless hours while inside—from the memories of what led to our incarceration and specific moments that could have altered the course our lives took in immeasurable ways to the family we find ourselves pulled far away from and increasingly out of touch with in all but the rarest of situations, given the challenges of maintaining the familial bonds necessary to survive inside and after release.

Yet this mental affliction—without the barbed wire gates and iron bars, without the towers in the sky manned by guards holding military-grade weapons, without the physical violence and inhumane isolation of solitary confinement in a six-by-nine cell—this condition that chose my brilliant and beloved mentor as its host aggressively began eroding these critical aspects of her life and world. If we were the proverbial canaries in the mine before, how much more did this ailment place her at the very center of her own analysis twenty years later? Given the exponential increase of people facing mental health challenges in American prisons, how much more traumatic is that experience of loss for those who are grappling with the dual crisis of mass incarceration and mental illness—under systems very intentionally designed to break our bodies and our minds?

These are among the experiences and issues I brought with me to a dialogue ("Critical Justice") I facilitated, joined by national experts and leaders of community-based justice movements, on May 24, 2018, as part of the annual We Rise Conference in Los Angeles. This conference is part of the Mental Health Awareness Month initiative of the Los Angeles

County Department of Mental Health, whose ongoing Why We Rise campaign is funded by Proposition 63 and a range of invaluable sponsors. Special thanks are due to each of these contributors, and particularly to Yosi Sergant of TaskForce, for this dialogue.

Mental illness was not the only concern we examined in this dialogue. Our dynamic discussion interrogated a diverse range of problems at the heart of the prison crisis. However, as I have learned from the challenges my mentor is facing in her ongoing battle with Alzheimer's (and now COVID-19), the impact of mental health challenges on individuals, families, and communities shares much in common with the trauma endured by those systematically dehumanized by America's *criminal* justice system. This trauma personally affected the four system-impacted activists I engaged in the critical conversation on justice that follows.

The comrades who joined me included living movement legends. Melina Abdullah is a founder of Black Lives Matter LA and chair of the Pan-African Studies Department at California State University, Los Angeles. Joel Aguilar is a formerly incarcerated program manager for Mass Liberation and a member of ARC's (Anti-Recidivism Coalition) leadership. Topeka K. Sam is the formerly incarcerated founder and executive director of the Ladies of Hope Ministries. Shaka Senghor is the best-selling author of *Writing My Wrongs*, a formerly incarcerated movement leader and former executive director of ARC.

.   .   .   .   .

BRYONN BAIN: We're here to talk about the impact of incarceration on our families. And I want to jump right in. You know, as a parent and as someone who just this morning—like, I spend several mornings every week at the juvenile hall in Sylmar [LA's northernmost neighborhood] at BJN [Barry J. Nidorf Juvenile Hall], where recently they had a young brother who was nine years old who was incarcerated at the facility. And it was devastating to realize that our babies are taken at that early age. So I want to ask each of my brothers and sisters here to tell us what, in your opinion, are the consequences that children face when they're caged behind bars. What are the consequences that the youngest of the young face when they experience incarceration?

JOEL AGUILAR: The cycle of trauma continues. I grew up a couple of miles away from here on the southwest area of Los Angeles. And you know, it's different. It's something normal to us. But it can be negative and destructive to the rest of America. So, you go to sleep hearing gunshots, helicopters. And if you want to make things worse, you know, if your parents are dealing with addiction, then maybe they cannot wake up to dress you, to feed you, to go to school. And if you want to make things a little bit grimmer. . . . What if they're addicted to crack? What if through their pregnancy, they used crack? And what do you have now? A crack baby? So it's very difficult—like, dehumanization begins from the very conception. And it just continues. It continues in the neighborhood. It continues in school. It continues in prison or in juvenile hall to prison.

MELINA ABDULLAH: I hesitate on this question because it's such an appalling question, right? What's the effect of incarceration on our children? The response that the city gives to our children—and we want to be real clear we're talking specifically about Black and Brown children and poor children who are targeted for incarceration. The notion that they can see them as something other than children is appalling. And it's shocking when you ask them.[11] And then I started to think, because before anything, I'm a mother, right? And I have three children. I have a daughter who's fourteen, another daughter that's eleven, and a son that's eight. And just kind of processing the question, I thought about the fact that two of my three children have already been targeted for criminalization.[12] Now I'm a college professor. I grew up in the 'hood. . . . But they have resources that many of our children don't have. My eleven-year-old daughter was seven years old the first time the police were called on her in school. And they came. The principal told me if I didn't beat the police there, they were going to take her into custody for bringing vitamin C to campus because they have a zero tolerance policy, right?[13] . . . right before the end of first grade, we got a visit to my house from the gang unit for my first-grade son, right? So when we talk about what's happening to our children . . . I think that there was a report that came out at the beginning of this year by the Economic Policy Institute. And it looked at comparatively where we are as Black people now in 2018 as opposed to where we were in 1968. It found that by every measure, we're worse off now than we were in 1968.[14] If anybody knows anything about the Economic Policy Institute, it is not a radical think tank, right?

The conclusion they reached is that the reason we're worse off is because of this society's failure. I'll say it's worse than that. It's a refusal to directly address racism. . . . What we're experiencing is what we've been experiencing since the moment we were stolen from Africa, since the moment we were told that we were chattel. They tried to create us into these dehumanized beings instead of people, right? They're treating our children exactly the way that they treated them when we were enslaved. And so this is why they can take our children and lock them in cages, take our children and treat them like they're not people. And I think that that's why we're appalled because we've been told that we've been done with slavery, right? But not really.

BRYONN: What is the impact not only on our young people, but on the families of these young people? The parents, the brothers and sisters? How are the folks who are experiencing incarceration by losing their child to the system for the period of time that they're incarcerated? What's *that* impact? What's *that* effect?

SHAKA SENGHOR: So when you ask that question, the first thing that came to mind was Khalif Browder. That's what prison does to kids.

BRYONN: Can you explain for folks who aren't familiar with his case?

SHAKA: So Khalif Browder was a young man in New York who was arrested for a crime he didn't commit. At age fifteen, he was incarcerated on Rikers Island, where he remained for three years, two of which was in solitary confinement. The crushing weight and reality of solitary confinement damaged him to such a point that when he got released, he ended up committing suicide.[15] The reality is, when kids go into that environment, the trauma is so penetrating and so deep that they'd never come out the same. I'm very fortunate to work in a space that allows us to actually go inside and work with these young men and women to ensure that they're not broken beyond repair. But this is what our system does to young people. And the impact it has on families is devastating. I was a producer on a show called *Released*, which some of you guys may have seen. And it showed the other side of coming home. It showed the other side of the impact of incarceration that it has on families and how devastating it is to try to go see your loved one when you can't afford to. To try to take those phone calls that oftentimes cost more than mortgages, cost more than rent. To try to go see your loved one in prisons so far from home that they might as well be in another country.

This is what we do to people in this country. In Germany, where I went and studied their prison system, they're very intentional about ensuring that if you happen to be incarcerated, you maintain a relationship with your family and your loved ones. It's part of their constitution, because they recognize the men and women who want to follow the law as their fellow citizens. In this country we recognize them as those people over there. And that's problematic.

BRYONN: Thank you, Shaka. Topeka?

TOPEKA SAM: I think the only thing that I would add is, when I think about young people, when I think about youth incarceration, I think about our young girls. And I think about how, you know, 86 percent of women who are incarcerated are women who suffered sexual trauma, abuse, or violence.[16] And that's reported, right? Because some people don't talk about the trauma that they've experienced, so I think about that woman who was a young girl. And when young girls are abused and victimized and criminalized and how they're ripped out of schools and put in prisons or baby jails. And I think about how Black women and women of color are always looked at as criminal just because of the color of our skin. And it's just such a heavy question. I think that's why I kind of waited, you know, because our girls turn into women. And then when women end up in prison, they end up in relationships that have them suffering. You know our sisters are dying in prison based on just the systems and these abuses and just the decades of trauma. So I just want to lift up all of our young girls and our women that's in this space. Just like the young sisters who came on just a moment ago, we have to love each other. We have to recognize beauty in each other. And when we see each other struggling, we have to be there to lift each other up.

BRYONN: There is somewhat of a taboo, especially with Black folks and talking about mental health, in some circles, right? There's a lot of folks who don't like to talk about mental health issues. And it's so critical that we do talk about it because it's something that so many of us are facing on a daily basis. One thing I have said before, but hasn't been said nearly enough: more people in this country are struggling with mental health challenges in prisons than in mental health institutions.[17] And over the last several decades, we have seen nationwide the closing of mental health facilities because of the unspeakable abuses in these institutions around the country. We've also seen the unprecedented expansion of the prison industrial complex.[18] Neither one of these is an acceptable way to deal with the mental health issues we're facing in our communities, even as we see the criminalization of those with mental ailments in our communities. Why has this happened? What strategies should we be pursuing to address this crisis?

MELINA: It's happened because we've allowed it to happen. It's happened because we've given people power or submitted to their power. We've given the folks power who were invested in creating these conditions, right? So here in Los Angeles, 53 percent of the city's general fund goes to LAPD directly, right? But then there's more than that, because there's money that's hidden. So yesterday, every week we go to the police commission meeting. . . . We, just as voters, as Angelenos, voted for these funds to address homelessness. Do you know where the city directed those funds? To LAPD, because LAPD is seen by this city's governance as the front line for everything, right? LAPD for the city and the jails for the county, right? They're proposing to spend three and a half billion dollars on a new jail in Los Angeles.

We already know the LA county jail system is the largest mental health provider. Not that jails can provide mental health [care treatment] because we know that folks who go into jails and prisons with mental health conditions have those conditions exacerbated when they're on the inside because they're traumatized. And that's what brother Shaka was talking about that happened with Khalif, but you also see it in the Central Park 5.[19] When you talk to them, when you see them, you know that these conditions have been exacerbated. So we have allowed our so-called leaders to prioritize things in a way that works for the few. Jails, prisons, police work for the few. The rest of us, especially if you're seen as not quite human, if you're black, if you're brown, if you're poor, if you're houseless, if you suffer from mental health challenges, are seen as kind of food for that system. So we have a choice to claim power. We have a choice to say we are the leaders we've been waiting for.

We have the capacity to shift things . . . I hope that you have all been signing the Reform LA County Jails petition. We're saying we want to divest from jails.[20] We want to invest in real mental health services. We want to invest in rehabilitative services. We want to invest in the answer to homelessness. Not more police on the streets. House keys, not handcuffs, right? And so we have to commit ourselves to fighting against the very same system that evolved from what you opened with. This country is based on genocide and the stealing of Indigenous land and unpaid Black labor and the dehumanization of Black people, right? That's what's evolved. That's what's in power. We can see it in DC like we can see nowhere else, right? So what is our response? What is the new antislavery movement? The new antilynching movement? The new Black Power movement? The new Chicano power movement? What does that look like? And what are we committed to do to make sure that we tackle this kind of system once and for all?

BRYONN: I've had a chance to do some work at the California Institute for Women, CIW, the oldest prison for women, still working, still functioning in California. And 90 percent of the women incarcerated there have experienced some form of abuse, intimate partner violence, domestic violence, often at the hands of a man who they retaliated against. And I know at least one or two of the students who were in my classes are here tonight, and I want to give it up for them for making it out and being here—Wendy Staggs . . . on the crew here tonight for We Rise. . . . Part of what's happened [at CIW] also is that they have the highest suicide rate in the country—five times the national average and eight times the state average.[21] So, what has been your experience in coming into contact with mental health issues with the women you work with? And what are some strategies that your organization has been pursuing?

TOPEKA: When I think about my direct experiences when I was incarcerated, I think about the women, or the women that I would see, people who've been incarcerated. You all know about pill line, right?[22] And I remember just hearing the pill line call and seeing probably more than

50 percent of the women who were in places that I was going to line up for a pill. And I remember not really understanding what that looked like and why, right? It was like, "Okay, why is everybody going to get something just to take themselves out of a situation that they just come from?" And I will continue to ask these questions. And then I started to find out that people were just being medicated. And they were being pushed into a different level of addiction. And then they will go out. And then they would be looking for the same things that they were on. And then they would be having to cope and substitute that with the same drugs that they were addicted to before they went in. And then it will be . . . you know, they couldn't get jobs because of the criminal conviction. They couldn't get housing because of all these barriers. And then it would be back to just what they knew that landed them back in prison.

And so the work that I do specifically at the Ladies of Hope Ministries, we help women through education, entrepreneurship, advocacy, and spiritual empowerment. And when I think about mental health, and I know you had said earlier we don't talk about it, and in a lot of our communities, specifically in communities of color, a lot of times . . . I know even when I think of traumas and things that I had been through, it was like we talked about it internally. Then you don't talk about it again, and you pray. And that's the way they were supposed to handle things. And you know, I am a firm believer in prayer. And prayer does change things. But I also know through my experience that if I had gone to someone, to a specialist, and talked through some of the issues that I had been through in my life as it related to relationships and things, that I had been in abusive relationships . . . the cycle of abuse that I found myself in wouldn't have landed me through all of the victimizations and things that I had in my own life. And so I tried to help women and really giving them these assets so they can tap into their spiritual self. And once they really understanding what that looks like, then also tap them into different services, whether it is speaking to a social worker that actually is faith-based. And it doesn't matter to me who you're connected to. I know for my journey that I connect with God. And that's what got me through. If a person is able to connect to whatever higher power that also helps them through different treatments, and that can also give them a level of accountability. That's a lot of the stuff we do.

BRYONN: Joel and Shaka, you both spent time behind the walls and have come home as activists, as leaders in this movement. I really want to get your sense of what are the resources and services that are available to folks when they come home? What was your experience of mental health issues inside? What you experienced firsthand and then coming home? What are the greatest resources and the greatest gaps in resources for folks when they come home?

JOEL: I think that's something that's not being said. You know, there's an emotional and spiritual aspect to this as well. And that comes through volunteers. Like in prison, for example, we get help because volunteers come. And they spend time and that's something that's very essential for a person to be humanized, to be heard, to be seen. And this is what we do out here with ARC as well. It's like a family. It is the human contact. It is to be present. And I think that we need that. I think that's very essential.

Look, I think you know there's a psychological factor to this. There's also biological, if there's genetic, I don't know. But there's also societal factors. And I think that we as a community, we need to be involved. And we need to spend time, quick numbers by this, by the age of eighteen. Once you turn eighteen, you spent 158 [thousand] hours on earth. 158. So, if you go to school every day, 180 days for six days a week [including Sabbath and Sunday Schools], the number totals 13,000 hours. When you combine that . . . just think about that, that's 9 percent of time that you're under the leverage or under the influence of education of a school. Now the other 91 percent, who's influencing you? And when you add, you know, like I said, the negative, the destructive, the destruction in our neighborhoods, in our homes. I mean, who's influencing our children? 91 percent. I was amazed. But that's what exactly . . . that's my life. That's what led me to this criminal lifestyle that led me to prison. And in there, it was a shift. Something happened because people took interest groups, process groups. For example, the chapel, spirituality. And I think that's the element that we're missing. A lot of our mental health brothers in prison are neglected. . . . But if you offer them coffee, a piece of bread, all of a sudden they just kind of react. And they're responsive. When I was a kid, I used to model my father because I looked up to him. And I think that, as humans, we model each other in the same way.

BRYONN: Thank you. Shaka?

SHAKA: I spent a total of nineteen years in prison, seven of those years in solitary confinement. What I witnessed in solitary confinement was unimaginable: the intentional breaking and destroying of the human mind. I watched man after man lose their mental faculties up under the strict watch of the state. To me it's one of America's blind spots. As a country we've fallen asleep at the wheel. And we've allowed a level of suffering, dehumanization, degradation of our fellow citizens, our brothers, our sisters, our mothers, our cousins; our loved ones are suffering.

Anytime that you lock a human being in the cell for twenty-three hours a day, for extended periods of time, that's intentional torture.[23] They say that the majority of people begin to lose their mind within the first ninety days of being in solitary confinement. I've watched that happen in the first ninety hours, because a lot of these men that I was around, they had already suffered adverse childhood experiences [aka ACEs] early in their childhood. Most of us went to prison with PTSD and came out with compounded PTSD, because we never got treated for the things that we deal with in our community. To be black, to be brown, to be poor and white in America is to have a mental illness, is to be afflicted by the trauma that you see around you and your everyday interactions as a human being. You can't exist in this country when you fall under one of those *otherings*. It's not healthy that, when you drive [and] you see police, you automatic shrink as a human being. That impacts you psychologically. It's not okay when you were a child, you experienced the first murder before you experienced the first graduation. That's mental trauma.

We expect our children to see life through a lens that oftentimes isn't that clear. For people who have never been traumatized, who have never been around gun violence, who have never been around police brutality, they're seeing the world through these crystal-clear lenses. For our kids, who the first time they were struck and saw that it was done out of love even though it was hurtful and it was harmful, they begin to see that life from that point forward through those same glasses that have been dipped in the mud of abuse, harm, and hurt. From that point forward, you can't see life clearly. And so what's happening in our prisons in what

we're seeing is the normalization of the abnormal. We don't think nothing about a human being trapped in solitary confinement for seven years.
Sometime our first response is, "What did he do?" [But] what did the
system actually do? You know, when we see our children being dragged
out of classrooms, and we're justifying that as adults, that's mental illness. When . . . a person being shot in the back in this country, and our
first reaction is, "What if he just didn't resist?" that's our collective mental illness. In a way that it shows up is the normalization of this idea that
we will turn in and out of prison.

I'm fortunate to work with amazing human beings. We have thera-
pists, because we realize that you can't go through that traumatic experience and walk the path of freedom alone. We have life coaches, because
we know that we all need a little bit of help to get to that next level. But
more importantly, we have a common sense of community. So when I
look at this brother, we can communicate without even talking. When I
look at this sister who has been through some of the most harmful,
degrading experiences, and we have an understanding that you just don't
have if you've never walked in our shoes, that's a model that should be
replicated in every community throughout this country. In order for that
to happen, we have to be honest about what we're intentionally doing to
the people in this country. It is not okay to lock kids up for the rest of
their lives. It's not okay to lock people in cages for hours upon hours
upon hours when, if you did that to an animal, if you did that to a little
Sparky, you put little Sparky's ass in the cage for seven days straight,
twenty-three hours [a day], without letting him out, PETA [People for
the Ethical Treatment of Animals] will be at your door! But you can do it
to Sam. You can do it to Samantha. You can do it to Terrence. You can do
it to Shaka. Until we change that reality, we will always be dealing with
these issues.

BRYONN: Shaka touched on this eloquently. And I want to put it out
there to everyone before we begin opening up for questions. There's deep
structural forces at the root of much of the harm in Black and Brown
communities. I want to open up the space to talk about what those structural forces are. We talked about a little bit, but I want to explicitly call
out the largest structural, institutional forces that are behind not just
poverty, but everything that's linked to leading us to incarceration. The

second part of this is, What are the most effective alternatives to prisons and to police that you see in your work and would recommend we take a more serious look at? How do we avoid using those tactics to deal with the problems in our communities that police and prisons only make worse and don't do anything to really solve?

MELINA: I think we need to be real explicit, right? We live under a system of white supremacist, patriarchal, heteronormative capitalism. That is the structure we live under. We can't pretend like the system isn't racist, like the system is color-blind, like Black people are treated like everybody else. And we need to also be clear. And I'm processing and talking at the same time so that's never a good idea but I'm still going to do it. So I pray that the words that come out are right. I think it's important to look at the way in which white supremacy affects different communities differently, right? Anti-Blackness is a particular form of white supremacy. So we have to be very clear about the ways in which Black people are targeted by the state. This doesn't mean that poor white folks aren't targeted by the state. It doesn't mean that Latino folks aren't targeted by the state, but I think that we need to look at how that targeting looks different for each community, because that also means that even though there's lots of solidarity, there's also very clear ways in which we have to resist. We have to recognize we live under a white supremacist state. And I don't think anybody can miss it right now, because we have a blatant white supremacist patriarchal capitalist in the damn White House, right? And he's doing it, and this regime is doing it, in every single way. They're carrying out that mission in every single way, right? So if we think about the rhetoric that comes out—what did he say yesterday about the national anthem? If you don't want to stand for the national anthem, maybe you don't need to be in this country. Maybe *you* don't need to be in this country, homie! Right?

So there's the rhetoric, but we also need to think about how that rhetoric translates into both policies and also violence on the ground. Policy—in terms of how the prison system and police harass and abuse our folks, right? We're seeing, for one of the first times actually, the highest number to date of police killings, in terms of keeping record of . . . numbers of people who are killed by police. This year exceeds previous years, right?[24] We're also seeing a surge for the first time on record in hate crimes, right?[25] So, since hate crime statistics have been kept, there's always been a downward trend. This is the first time . . . actually this isn't the first time. It was the months that, right before the election took place, you saw a surge in hate crimes. So that rhetoric empowers violent white supremacy.

We also need to think about the way that patriarchy plays in. So often-times we talk about the men who are imprisoned, but I'm glad that you're here, Sis, because we need to talk about the way in which Black women are targeted for imprisonment, right? We need to think about that the vast majority of those of us who were in prison have mental health conditions. And it's gendered. Black women who were imprisoned suffer with mental health conditions. It is at an even higher rates than Black men, right?[26] We need to also think about capitalism. And I know that some people like to do two things. They like to sum everything up. You know those on the left say everything is just about class: "It's just about class. And if we just engage in class struggle, we'd be free." Right? But then there's people on the other side who say, "You know, we can neglect it."

We have to understand Manning Marable. If you haven't read the book *How Capitalism Underdeveloped Black America*,[27] that needs to be on your summer reading list. At the conclusion of that book, he says, "The road to black liberation must also be the road to socialist revolu-tion." Right? And what he's talking about is the intertwining of racism. He doesn't talk explicitly about sexism, but sexism is in there along with class struggle. And so when you talk about these systems, these systems are what created policing. These systems are what is expanding the prison industrial complex. That's trying to expand LA jails, right? That's what the system is doing.

And then we need to think about how do we resist, and that resistance needs to take place in many different forms. So we have to vote. We have to engage in that, and I know that's not always popular. I don't happen to vote for mainstream candidates very often, but you know we do have to elect folks. And voting can make a difference. We can think about cities like Newark, New Jersey, that elected Ras Baraka. We can think about Jackson, Mississippi, where we elected Chokwe Antar. And Cat Brooks, the cofounder of the antipolice terror project, is running for mayor of Oakland, right? We can think about these opportunities to elect folks. And some people go, "We shouldn't vote." Look: the Black Panther Party ran Elaine Brown and Bobby Seale for office. So don't buy this thing about it's not revolutionary to run for office, right? It's part of our history, but this is what we've done: we've left it in the hands of these elected folks to lead us. We've never won that way. You can't give up the struggle on the ground. So I know y'all want to come to the forums or say, "I voted and now I'm done." Put that little sticker, you know, that stupid sticker they give you when you vote, right? Okay, maybe wear the sticker, right? But you aren't done. You're not finished with your work because you have an "I voted" sticker on, right?

You're finished with your work when you've given everything you can to honor our ancestors. When you've given everything that you can to honor those warriors who've walked before us, by giving all that you can to the struggle for our liberation. And that means signing petitions. That means voting. But it also means . . . it's Ramadan, so I'm gonna just say, "Shut stuff down." That's not actually our chant, right? But "Shut stuff down!" We got to shut stuff down. As long as we allow white supremacist, patriarchal, heteronormative capitalism to churn as if there's nothing happening, they're going to keep doing what they're doing and pour more into the system that keeps us oppressed.

SHAKA: She always just drops so many jewels. I think it's so important. So, my personal belief is that, all too often, we allow people to control our energy through their unhealthy narratives. Every time the current administration says something, we find ourselves in emotional turmoil. To me, there's nothing more disempowering than playing pity politics. Meaning that you're looking for people to pity you because you're allowing somebody to hurt your feelings. I believe empowerment is what disrupts and turns over systems. We have to stop wasting so much of our energy worrying about what *they* are not doing and worry about what *we* can do. Period. The world wasn't changed by somebody whining about somebody else. It's changed because people actually got up and did something and made it happen. We recently had a relief concert around a bill that's currently sitting in the [US] House [of Representatives].

And this bill is a criminal justice reform bill. And some of my esteemed colleagues were invited to the White House. And because we're so emotional around the issue, people attacked these men and women who fight every day against the system. No sleep.

This sister Topeka sitting right here is one of my personal heroines. She fights every day for dignity for women who are incarcerated. Every day. When she walked into that White House, people judged her. And it pissed me off because I know her spirit, I know her heart, I know her commitment, I know her passion, and I know her wisdom. And she's wise enough to know that when there are these moments, where these conversations are being had, we have a responsibility to step in those rooms, even when we dislike the company that we know we'll be keeping—that is our responsibility. We have to push the envelope. We have to challenge these systems by actually doing the real work. Making a tweet that sound fancy and sound smart, it's not real work. You probably didn't even get off the bed or off the toilet to do that. Real talk. I know y'all be up in the morning. Let's be honest. We all get up and go.

But I'm serious, in the sense that that we have to be mindful of what we're doing to people. It was unfair for them to treat my colleagues like that. I was actually invited. Had I not had a prior commitment I would have gone because it's my responsibility. We have been duped into believing that people who haven't worked in our best interest are serving us while we criticize this system. And the rest of my colleagues, we celebrated Bill Clinton, we celebrated Hillary Clinton when they passed some of the worst criminal justice bills in the history of this country. So we have to stop playing petty politics. We have to develop more critical thinkers. We have to have more critical analysis. But most importantly, when you don't like what's happening, we got to get off our ass and get out there and make it happen, and build the shit that we want to see.

BRYONN: Before we open up, I want to ask Joel and Topeka to jump in on this, but I want to focus the question in a very specific way. Part of what I've heard from Melina and Shaka is this sentiment challenging the popular idea that the system is broken, and if we just fix it and make it work better, if we could just tape up the edges and bandage it up, when in fact the system is actually working exactly as it was designed to work.

And so we need to shift the paradigm of our thinking and begin thinking about how do we actually break it? Or *disrupt and dismantle* a system functioning just as it was designed to? How do we transform it into something humane? Because it was not designed to be humane and never functioned that way.

So my specific question for you, Joel and Topeka, is: what are the skills that the folks in this room coming into this work need to have? What are the skills that are most needed right now in terms of the training and preparation? We got a lot of spirit being willing but if the flesh is weak, if the flesh is not prepared, if folks are not properly set up to actually do the work, then the work can't get done the way it needs to be done. And y'all are on the front lines, work every day. What are the skills you need to see more of in terms of preparation for folks who are engaging in this movement that y'all are in the leadership of today?

TOPEKA: First, I want to thank you, Shaka, for those words, because it has been incredibly difficult over the last week. And thank you for acknowledging that. I really appreciate that. I love you. And so when I think about the skills that are needed, I think about . . . I mean I'm a spirit animal, right? So I think about just having the spirit of humility. I think in doing this work you have to remain humble. You have to learn how to put your ego aside. And you have to always check your own intentions. I've learned in the last three years because I'm new to just this movement. I'm new to this work. Since my release from prison in 2015 is when I really got involved. And it's been these different times. It's times when people want to come together. And you want to build coalition. You want to collaborate. When you believe that you're following the same mission and goals. And then, when people start to elevate based on their learning and understanding, then we want to pull and hold each other back and criticize people.

I think we need to start to look at this beast as a beast. And we need to understand that each of us up here have a different lane. Each of you in here have a different lane. And you just need to find what that lane is, right? If it's not your lane, then you have to learn how to cede and to give it to someone else. Like this sister was kicking and dropping jewels. There's no need for me to add anything to what she's saying, right?

Because she got it. And then sometimes when you just sit back and you listen, you can learn. And then when you learn, you can develop a different way of critical thinking. You know? And then I think what's incredibly important, too, and learning through this last week, is the adage of reading is fundamental. I'm gonna go back into a course I took when I first came home. It was Biblical Exegesis. And I remember being in this course, and there were all these theologians and PhDs, and I'm just new. And I'm like, "Wow, I don't know how I'm gonna make it through this class." All these brilliant minds. The professor was like, "You are going to be one of the best people in this class because you come in here with an open heart and open mind." I wasn't coming in there with these beliefs based on things that I had learned before. But it was also about not just . . . "because the Bible says this." You need to read it for yourself.

BRYONN: How does that dynamic impact your justice movement work?

TOPEKA: I think about these bills and I think about these laws, and I know that I have been doing my work based on spirit work. But also in learning and moving in this work, you depend on your elders and your allies a lot of times in the work. And sometimes we just go ahead, and we sign off on things. And we don't look at it because we believe that the person who was teaching us is telling us the right thing to do. And then you soon learn that people have their own political agendas, their own intentions. And a lot of times it's not even for the people that they're supposed to be serving. So what I've learned is that it is incredibly important for you to do your own due diligence, to take your time, whether it's to read to understand, whether it's to learn to heal. Because we can't lead unless we really have healed ourselves. Because then what you end up doing is pouring your trauma into someone else's trauma and that perpetuates trauma. And you know, we have a big mess. So I think that's how to dismantle a system, because we're not trying to fix it. It is really to transform yourself. And it starts from within.

BRYONN: Thank you. Joel, what needs do you see in your own movement work?

JOEL: Yeah, I'll start with what I said at the very beginning. We all have a stake at this. Just look at the model of ARC,[28] what ARC has done here in California, at the forefront of changing laws, of going into prisons and sponsoring education, higher learning groups. And it's out here preparing. It's like there's a saying in recovery that "you clean your own side of the street." And the men that are coming home are being received with open arms from their brothers who were in there. What we do out here, we do for the next man who's sitting in that cell, thinking what he's going to do when he gets out. And it's about being involved. Mobility. I mean the civil rights movement started with people. We begin this change because we all have a stake in this. This is a national defense crisis. If another foreign country was doing this to us, this would be deemed as an act of war. So we all have to mobilize. We all have to be part of this solution. And look, if we shift the blame just on one entity, then the implication is that that one entity is going to fix our problems. And that's not true. It never happened. I take responsibility. That's what I learned in prison. And I'm out here, paying it forward.

BRYONN: As we close, I want to acknowledge some of the other folks I know who have been doing this work for a very long time: A New Way of Life, Dignity and Power Now, Youth Justice Coalition, Black Lives Matter, InsideOUT Writers, among many more than I can name here. There's a lot of folks out here doing this work. I see you. We see you.

AUDIENCE QUESTION #1: . . . I represent A New Way of Life. . . . I want to say to the audience, I'm a numbers person, and . . . I've been following the numbers. And as a tax-paying citizen what scares me the most in California is that we have our governor spending eleven and a half billion dollars to fund thirty prisons in California. That's at a cost of about $76,000 per prisoner.[29] And we are funding that as tax-paying citizens. They're taking money away from everything. And what bothers me is *what we don't have*. We are getting that information out, but I would like for us to be aware of the monies that are being spent . . . the money we can divert to other programs and other things that will help people instead of incarcerating people. We're spending $76,000—the amount that it costs to send somebody to Harvard—just to lock somebody up every day. All day long.

BRYONN: That's an incredibly important point. Thank you.

MELINA: There is this website called Million Dollar Hoods that your colleague [to Bryonn] Kelly Lytle Hernandez developed. Please check it out because it is about the choices we're making. What could we be doing with that money if we weren't spending it on incarceration?

BRYONN: Yes! Thank you. I see your hand there.

AUDIENCE QUESTION #2: With mass incarceration, it seems like a lot of it stems from stigmatizing stereotypes by people that are decision makers. They make decisions off of presumptions about people. Groups. Things like that. So how much do you think miseducation with American history plays a part? It seems like a lot of people don't know about convict leasing. They don't know about destruction of Tulsa, Oklahoma—Black Wall Street. And so, if the school system isn't teaching proper American history, accurate and inclusive American history, people grow up not knowing that these stereotypes are rooted in history. They were made by people in power. Do you think we could ever change the American history classes or implement implicit bias training? Something that addresses the stigmatizing stereotypes that lead to mass incarceration?

BRYONN: Great question. Miseducation, stigmatization, stereotypes—how much of that is related to what we are talking about?

SHAKA: Thank you for asking a great question. One of my mentors, Joi Ito at MIT Media Lab says, "Education is what they do to you. Learning is what you do for yourself." I say that to say this: Ava DuVernay and her artistic brilliance directed the film *13th*. It gave the most accurate historical breakdown of our current prison system. Is what it is. It's not just stereotypes. It's actually written into the Constitution that nobody should be subjected to involuntary servitude except for those duly convicted of a crime. So basically, through the Constitution, slavery was reinvented in its modern form—also known as mass incarceration.[30] So it's not so much a stereotype as it is legislation, which is why it's so important for us to be in those rooms when it comes to trying to change policies and trying to undo the harm that the Constitution, which is the fabric of this country, has done over the course of many decades.

The more we learn . . . we don't have to be relying on educational institutions, which are basically like cousins of the prison industrial complex, so to speak. I mean, sometimes you walk in one and you can't tell the difference which one you are walking in—especially if you come from the 'hood. I'm from Detroit, so walking in our schools is like walking in San Quentin or Folsom because it's real out there. But also the intention behind the school is just as catastrophic in terms of the outcome that it is producing where we're basically just training people not to think for themselves. You can't think for yourself, you can't empower yourself. Therefore, you can't change the environment in a way that honors who you are. So it's all about learning. We have to stop relying on these broken institutions to inform us of what are the things that we need to know. Instead, let's take this opportunity to really build. Go watch the film *13th*. Start a conversation online. . . . It's still restricted, but it's not as restrictive as the past where we couldn't communicate across all these spaces. So those are the opportunities that we have right in front of us that we have to take advantage of.

MELINA: Can I just quickly add to that? I'll say there's also a difference between schooling and education. . . . I think brother Shaka is absolutely right. . . . Everybody read Paulo Freire's work . . . we need to think about how do we build educational models that are liberatory. We're coming up on the fiftieth anniversary of Black studies/ethnic studies. We need to think about what my discipline was created to do. It wasn't created by the institution . . . Black folks and Brown folks, and the Third World Liberation front . . . demanded that the institutions be shut down so that we can build models of education that are actually liberatory. In LAUSD [LA Unified School District]—and this is about the power of people, right?—just a couple years ago, it was students and teachers and community organizers who demanded that within LAUSD we have an ethnic studies requirement. And so my daughter, who's now a ninth grader, is going to be the first class of students who graduate [high school] with an ethnic studies requirement. Now it doesn't fix everything that happens in the classroom, but it's very different. It adds tremendously to what they've been learning. And what it does is that it teaches them that they have the power. That *we* have the power to transform systems—to topple systems that are oppressive and build something new.

BRYONN: Brilliant! Thank you.

AUDIENCE QUESTION #3: This is an amazing night! Thank you so much. My son was in Twin Towers and it's like being in a sardine can. If anyone's ever seen what it's like . . . there's nothing for the inmates to do. And he was in jail for mental health. I thought I heard about EBI [educational-based incarceration].[31] And I asked him if he could be part of that. I found out that none of the mentally ill—mental health inmates— were allowed to even be considered for EBI. And I just want to encourage you all to try to see if you could get more, because I did a lot of activism about that. And now they do have it, but not enough. So I really think when they're in jail, try to help them move forward because otherwise they get sicker. . . . Do you have any other ideas about that? I'd love to know.

BRYONN: Topeka? Joel? Either of you have a response? More of these kinds of services inside facilities? Were there particular programs that you participated in that were more than just the usual okeydoke programs inside the facility? Programs that actually made a difference? Made an impact that you would like to see more of an investment in—for folks who are in this room and committed to doing that kind of work?

TOPEKA: For me, there were none. I was in federal prison. And then the two federal prisons that I was in . . . if you did not have your GED, then they offer the GED course. There were no Pell Grants.[32] So if a person wanted to do any college courses, they didn't offer them in the prison, and you had to do a correspondence course—which you had to pay for. And you all know that people are making five dollars a month. So there's no way they could pay for a college course. This is in federal prison. For women, they offered us knitting and crocheting and beading and plastic canvasing. I mean, it was really a joke.

I always say that for me, in my experience, that prison didn't change me. It was the women that were in there that did. So your resources for me were right there through the sisters. Through the books and things that they would tell me to read . . . I was very fortunate; I had a support network at home. I had a mentor that came in and saw me. I had visits every week. So I had a plan. I was very spiritually grounded. I knew what I wanted to do. But it had nothing to do with the prison. That's why it's very important for us to think about alternatives to incarceration and how do we reinvest that into community-based organizations that are led by formerly incarcerated people and directly impacted people.

BRYONN: On point. Thank you, Topeka.

SHAKA: When I was inside, I was fortunate. I just had incredible mentors. . . . They're currently dying in prison. They've been in prison for forty, fifty years now. But one of the things I really want to lift up is the model that ARC has. Seriously. And I'm not just saying that because I'm the executive director. I'm serious and very intentional about this. We have very important "in-reach" programs. A lot of people do outreach. We have a member team called Hope and Redemption. The leader of that team is our director, Sam Lewis. . . . He's dealing with some things. We sent a prayer up for Sam. These are lifers—men who literally have gotten out of prison after thirtysomething years. Twenty years. Thirty years. They go back into prison four times a week—four times a week to provide hope and love to men who hope to be them one day. We have a team that goes into several juvenile halls and spends time with the young men to make sure that they don't end up graduating to the prison system. Those models can be replicated because it's peer to peer. It's people who've lived through it. And the crazy thing is that people are resistant to that outside of California. And I couldn't share this information without acknowledging the founder of ARC who's actually here, Scott Budnick.

This organization serves hundreds of members and was sparked by him just going inside and having proximity to young men who were suffering. And he decided to do something about it. Now, nearly five years later, hundreds of members serve . . . it is working. Super-low recidivism rate: 70 percent of people go back to prison; less than 10 percent of ARC members end up back in that environment. Literally just because somebody decided to do something different. Going inside, showing a little love, showing a little care produces different outcomes. Everybody in this room is capable of doing that. You don't have to join ARC to do it, but you can do it. A little bit of love, a little bit of care, and a lot of hope goes a long way.

BRYONN: I have to underscore what you said by mentioning that two summers ago, ARC did a survey of its more than 250 formerly incarcerated members in which they asked what were the top three things you need when you come home from prison. On that top three list, housing and employment were two and three. But number one, if I recall correctly—and I'm sure I'll be corrected if I'm mistaken, but I think I'm not—number one was mentors. Mentors! Folks who've been through what brothers and sisters inside are going through and have not forgotten about this struggle and remain committed to making sure they give a guiding light and a pathway to freedom on the path that they're on. So I want to acknowledge and celebrate what you just said as well, Shaka. Thank you. Someone in the back had a hand up?

AUDIENCE QUESTION #4: Hi. . . . I'm currently in the United States Navy. . . . I just wanted to get your opinion about how you feel about people who serve in the military, especially those of color. And my other question was, with me, all my life since 2008, when I was eighteen, I've always been a libertarian. I don't agree with what Democrats or Republicans were saying. So how do I go off . . . and find a party that represents what I feel?

BRYONN: I want to make sure I heard the question correctly. I think it is was, What do you think about the military industrial complex? People of color in the military? Any thoughts?

SHAKA: They probably got PTSD too.

BRYONN: I'll say this: I spent a lot of time on Rikers Island. I'm from Brooklyn, New York. The East Coast. Been here for less than three years. LA has the most folks incarcerated in any jail system in the world, but New York and Rikers Island is the largest penal colony. One space with ten jails—more than 15,000 people when I started teaching the young folks there. And inside the largest high school at Rikers, because there are several, there is a big sign when you first walked into Island Academy High School. They have a picture of a man who was split in half. And on the back half he has his green prison outfit on, and the front half, he has a camouflage military outfit on—holding an M16 [rifle]. And over the top it says "choose your green." As if to say for the sixteen- to nineteen-year-olds—more than 4,000 or 5,000 every year are at Rikers—these are your options. These are your choices. Choose to be in prison. Or choose to go give your life and pledge allegiance to the flag of a country that has never pledged allegiance to you.

I say that as the son of an Army veteran who, with a medical disability, had to fight just to get the basic minimum disability he was promised, because after experiencing the trauma that he experienced in the US Army, he came home and did not get the basic dignity and respect that any human being deserves. Alright? Especially one who's put their life on the line. . . . So I think there's a lot of parallels for us to think about in terms of the experience of folks who are incarcerated—folks who experience the prison industrial complex and folks [who] experience the military industrial complex.

Last thing I'll say is this: before [President] Eisenhower left office, one of the things I recall he had to say was that you should beware conflating your interest in security and safety with the profit motive.[33] Beware of allowing your interest in generating capital and profits with being mixed up with the idea of national security. Because, ultimately, that's what happened. We've seen it not just with the military industrial complex but with the prison industrial complex. We know both are driven by this idea that they can generate huge profits off our suffering and on the backs of other people. I don't lay blame [on] folks who feel like they have few options and few choices and feel forced into these small spaces where their lives are not respected and given dignity and fundamental decency. I don't blame folks, but I want to call for a sense of critical consciousness and thinking about those choices within the broader context of what our communities are facing. I see we have another hand. We have a microphone back there?

AUDIENCE QUESTION #5: Thank you very much. Listening to you guys and following the current events, I cannot stop and think about Palestine. I just came back three weeks ago, so everything is fresh in my mind. In Palestine, they arrest young children. They have administrative detention. Kids are tortured. You guys heard about Ahed Tamimi? You guys know what happened to her when she slapped a soldier? It's not in the news, but an Israeli soldier shot her fifteen-year-old cousin. Almost blew his brains out. Once Ahed Tamimi found out that her fifteen-year-old cousin got his brains blown out, she reacted like anyone else would react, and she slapped the soldier. So the news came out that "why is this Palestinian slapping an Israeli soldier?" That was the news. And then she is incarcerated. Her mom recorded that slap, and because she uploaded that video on Facebook, she has been detained for that.[34] So there's a lot of connections to the way Palestinians are treated to the way that our

Black and Brown brothers and sisters are treated here. Add to that the fact that this country—your country, America—gave Israel $38 billion to support Israeli apartheid.

Now, if we bring it on a local level . . . thirty-eight billion dollars to Israel to continue this same type of torture—the way the city of LA put a lot of money to the police department. We got to change the way this country puts a lot of money in the defense budget. We got to shift our narrative from security to criminalizing our people—defense budget to bombing other countries—in order for us to secure and have public safety. To ensure public safety means that our children have to have a good education. Our elders should have senior housing. We have to talk about the basic human rights. And that is how you have public safety on a local level. That's how you have social national security on a national level. So let's shift the security aspect and make it more humane.

BRYONN: That was more of a comment, but I'm grateful for it.

AUDIENCE QUESTION #6: How are you doing? I'm from a program called Repent Atlantic City, New Jersey. Yeah, give me a clap. I have had the unfortunate experience of going through the incarceration process. I have been in that Twin Towers, unfortunately. I did over ten years in prison in New Jersey. I found ways to try to overcome those obstacles in getting out—and doing so, diligently striving to do so—the obstacles that I found most is with some of the programs in that "nonprofit" system. That is really not set up for us to be able to do peer to peer because they really don't recognize our value. How do we overcome these obstacles that are set up among us? . . . We already deal with all the other problems when we're trying to get out there and really help. You got people who have monies that are intentionally blocking these avenues. How can we reach out to brothers who are like yourself? Sisters who are like yourselves? Who have been there and know how to do it? And be able to replicate that elsewhere? Because right now the struggle is serious and we need your help.

TOPEKA: Thank you for that question. I could just talk about it from my experience. When you talk about systems and funding and how do you do replicate models. I have Hope House—which is a safe housing space for women and girls in the Bronx. And my house is a replication model of A New Way of Life, which is Susan Burton's housing, and we started off of a grant from Susan Burton. And so, I share that because that's another formerly incarcerated woman that I had reached out to, who I heard was doing the work that I wanted to do. And after having conversations with her, she invested and poured into me, right? So that I can do what I needed to do. And that helped me get started. And once I started to move, I was able to get the house full. And through all the adversities that we have in the community, I was still able to go to different foundations because I had tangible work. And then the foundation started to fund us.

So I think first, again, when we think about the network, and we got to think about it, you know? Also, before I was incarcerated I was an entrepreneur. I always think about, like, diversifying portfolios. You don't always have to go after the same foundations in the same ways of funding that you see everyone else doing. It's how do you find different creative ways in order to fund the work that you do. But it also starts with building community and within your network. So yes, you can do replication models. And maybe that's something that you can talk about with ARC—with the brothers up here—because there might be something that's working or that can work in Atlantic City. And also look for other things that are happening within your community. There's a large national movement of formerly incarcerated leaders. And so, tap in . . . there's a few up there in Jersey, so we can always connect you too. But social media has given us the ability to really connect in ways that we wouldn't have before. So I think it's really not as difficult. I'm just saying this based on my experience, right? I think the difficulty is that we always go after what we see other people doing and not necessarily doing our research and due diligence to see, like, "Hey, how can I get something done?" . . . You don't want to be tied into a lot of these foundations anyway, to be honest. . . . We can talk afterward.

BRYONN: Thank you. We have time for just one more question. Right here, please?

AUDIENCE QUESTION #7: . . . I'm part of Transitions Collective, a student organization at Cal State San Marcos. We are composed of formerly incarcerated students and students who have family members who have been impacted by the criminal injustice system and allies. And my question for you is, We just started about a year ago at the university—how can we better assist in offering our services and our help and guidance for folks who are coming out of the prison system—to better reintegrate and succeed in higher education?

JOEL: Yeah, I'll share a little bit. So I'm back in college. I just finished my semester maybe two weeks ago. And I think that, you know a lot of the times I think with me, for example, I had to deal with the aspect of shame of not coming out in a sense. I was in a closet. So I was going to school and no one knew . . . no one knows that I'm formerly incarcerated. And that was just psychological. It was probably a defense for me to protect myself because I didn't want to be judged. So I think your first approach . . . that it should be kind of like very sensitive. Every case is different. I don't think we're going to find something that's categorical, that's going to fit everyone. So I would just kind of like approach it individually. Each person is different, at a different stage in their life. . . . For example, I wasn't sure what I really wanted to major in. And it was me just going in school and figuring that out. And what was truly my passion was, for example, having mentors. I have mentors that aren't just formerly incarcerated. I have mentors who are attorneys—like Elizabeth Calvin . . . Efty Sharoni. These are the people that I go to and I ask, "What do you think I should do?" And they guide me. So like I said, and for the brother . . . it applies for him, too. We're fortunate here in California that we have an organization like ARC and a lot of nonprofits who are allies with ARC and are part of this work that we do. But to affect the life, you don't need ARC. You don't need all these other allies. You can do it on your own. You can impact one life and that's enough. You're saving a life. This is a human crisis. You're saving one life. And I think that's enough.

BRYONN: I'm getting the signal that we are at time, so I want to close out by thanking our powerful guests: Topeka Sam, Melina Abdullah, Joel Aguilar, and Shaka Senghor. Please give them a big round of applause. I want to thank Gina Belafonte [Sankofa.org] and Cristina Pacheco [the Underground Museum] for their leadership and work to pull this together. All of the We Rise organizing staff, the team, everybody involved in doing all the work. I want to end by sharing words given to me by a mentor of mine, Harry Belafonte, who told me a worker's anthem that I will never forget:

> Calculate carefully and ponder it well
> And remember this when you do
> My two hands are mine to sell
> They built your machines
> They can stop them too

LINER NOTES

Track #4 is excerpted from a panel discussion titled "Critical Justice" at the We Rise Conference in Los Angeles, May 24, 2018. The conference was part of the Mental Health Awareness Month initiative of the Los Angeles County Department of Mental Health. Special thanks to Yosi Sergant of the LACDMH TaskForce, published courtesy of TaskForce.

1. Derrick Bell authored a number of groundbreaking books on race and racism in the US—for instance, *Race, Racism, and American Law,* 6th ed. (New York: Aspen, 2008), and *Faces at the Bottom of the Well: The Performance of Racism* (New York: Basic Books, 1992).

2. Gerald Torres is a professor of environmental justice at the Yale School of the Environment and on the faculty of the Yale Law School.

3. In 1999 New York governor George Pataki vetoed a $500 million investment in school construction and instead proposed to spend $180 million for constructing a new maximum-security prison, which was on top of another $180 million already allocated to prison construction by summer 2000. Tracy L Huling, "Prisons as a Growth Industry in Rural America: An Exploratory Discussion of the Effects on Young African American Men in the Inner Cities," Prison Policy, 1999, www.prisonpolicy.org/scans/prisons_as_rural_growth.shtml.

4. Guinier uses "canary in the coalmine" as a metaphor for the experiences of people of color in higher education. It embodies the challenge to "rethink race and the role of those who have been excluded from, or underrepresented in, positions of authority or decision making in society." Lani Guinier and Gerald Torres, *The Miner's Canary: Enlisting Race, Resisting Power, Transforming Democracy* (Cambridge, MA: Harvard University Press, 2002).

5. In July 2014 Eric Garner, a Black man, was killed by a New York City police officer in a prohibited choke hold after calling out eleven times "I can't breathe." The incident generated wide national attention and massive protests and ignited debates over race and policing. Garner's death has been cited as one of many police killings

of Black Americans protested by the #BlackLivesMatter movement. Al Baker, J. David Goodman, and Benjamin Miller, "Beyond the Chokehold: The Path to Eric Garner's Death," *New York Times*, June 13, 2015, www.nytimes.com/2015/06/14 /nyregion/eric-garner-police-chokehold-staten-island.html. The killings of George Floyd and Breonna Taylor in 2020 continue to expose violence against people of color from law enforcement, leading to ongoing massive protests. "George Floyd Death Homicide, Official Post-Mortem Declares," *BBC News*, June 2, 2020, www .bbc.com/news/world-us-canada-52886593; Darcy Costello and Tessa Duvall, "Minute by Minute: What Happened the Night Louisville Police Fatally Shot Breonna Taylor," *USA Today*, May 15, 2020, www.usatoday.com/story/news /nation/2020/05/15/minute-minute-account-breonna-taylor-fatal-shooting-louisville-police/5196867002.

6. "Alzheimer's Disease and Healthy Aging," Centers for Disease Control and Prevention, accessed August 23, 2021, www.cdc.gov/aging/aginginfo/alzheimers .htm.

7. Biogen, "The Importance of Early Detection of Alzheimer's Disease," based in part on the Alzheimer's Association Report 2018 published in *Alzheimers Dementia* 14 (2018): 367–429, accessed August 23, 2021, www.identifyalz.com/en_us /home/diagnosing-mild-cognitive-impairment.html.

8. The Tuskegee Experiment was an unethical medical experiment on syphilis disease that began in 1932 and lasted for forty years. The experiment recruited six hundred Black men without informing them of the real purpose of the study and without treating their conditions as promised—even when the treatment became available. The study caused needless suffering for participants and their families. It serves as a case in point for the exploitation of people of color through medical experiments. "The Tuskegee Timeline," Centers for Disease Control and Prevention, accessed August 23, 2021, www.cdc.gov/tuskegee/timeline.htm; "The US Public Health Service Study at Tuskegee," Centers for Disease Control and Prevention, updated April 22, 2021, www.cdc.gov/tuskegee/index.html. See also "The Legacy of Henrietta Lacks," John Hopkins Medicine, accessed September 16, 2021, www .hopkinsmedicine.org/henriettalacks.

9. In 2017 a two-year study with more than two hundred individuals with mental illness found greater self-stigma associated with poorer recovery form mental illness after one to two years. "Stigma, Prejudice, and Discrimination against People with Mental Illness," American Psychiatric Association, accessed September 16, 2021, www.psychiatry.org/patients-families/stigma-and-discrimination.

10. The convening was filled with Lani's colleagues and friends. Niko recognized that he was, in fact, surrounded by family, from critical race studies luminaries like Patricia Williams to lifelong collaborators like legal scholars Susan Sturm and Gerald Torres and colleagues in a range of fields like theater guru Tim Mitchell and political scientists like Phillip Thompson, who gave me Lani's *Tyranny of the Majority* when I took a Contemporary Black Politics course with him as a sophomore.

11. According to a study published by the Economic Policy Institute, "Young African American men are no more likely to use or sell drugs than young white men," but are "nearly three times as likely to be arrested for drug use or sale; once arrested, they are more likely to be sentenced; and, once sentenced, their jail or prison terms are 50 percent longer on average." Leila Morsy and Richard Rothstein, "Mass Incarceration and Children's Outcomes: Criminal Justice Policy Is Education Policy," Economic Policy Institute, December 15, 2016, www.epi.org/publication /mass-incarceration-and-childrens-outcomes.

12. Numerous books and articles have exposed the discriminatory practices of criminalizing children of color. For instance, see Bernadine Dohrn, "'Look Out, Kid, It's Something You did': The Criminalization of Children," in *The Public Assault on America's Children: Poverty, Violence, and Juvenile Injustice*, edited by Valerie Polakow, 157–87 (New York: Teachers College Press, 2000), and Monique W. Morris, *Pushout: The Criminalization of Black Girls in Schools* (New York: New Press, 2016).

13. "Zero-tolerance" rules have led to some of the harshest forms of school discipline today. These policies were originated in the 1990s in response to the surge in school violence and to confront the presence of firearms brought to school by students. Nowadays, zero-tolerance rules have been expanded beyond expulsion of students for bringing firearms. It also applies to "suspension or expulsion of children from school for everything from weapons to drugs to smoking to fighting." In addition, the rules also apply to dress-code violations, truancy, or tardiness. Catherine Y. Kim, Daniel J. Losen, and Damon T. Hewitt, *The School-to-Prison Pipeline: Structuring Legal Reform* (New York: NYU Press, 2012), 79–82.

14. Based on research published by the Economic Policy Institute, African Americans today are better off in some ways but are worse off in others. First, African Americans today are better educated than they were in 1968. Second, the higher educational attainment of African Americans also resulted in higher incomes and better health within the population compared to that in 1968. Third, there has been no progress but regression when it comes to home ownership, unemployment, and incarceration for African Americans. See Janelle Jones, John Schmitt, and Valerie Wilson, "Fifty Years after the Kerner Commission: African Americans Are Better Off in Many Ways but Are Still Disadvantaged by Racial Inequality," Economic Policy Institute, February 26, 2018, www.epi.org /publication/50-years-after-the-kerner-commission.

15. For more detail, see Jennifer Gonnerman, "Khalif Browder, 1993-2015," *The New Yorker*, June 7, 2015, www.newyorker.com/news/news-desk/kalief-browder-1993-2015.

16. Shannon Lynch, Dana DeHart, Joanne Belknap, and Bonnie Green, "Women's Pathway to Jail: The Roles and Intersections of Serious Mental Illness and Trauma," US Bureau of Justice Assistance, September 2012, 32.

17. E. Fuller Torrey et al., "More Mentally Ill Persons Are in Jails and Prisons Than Hospitals: A Survey of the States," Treatment Advocacy Center, May 2010, www.treatmentadvocacycenter.org/storage/documents/final_jails_v_hospitals_ study.pdf?utm_source=April+2016+Newsletter&utm_campaign=April+ 2016&utm_medium=email.

18. The number of US residents incarcerated per 100,000 grew from 161 in 1972 to 707 in 2012. Jeremy Travis, Bruce Western, and Steve Redburn, eds., *Growth of Incarceration in the US: Exploring Causes and Consequences* (Washington, DC: National Academies Press, 2014), 33.

19. The Central Park 5 were five teenage boys who were wrongfully charged for attempted murder, rape, and assault of a white female jogger in 1989. Each ended up in prison for between six and thirteen-plus years. Aisha Harris, "The Central Park 5: 'We Were Just Baby Boys,'" *New York Times*, May 30, 2019, www.nytimes .com/2019/05/30/arts/television/when-they-see-us.html.

20. See "Summary of the Reform Jails and Community Reinvestment Initiative Ballot initiative," Reform LA County Jails, accessed August 23, 2021, http:// reformlajails.com/summary.

21. "Although incarcerated women made up about 4 percent of California's prison population from 2014 through 2016, they accounted for about 11 percent of the suicides. Almost all the suicides during this period occurred at the California Institution for Women (CIW)." California State Auditor, *California Department of Corrections and Rehabilitation: It Must Increase Its Efforts to Prevent and Respond to Inmate Suicides*, Report 2016-131, 9, www.auditor.ca.gov/pdfs /reports/2016-131.pdf. See also Hillel Aron, "Why Are So Many Inmates Attempting Suicide at the California Institution for Women?" *LA Weekly*, July 20, 2016, www.laweekly.com/news/why-are-so-many-inmates-attempting-suicide- at-the-california-institution-for-women.

22. *Pill line* is the queue to receive medication before being allowed to return to a prison housing unit.

23. "Solitary Confinement: Torture in US Prisons," Center for Constitutional Rights, May 31, 2012, https://ccrjustice.org/home/get-involved/tools-resources /fact-sheets-and-faqs/torture-use-solitary-confinement-us-prisons. See also Jeffrey L. Metzner and Jamie Fellner, "Solitary Confinement and Mental Illness in US Prisons: A Challenge for Medical Ethics," in *Health and Human Rights in a Changing World*, edited by Michael Grodin et al., 316–21 (New York: Routledge, 2013).

24. The number of fatal police shootings grew from 996 in 2018 to 1,004 in 2019. The number among Black Americans is disproportionately higher than that for any other ethnicity—31 fatal shootings per million as of August 2020. "Number of People Shot to Death by the Police in the United States from 2017 to 2020, by Race," Statistics Research Department, August 31, 2020, www.statista.com /statistics/585152/people-shot-to-death-by-us-police-by-race.

25. Adeel Hassan, "Hate-Crime Violence Hits 16-Year High, FBI Reports," *New York Times*, November 12, 2019, www.nytimes.com/2019/11/12/us/hate-crimes-fbi-report.html.

26. According to a study conducted by the Bureau of Justice Statistics in 2017, more than two-thirds of incarcerated women have reported a history of mental health issues, which significantly outnumbers their male counterparts. "More Incarcerated Women than Men Report Mental Health Problems," Equal Justice Initiative, July 10, 2017, https://eji.org/news/more-incarcerated-women-report-mental-health-problems.

27. Manning Marable, *How Capitalism Underdeveloped Black America* (Boston: South End Press, 1983).

28. ARC is the Anti-Recidivism Coalition, a nonprofit organization founded by Scott Budnick, James Anderson, and other formerly incarcerated activists in 2013, working to end mass incarceration in California. The organization provides support networks, comprehensive reentry services, and opportunities to advocate for policy change. "ARC—About Us," accessed August 23, 2021, https://antirecidivism.org/about-us.

29. More recent data show that the annual cost to incarcerate an inmate in California is even higher—$81,203 per person per year. "California's Annual Costs to Incarcerate an Inmate in Prison," California Legislative Analyst's Office, January 2019, https://lao.ca.gov/policyareas/cj/6_cj_inmatecost.

30. Michele Goodwin, "The Thirteenth Amendment: Modern Slavery, Capitalism, and Mass Incarceration," *Cornell Law Review* 104 (2019): 899–990, www.lawschool.cornell.edu/research/cornell-law-review/Print-Edition/upload/Goodwin-final.pdf. See also Whitney Benns, "American Slavery, Reinvented," *The Atlantic*, September 21, 2015, www.theatlantic.com/business/archive/2015/09/prison-labor-in-america/406177.

31. For more on education-based incarceration (EBI), see Bria D. Fitch and Anthony H. Normore, eds., *Education-Based Incarceration and Recidivism: The Ultimate Social Justice Crime-Fighting Tool* (Charlotte, NC: Information Age Publishing, 2012).

32. The Pell Grant is a federal financial aid award given only to undergraduate students with exceptional financial needs who "have not earned a bachelor's, graduate, or professional degree." The grant usually does not need to be repaid. Federal Student Aid, accessed August 23, 2021, https://studentaid.gov/understand-aid/types/grants/pell.

33. In President Dwight D. Eisenhower's farewell address in 1961, he urged the need to seek balance among a range of different interests, stating that " each proposal must be weighed in the light of a broader consideration: the need to maintain balance in and among national programs—balance between the private and the public economy, balance between cost and hoped for advantage—balance between the clearly necessary and the comfortably desirable; balance between our

essential requirements as a nation and the duties imposed by the nation upon the individual; balance between action of the moment and the national welfare of the future. Good judgment seeks balance and progress; lack of it eventually finds imbalance and frustration." Dwight Eisenhower, "Transcript of President Dwight D. Eisenhower's Farewell Address (1961)," www.ourdocuments.gov/doc .php?flash=false&doc=90&page=transcript.

34. Ahed Tamimi is a teenage activist in Palestine who was incarcerated for confronting Israeli soldiers. The incident was filmed and went viral internationally. She is seen as a symbol of the Palestinian resistance. Yasmeen Serhan, "A Symbol of the Palestinian Resistance for the Internet Age," *The Atlantic*, January 5, 2018, www.theatlantic.com/international/archive/2018/01/internet-famous-in-the-west-bank/549557. See also Oliver Holmes and Sufian Taha, "Ahed Tamimi: 'I Am a Freedom Fighter. I Will Not Be the Victim,'" *The Guardian*, July 30, 2018, www.theguardian.com/world/2018/jul/30/ahed-tamimi-i-am-a-freedom-fighter-i-will-not-be-the-victim-palestinian-israel.

TRACK #5
BEYOND THE BARS

WENDY + JENNIFER

#5 Beyond the Bars

JENNIFER CLAYPOOL AND WENDY STAGGS
ON LIFE AFTER LOCKDOWN

Jennifer Claypool and Wendy Staggs are inspiring artists, college students, and mothers. They are both returning citizens, who came home from prison just months apart in 2017. We met and began working together while they were incarcerated at the oldest women's prison in the state: the California Institution for Women (CIW).[1] Women have long been the fastest-growing population behind bars in the United States. Between 1970 and 2015, the number of women behind bars grew from under 8,000 to almost 110,000—a fourteenfold increase primarily for drug-related crimes.[2] There is an abundance of social science research highlighting that women in prison have a history of trauma that plays an undeniable role in their incarceration. We know incarcerated women are often the survivors of psychological, physical, and sexual abuse.[3]

In 2015 I joined the faculty of the University of California, LA, and worked with incarcerated and university students, faculty, staff, and community partner organizations to launch the UCLA Prison Education Program. By the following spring, I taught the university's first pilot course at CIW. The following dialogue focuses on the experiences of Jennifer Claypool and Wendy Staggs, two of the women I met while teaching at CIW during the first year of the program. Jennifer, Wendy, and I worked together with a group of visionary incarcerated women to develop the CIW Think Tank—a committee of women at the prison committed to guiding UCLA in the development of educational opportunities. At least 95 percent of those incarcerated in state prisons in the United States will return to society.[4] Evidence overwhelmingly suggests higher education is a leading factor keeping those released from prison from returning to the inside of a cell.[5]

Back in 2016, during the early days of developing the UCLA program at CIW prison, the Creative Writing Workshop Wendy and Jennifer participated in was one of the most unforgettable experiences. Not only was I able to hear them share poems, songs, free writing exercises, and theatrical readings, but we also collaborated on the adaptation of a hip hop theater, prison abolition remix of *The Wiz*. As we worked every other Friday to reimagine *What It Iz: The Spoken Wordical*, we had no idea they would both be released from prison in time to see it staged at UCLA the following year. That extraordinary night began with an opening performance by living spoken-word legends The Last Poets, ended with a set by pioneering hip hop DJ Kool Herc, and was further magnified by a cameo appearance by actress-activist Rosario Dawson. Yet none of those priceless moments compared to the look on Wendy's and Jennifer's faces after a cast of a dozen actors brought to life the play they'd worked on for so long, to the thunderous applause of hundreds offering a standing ovation.

1. TRAUMA BEFORE PRISON

BRYONN BAIN: I am looking forward to speaking with you about your experiences and your journey on what has brought you to this point. We met two years ago at the California Institution for Women, and I have to ask you about that, but first I want to ask about your life before CIW. Let's talk about your childhood. In the early years of your life, what kinds of relationships were most important to you? In your first decade or so? Jennifer?

JENNIFER CLAYPOOL: It was rough growing up. I was very lonely. I feel like I envied my other friends because their parents were totally involved in their kids' lives, and my parents weren't. I tried to do any-thing I could to get positive attention from them: I got straight As. I got better grades than my brother did. My grades were never put up on the refrigerator, while my brother's grades were. I missed a lot of school growing up, the older I got, especially because if I'm not getting rewarded for getting good grades and going to school, then why do I? My parents did not put a heavy emphasis on education; it was like this doesn't even matter.

My younger brother was born when I was almost eight, and then it became my responsibility to take care of him. So I had to feed him and change diapers, and if I went to go hang out with my friends, he had to come with me. The older I got, the less kind of attention I was receiving. So, I was on my own a lot. My mom wasn't there. I started to go to school. I hated taking care of my little brother, but I had to do it. It's just part of every day. My mom wasn't there. And then I would do anything I could to make money. My grandma would give me chores. I would be babysitting. I would do something for my grandpa so I could make my money so I could buy my own things.

I learned very young that I needed to support myself. I need to be independent. I control my emotions so my relationships don't control me, which started off a really bad path for me because then I was closed off from any kind of real connection with people except a couple of friends I had. I was going to parties. I was going to raves. I mean, I was into ecstasy. I started drinking at a very young age with [my parents]. My parents knew [about the drinking] and it was kind of just like, "As long as you are home drinking, it's okay." But my family just didn't know anything was happening with me. They didn't realize that I was starting to get really depressed because I didn't have—I wasn't getting, like—you know, it sounds really silly cliché, but I wasn't getting that love and affec-tion I needed at home. So, I sought it with friends and drugs and then I got into a really bad relationship. It wasn't until my senior year—my par-ents wouldn't let me work until my senior year, and they still didn't let me work, but I went and got a job anyways. They didn't know for the first month just because I was just like, "Oh, I have this to do, I'm going to my friend's house," and because I wasn't home a lot . . . that's when I was grounded.

BRYONN: What was the job?

JENNIFER: I worked in a pet store. Petland in Orange County. My best friend worked there, then she said, "Hey, you could work here too." I was seventeen. I started working there. It was like right before my senior year, and it was awesome. My parents didn't know about it for a while. They didn't want me [to] have a job because they said they wanted me to focus on school.

BRYONN: What were your hours? What was that routine like?

JENNIFER: I would get out of school, if I actually went to school that day or stayed [in school] the whole day. I would go to school; I might be at work by 3:00 or 3:30. So I usually take a bus or walk because my parents just . . . if they had a car, they weren't going to take me anywhere. And then I'd go to work until about 9:30 at night, which I just loved it. So, in the beginning I just, like, cleaned up the dog poop and stuff and fed them, and then within about a month, maybe, they promoted me to the vet tech. So, I gave them their medications. I'd give them their shots. It was really cool. I felt powerful and independent—like I was a strong woman who can go conquer the world now.

BRYONN: Where did your parents think you were?

JENNIFER: A friend's house or whatever, yeah, because that's where . . . I learned to manipulate, you know. . . . But they weren't home. So, a lot of time, they didn't even know that I wasn't going to school. I forged signatures. They didn't have a phone line for a while, so that totally works for my benefit because if the school is going to call, they can't tell them.

We finally moved out of my grandma's house and they rented a house at the end of my eighth-grade year, which kind of shook my whole world because I should have gone to the high school that I went to middle school and elementary school with all of my friends, but they started me off at a high school that I knew absolutely no one. They let my brother go to the same high school and if we would have taken, like, the bus together. . . . But they said we were grown up. So, they said, "We don't want you guys to take the bus that far." So, then that kind of just started rebellion for me.

BRYONN: How about you, Wendy?

WENDY STAGGS: I'm going to say from the earliest age that I can remember, which was three years old, I experienced loss and trauma. My first memory was my Irish setter, named Penny, laying on our garage floor and I was laying on her stomach crying, telling her that I wouldn't let them take her away. The Humane Society was coming to pick her up because she had a blood disease that was incurable. Then, shortly after that, and I know this sounds trivial, but this is a buildup of all the trauma that ended up happening. My dad was a tour bus driver, so he was gone a lot and it was just my mom and I. When I was around four years old, my mother decided that she wanted to wash my favorite stuffed animal, which was called Fido. I stood at the washing machine and waited. When the washing machine finished and my mother opened it, all that was left of Fido was stuffing. I remember feeling so alone. First, I've lost my dog. Now, I've lost Fido, and my dad's never home.

My father left when I was seven. When he was home, my parents never fought or anything, so I didn't know there were issues going on. I didn't understand why he had left us. The day he left was very devastating for my mom and myself. Shortly after that, one of my mom's fellow coworkers' husband molested me. We were at their house for dinner that day and my mom and I had left to get something from the store. In the car I said, "Hey, what would you do if I told you that Hank touched me?" My mom said, "Oh, that son of a gun. Just stay away from him!" and when we got back to their house, she went right back into the kitchen and he just proceeded to touch me. I may not have realized at that point, but for me that was a sign that I've already told and nobody is going to help me.[6]

There was a girl who lived across the street from me when I was growing up. I remember her telling me that her dad was molesting her and she said, "It's a secret only you know. You can't tell anybody." One night her father fell through the glass shower door when he was drunk and her mother called my mom over to help with him. So, even in the only friend that I really had I was experiencing trauma, in her life as well as mine. My life started to consist of secrets. It's just crazy. As far back as I can remember in my childhood. Let's just say from three to twelve it was loss, secrets, and trauma. There was signs long ago, but I was so broken and so filled with trauma that I just wasn't able to find an outlet for the pain, and I got caught up in drugs and all the nonsense that comes with that life.[7]

As time passed, I was never accepted in school. I went to a very rich school district; my backyard fence was the borderline of that district, so I lived on the outskirts of this district. My mom came from a farm environment, you know; she's an outdoors type of person. She doesn't like makeup or fancy clothes or any of that stuff, and she's a Christian so she's very simple. I was short, heavyset, and wore glasses. I was made fun of, kicked on and spit on, and all these horrible things that children do to each other. I was alone, no siblings, and to be honest, food became my friend. It was the thing that comforted me. At ten years old, my mom used to sing in the choir and I was . . .

BRYONN: It's okay, take your time.

WENDY: . . . molested by my church janitor. That went on for over a year.[8] I can honestly say that I never held God responsible. I blamed myself because I liked it. It was a form of attention, and I sought it out and I thought it was sick because of that, but it was the only attention that felt good. I didn't tell anybody for sixteen years, I didn't tell anybody that had happened. In fact, I didn't tell my mom until I was in jail on my way to my first prison trip, which was at the age of twenty-five.

At thirteen I started experimenting with drugs. Weed first. Actually, at twelve I got drunk for my first time on the parent-teacher conference day. My mom was a teacher, so I knew that she was going to be gone too. That was my first time getting drunk, but then I started to experiment. And the funny thing about my life was that I became very angry. Because I was molested, I had an age-inappropriate knowledge of sex. And so by the time I was thirteen, I had lost my virginity and I started to seek out men. I was a tomboy, I was one of the guys, but I also was very promiscuous, I guess you could say, at a young age. I needed to be acknowledged, and in junior high I went from being a scum because I was short and ugly wore glasses, or so they say, and then I grew into my weight, stopped wearing glasses, and I was very attractive. But they didn't know how to accept me, so they start calling me a slut and I had never even kissed a guy.

I had some anger things going on inside of me—resentment, bitterness. By the time I was in high school, I was using drugs. Of course, I was on the down low, but the one part that was really hard for me: I lived like a double life. I never told my mom the things that went on in school, so my mom didn't know that I had those struggles. I didn't tell my mom that the church janitor molested me. I played varsity volleyball and I played in league softball for many years, and I did all these activities acting as if everything was okay. So, it's kind of strange because I had a normal life, and the fact that I lived in the same home my whole life and that my mom was off for the summer, we'd always go travel somewhere. I've been all over the United States. I feel blessed in that aspect, and my mom always showed me that she loved me.

My grandfather was a very violent alcoholic and my mom's mom died when [mom] was ten. She learned how to do everything just to stay outside the house. She became very successful. She got the Women's Athletic Association award when she graduated and an award for not missing one day of high school. Like I said, she did everything she could to stay out of the house. Unfortunately, I wasn't built like her. I can literally count on one hand the times I've seen my mom cry. There's no way she can count to the number of times she's seen me cry, because I'm a crier. I learned somewhere along the way on my mission or journey of self-discovery that it's okay to cry, you know; it really doesn't matter if I have to cry to get it out, it's okay. And I find that today I feel so well or healthy inside that I don't cry as much as I used to.

My mom kicked me out at nineteen. She kicked me and my stuff out, and I remember going to a friend's house and putting all my stuff in their carport and the next day I went down there, somebody had gone through everything. I was devastated. Why would somebody do that? I grew up an only child and I always wanted my friends, I always wanted to be around somebody, and I just didn't know yet that that was part of the drug life, that that's the things that happen. And I was just so hurt and so crushed, and how can people do this to each other? My mom always taught me about trust and about believing in people and, you know, never judging somebody because they had a mohawk or because they had tattoos. She was a high school teacher, so she taught me good morals and good ethics, and I loved that about her and loved that she always has been the forgiving person and I in turn had that trait, but it was hard. At twenty-five, I was on my way to prison. I guess we will talk about that next.

BRYONN: How did your relationships change? Did the relationships help to address the trauma? Or did they add to the trauma between your teenage years and your adult years?

WENDY: I think they added to the trauma. . . . So, my freshman year I got kicked out of school for smoking pot on campus at this rich school, and the two boys that I got kicked out with, one chose one of the other district's schools and the other boy chose the other one.[9] So, there was no other school and they wouldn't send us to the same school. So, I remember the dean saying, "Well, we'll just send you to West Covina High School where your mom can keep an eye on you." I thought my life was over. But I just learned how to be a manipulator very early on, you know, because that's what was going to get me what I needed. So, I thought my life was over, and little did I know it just began. I was able to miss classes sometimes or whatever and just manipulate because all the teachers knew me. All these teachers knew me from the time that I was a baby. . . . I remember all the other broken kids there were. I mean this is the hard part—I had trauma, but I had a stable home. I had a mother that loved me. I didn't want for anything, really. . . . I had everything I needed. I didn't lack anything. But all the children that I hung with that were all broken and their parents using and divorce. There was always this brokenness around my life. We were all a motley crew, let's say.

By the time I was in high school, that's when I had become very angry. Very angry! It came to where I was supposed to graduate and I was short on credit, so I had to go to night school and I picked up the missing credits. I did graduate the year that I was supposed to—barely, I'm going to say. Then I just kind of started using more and demanding my freedom and my mom's like, "Listen, if you aren't going to follow the rules, you can just leave. You know?" And one night I said I'd be back in an hour. I wasn't and I got home, all my stuff was out on the porch—everything. And much later, she told me she stood on the other side of the door just crying, but she had been going to tough love classes. That was what they had taught her. You have to stand for what you believe in, and that would be the last time I would live with her except for a couple short periods of, like, a month or two after I'd gotten out of county jails. But I never really have lived with my mom since. I just discovered my own.

I got a prison term when I was twenty-five. I got out when I was twenty-eight. I was expected to be an upstanding citizen, and I had never really worked a solid job for more than two or three months. So I went back to school and had my children. I had my daughter and twin boys. Never got married. I went back to school to be a drug and alcohol counselor, which I did. I went back into the prisons and taught as a counselor, and shortly after that I left and went into the community. It was during this job that I got into a domestic violence relationship[10] that, ultimately, after over a decade of having my life somewhat on track, sent me back out. I had never been in that type of relationship. So, ultimately that sent me back to prison ten years later.[11] So, I had a prison term twenty-one years ago, eleven years ago I worked in a prison, and then about ten years later I'm in prison again at CIW.

2. SURVIVING PRISON TRAUMA

BRYONN: The California Institution for Women's suicide rate is five times the state average and eight times the national average.[12] You've talked a little bit about your relationships and routine before you entered CIW. What were your expectations when you entered? And what were you experiencing emotionally during that very first day?

WENDY: Okay, I'm going to say that I have two moments, because I went to prison twenty years ago and at that time prison was way different. Well, first of all, it's a privilege being at CIW, the oldest women's prison in the state of California. When it was built, it was designed with the idea of it being like a college campus. It has trees and grass, and it has a circle, like a quad or courtyard, where the women used to socialize outside on these concrete tables, playing cards or crocheting, hanging out with their boom boxes and listening to music. I can still remember, twenty years ago, everybody being outside when O. J. Simpson was found innocent or found not guilty, and I can remember the whole yard just exploding because everybody had their radio on that news.

This time I wanted so bad to come back to CIW because I know that Chowchilla is built like a level-four prison. It's all brick and eight people to a room, which is a lot more difficult to deal with that many personalities. At CIW, it's two people to the room. When I finally got back down to CIW, there was this heaviness; the prison had changed. There was a warden that took away all of the women's clothes, you know, and everything was only white and gray now. You couldn't wear your personal clothes; you couldn't have pretty shirts. I mean, back then they would have balls, women had high-heeled shoes, they had formal dresses, they had—there used to be a pool there; there's all these things that were not there anymore, and this was more like prison, but there was also a heaviness, an evilness.[13] There was this Linus cloud hovering over CIW . . . this sadness; it was horrible. People were doing drugs way more than before. There was people all over the place just strung out on speed and heroin. It was really a changed environment. There was nothing like what my expectations were, and maybe that's what the problem was, is that I had an expectation that it would be the same as it was twenty years prior, but the women's population had changed completely. More gang activity in women, the brokenness and injury, just the rage that I saw across the whole facility was unbelievable. I was on a mission not to be like that. I did everything I could not to be like that, but yeah, it was a struggle.

BRYONN: What were you emotionally? There was a lot of suicide; emotionally, where were you on that first day?

WENDY: On the first day, I was emotionally better than I was because I'd already been at Chowchilla for three months. So, as far as like my mom not knowing I was going to prison, disappearing, and my kids not knowing where I was, all of that had kind of—I had had three months of being clean and so all of that had kind of already disappeared. I dealt with those.[14] Okay, this is what it is [that] nobody knows. When I arrived to CCWF [Central California Women's Facility] May 13, 2015, I was completely broken into a million little pieces. I knew that being sober and liberated from that horrible relationship . . . life could only go up from there. Now you got to just pick up the pieces. So, when I got there I had an expectation of it being a better environment, which it still was to me compared to the prison I had been in out there in that relationship, but it just wasn't what I expected. It was different, you know.

I, myself, was not going back to where I'd come from. I mean, I had never in my whole entire life been so broken by an individual, I'd never let anybody take my whole being before, and I just . . . had to change. My outlook was different. With my commitment to witness for God and serve others, I became free of having to worry about healing myself. Ironically, though, those two commitments are what drove me to put one foot in front of the other. I became very empowered. I was involved in everything I could get my hands on. The healing process was slowly occurring and I didn't even realize it.

BRYONN: Jennifer, on your first day at CIW, what were you expecting when you arrived? And what do you remember going through emotionally on that day?

JENNIFER: That first day I was a complete wreck. I was scared out of my mind. I thought I was going to have a heart attack. It was just completely scary. I was twenty-two years old. I was young. I was super naive. So, right before my incarceration, my daily life was just my children. I stayed home with them and they were my lives, and I took care of them and that was it. They were my environments. They were my world. My life. My relationship's everything. I had two boys and they became my world and my safety.

I actually had my daughter while I was incarcerated.[15] I was, like, two weeks pregnant when I got arrested and didn't know, so that . . . was just traumatic.

BRYONN: At CIW?

JENNIFER: No, in jail.

BRYONN: After you had your baby, how long were you with her before she was taken away?

JENNIFER: Six hours. At Orange County. At the jail they have—it was like a hospital. I was in the main part, and the deputy was sitting with me. As long as they were sitting with me, I could be with her, but then they wanted to go, so they brought me to the inmate section and took her from me.[16]

BRYONN: So you had her for six hours and then how long before you saw her again?

JENNIFER: A month and half, two months maybe.[17] I was completely distraught. Right before I had her, I got the plea bargain of how much time I would take, which was twelve years. I cried nonstop for two weeks. I mean that's all I did. I'm not exaggerating. I just cried for two weeks. And then after that, I kind of shut everything off. I was distraught and I had all this inner turmoil happening, but I wasn't expressing anything. I wasn't sharing with anybody. I wasn't laughing or crying . . . happy or sad or angry or anything. I just completely shut off all of my emotions.[18] My friends said jokes that I was just like a zombie, like a robot just going through the motions. It was really, really terrible, and then just being away from my boys.

But my daughter became my safety while I was in jail. It was just me and her, like we're a team, and even now it's hard for me to cry. I can feel it inside, but I struggle expressing it. I try to watch sad or heart-wrenching movies so I can make myself cry, but it just doesn't really happen. For so long and especially in that environment, I just taught myself to not cry because the tears would start and wouldn't stop. They opened the floodgates. I definitely experienced postpartum depression.[19] I was completely distraught. Lost in a very dark place with no hope of ever seeing light again. Or any kind of happiness. It took me years before I could even start to pull myself out. And even more years to start to see some kind of light or reason to keep on pushing, living. I didn't want to. I just wanted to shut everything off. I really didn't want anything. Nothing made me happy or gave me pleasure or made me smile. Same goes for anger, sadness, and fear. I was void of all emotion for a very long time. I've done a lot of work to come out of that darkness, but there are times that I can feel myself slip back in. Times I even wanted to fall back into it.

I didn't want to feel pain, even if that cost giving up any feelings of joy I had managed. But it was hard. So that first day, I was just so scared. Like I don't want to talk to anybody ever and I heard the worst things ever. People are going to, like, try to rape me or, you know, like I mean, it's just going to be terrible. The officers are going to be horrible to me, they're going to make me, I don't know, do horrible things or whatever. And then I was just like, "I just need to figure out what to do" . . . like I don't want to make any friends, but I don't want to be alone in this. And then I just kind of had, like, this resolved feeling: "Well, I'm just where I'm going to be, so I'm just going to have to do it and that works for me."

I met a friend on the bus. I was actually going from the VSPW [Valley State Prison for Women] and she was going from CCWF—they're two institutions right across the street from each other. The buses were together when we're going to CIW and so we met on the bus and then hit it off. We just hung out, talked a little bit. She told me her whole life story . . . I had made my mind up and told myself to just not get close to people. It didn't work out, and to this day we're still friends. It's been kind of crazy and unbelievable since I first got to CIW July 15, 2009, and it was scary.

BRYONN: You've been home now for how long?

JENNIFER: Almost six months. February 27, 2017, only six months.

BRYONN: And Wendy, you have three children too?

WENDY: Two boys and the daughter.

BRYONN: What was your mothering experience like during incarceration and after?

WENDY: During incarceration, I had no interaction with my children except the letters that I wrote to them. My daughter and I have totally rebuilt our relationship. She is nineteen and now in her first year of college at CSUSB [California State University, San Bernardino]. However, my twin boys, age sixteen, I've only seen once and are way more reserved about rebuilding our relationship.[20] They want to see me doing well for a period of time first.

JENNIFER: My children were young when I went to jail. They were two and six months old, and I was two weeks pregnant. They didn't know what was happening and were too young to understand. I saw them a few times while I was in jail, before I was sent to prison. As they got older, I couldn't see them anymore or talk to them on the phone, because they didn't know I was in prison. Needless to say, I really didn't have a mothering experience. I would speak with their grandma on the phone—

[my mom] was taking care of all three—and she would give me updates on what was happening with them. Every piece of information I was given, via phone call or letter, I have kept and written down in notebooks. This way I can try to know them in some way.

BRYONN: Before we transition into talking about what's happened since you came home, let's talk a little bit about the daily routine at CIW. Time in your cell, time in the yard, time for education programs and the arts, and how the routine and the relationships—like, what that experience was like for you.

WENDY: Women become conditioned to live with these distorted ideas . . . such as it's mandatory to shower three to five times a day, you carry bugs in your clothes or can't wear shoes on the cell floor. When someone is a lifer, I get that their cell is their home, but the way people live and these unwritten prison rules they follow only minimizes their ability to remember what the outside world is really like [and], in turn, making their transition from inside to outside much more difficult.

JENNIFER: Shoes, and you're out.

WENDY: People wax their floor and it's super shiny, and you leave your shoes at the door.

BRYONN: In the cell?

WENDY: Yes.

BRYONN: How big are these cells?

WENDY: Six by eight.

BRYONN: And it's two people to a cell?

WENDY: Two people, and there's a desk and two tall lockers, bunk bed, toilet, and sink.

JENNIFER: I used to joke that I can stand in the middle [of my] cell and I would be in the living room, bedroom, the bathroom, the kitchen, the office, and the garage.

BRYONN: The bathroom?

JENNIFER: Yeah, the bathroom, all right there.

BRYONN: Any privacy in the bathroom?

WENDY: None, absolutely none. But for me, I got up at five o'clock every morning. Because I got up at five o'clock, I went straight down onto the floor that nobody else would sit on, but I didn't care, and I did some yoga stretches, detoxifying stretch, and then I got up and I read my Bible, and I made my cup of coffee. Then I would sit and have time with the Lord before I would get dressed for work. I was in the construction PIA for a year, where I completed the PIA carpentry and laborer programs.

BRYONN: PIA?

JENNIFER: Prison Industry Authority. Yeah, if you have a Prison Industry Authority job, that means you haven't been in trouble. It's one of the better jobs. Yeah, everybody hates the sewing factories, but it's still good—either way, I had to start at 7:00 a.m.[21] So, I didn't go to the chow hall either. I would have one little thing of oatmeal. That was my gig, and then I would go and I would take my little lunch. I didn't eat bread, so the only thing I'd have is *chicharones* because there's still no carbs—lots of fat, but no carbs. We're very limited on food there. Everything that you buy is processed. Everything. Because you don't have a refrigerator.[22]

BRYONN: Were there experiences you had during your incarceration that related to trauma before? How did your prior experiences affect your experience while incarcerated?

WENDY: I was in a very violent relationship prior to my prison term. I then, while in prison, saw three girls slice a girl up and beat the dog snot out of her in a utility closet. Watching that brought an awareness of my abuse that I had never seen from an outside point of view. That drove me to find a way to liberate myself from that horrible trauma that I had experienced and search for avenues of healing. I found healing through the arts and lots of commitment from myself to get better.

BRYONN: Do you remember learning about the problem of suicides at the prison or when you first realized that [it] was something that was impacting the woman at CIW?

WENDY: I hadn't heard about the numerous attempts and the actual suicides that had taken place, but October 18, 2015, I found my twenty-six-year-old bunky hanging in the middle of the night. I was woken up by her feet hitting the wall and I can remember just getting up and going,

"Oh, babe!" and just lifting her up so the straps would loosen. There was twenty-seven straps that she had wrapped around her neck, some of them leather camp bootlaces. At that moment, it was what it was.

My mom was a PE teacher, so I had been taught health and first aid and CPR since the time I was nine. So your instinct kind of just kicks into overdrive. So, I did save her life, but after . . . it was the after that really got to me. I just didn't know how I felt about it. I couldn't focus. It just made me really sad. She never spoke to me again, but at that point I made a conscious decision that I never wanted my life to be that hopeless. I think there was three other suicides that happened in the time that I was there.

BRYONN: How did it feel to save her life and then have her not speak to you?

WENDY: At first I was kind of hurt. Not bitter. I was hurt, but then I realized that her three-year-old son still had a mom and that her parents still had a daughter and that I did what I did because it wouldn't matter who it was. Even if it was somebody that I didn't care for, I think the act of humanity everybody deserves. I tried really hard after I talked about it with the psychologist, telling him I didn't know how I felt.[23] I tried really hard not to personalize it because what she did had nothing to do with me. It's just I happen to be the one that helped her. My counselor had come to me and said, "You know, there's this thing called a meritorious act and if we can get it approved . . . you'll get a year off your sentence?" For five months, he searched and searched everywhere and could not find any information or record on it. None of the 7219s that were done, there wasn't any paperwork, nothing in the logbooks. The incident just mysteriously disappeared.

BRYONN: What's a 7219?

WENDY: A 7219 is a form that they do when you go to the infirmary or medical, where they check your body for any injuries. She lived in my room and she had been beaten up the night before. Her whole face was black and I was the roommate. So, they wanted to know if I had marks as well. Of course the spotlight was on me. I didn't have any marks. My counselor looked for five months and could not find any documentation whatsoever. All the paperwork had mysteriously disappeared.[24] And that, to me, was a sign of the administration and warden's desperation to cover up any attempts of suicide. CIW made international news because of how high the suicide rate was[25] . . . but I had to let it go and not take it personal. I know that the strength through me was God. It wasn't me, you know, it just was kind of a natural reaction, but I had to not personalize it. However, Mr. Chacon informed me that he interviewed my old cellmate. He said when asked, she replied, "I would not be here if it were not for Wendy's actions." When he told me that, I broke down in tears. That was all I needed to hear. You see, after the incident, she never spoke to me again. So to hear that she felt that way filled my heart.

3. EDUCATION AND THE ARTS

BRYONN: Education is the most effective preventative measure against recidivism. Not only is it proven to empower incarcerated students, it is empirically proven to lessen the negative effects of self-stigma.[26] How did much education impact your overall routine?

JENNIFER: In the end I was pretty active. I would get up first thing in the morning and I would tutor someone or I would help my roommate with her homework. She was also one of my students. I was helping the community resource center run a project called Project Me to help some of the women who had behavioral or drug problems, kind of like we belong in the mix. . . . They had some problems in the institution: they needed some guidance, maybe they couldn't sit for a five-hour program on a weekend or something. So, we came up with a curriculum to give them small doses of the different programs over there. I did that five days a week.

I did what is called AVP, Alternatives to Violence Project, and that's my passion, my love. AVP was also really big for me because I learned a lot about myself. I was a team coordinator for the nonprofit organization that works to build self-esteem in individuals and brainstorm ways to deal with conflict nonviolently. Community building is really important, team building, communication, and all this other wonderful stuff. And there's workshops, so I brought many workshops to Project Me. I did the workshops as a participant and sort of facilitating, so it made me rise to my own expectations of myself and be who I wanted to be, because if I wasn't, then how can I facilitate for the people? I would do that three times a week so the women can get their hours and get their completion. We also did, like, exercise. Once a week we would walk around the prison. So, at least just getting them moving. We also did, like, a goal planning one.

Chaffey College, getting my degree . . . was really huge for me.[27] I never put emphasis on education. I always loved school for the most part, but accepted that it wasn't for me, that getting a higher education wasn't for me. But school showed me that I may be a "criminal," but I can still be treated like a human being. The courses were amazing. The instructors didn't give us an easy time, like "Oh, because you're poor we will go easy on you." No. You have to work just as hard with less resources. And you can still do it. Your past doesn't have to make your future. You know? You can just be a component of it. So that was really huge.

I would definitely have to say when UCLA came in, that was just another life changer for me. Chaffey is a community college. So I still felt I was at a lower level, that I couldn't make it past anything great. I could never be anything great. I couldn't do great things. I could do mediocre, but then the UCLA Prison Education Program[28] came in and I was doing Actors' Gang.[29]

BRYONN: And I know Actors' Gang very well, but for those who don't?

WENDY: Actors' Gang is also a program that is in there. It's a prison project that came from a theater called the Actors' Gang. Actor Tim Robbins and some other UCLA students that he graduated with thirty-five years ago put together the theater. Sabra Williams, also an actor, became a member of the theater and founded the Actors' Gang Prison Project, and they've been in the prison system for twelve years now. They're also in some juvenile camps and have more recently started two reentry programs as well.

BRYONN: Tim Robbins produced my show there two years in a row.

JENNIFER: Actors' Gang was also really important because it made me deal with my emotions, made me actually feel. It made me start to become more emotionally aware. I will talk all day long to other people and help them and facilitate them working with their own emotions, but I wouldn't do the same, so it forced me to. It forced me to identify my emotions inside of me, deal with them, manage them, and then push on from them, you know, like not get stuck inside of them and kind of just let them control me, and that was really huge.

The CIW Think Tank gave me purpose. It made me feel good about myself and confident that I could keep up with the other women in the Think Tank. Their education levels. They're just really freaking amazing, and like I can rise. Some of the time I can rise to them and I can work with them.[30] And so, I must have these good qualities in me, and it was really cool for me and it pushed me because they accepted me, and you accepted me, and UCLA accepted me and CIW accepted me, but I wasn't accepting. So I pushed myself working with these women and everybody else with UCLA and CIW who had really amazing educational backgrounds.

Working on *What It Iz* was really, really fun and it was more than fun.[31] Adapting it became a part of who I was. It's just another thing to add to all the things I was doing, and it was just something that I really looked forward to. I got to hang out with people. We went over this script and it was just really cool working through ideas—like, "Okay, will this work?" and then hearing someone else say, "Oh gosh, you're totally right. This would work better!" and it was cool how there were so many different people in the room. So many different ideas and brains and thoughts and emotion could come together to put something together and we didn't have any conflict. We didn't have any kind of BS. It was fun, but it gave me a sense of fulfillment, like I'm doing something, not just working.

I have no idea what I wanted to be when I grow up, but it's a good feeling because now I have options. Now there's so many different things that I can do because of all the work that I do while I was incarcerated. I stayed busy. I did so many different programs. I was in education. I was in fun, silly stuff like creative writing and *What It Iz*. I did nonviolence workshops. I did anything under the sun. I found out that I'm an amazing painter. I had no clue. Just took a superb, random painting class and it was beautiful. I'm 100 percent satisfied with my life and what I'm capable of. I wouldn't have known that if I wouldn't try it.

WENDY: The second day I was there, I was already singing in the choir! I literally found everything I can possibly do to keep myself from being locked up. Even though I was out and in a relationship, I was locked up in the middle of the desert without a friend in sight. I didn't want to be locked in a little cell either, and I just wanted to be a part of things. I did things that didn't normally have to do with me, like the Black education awareness team. I became a big part of that. I was gone out of my cell all the time. I became a Women's Advisory Council member. I was the white representative in my unit. There are four reps to a unit: white, Black, Hispanic, and other; we were between the population and the staff. When there were concerns, we were the people that were the liaisons, I guess you could say. I kept myself busy in tons of positive things and I think, you know, ultimately Jen and I were in the same unit, but the reason that we met was through Actors' Gang. . . .

It's absolutely imperative to discuss the arts in my life and the effect they had in my life. The arts became my number-one vessel where I discovered healing. I was in a singing group, I was in the Actors' Gang, and I was in Annie Buckley's Community Based Art Program from Cal State San Bernardino, where we would use all different types of mediums to create art. Then, really finding this place of safety in my writing and being able to actually share it. Not only share it, but to hear other things that people had written and their pain and it being so raw and feeling so a part that I was writing about things that had happened to me. I feel like I had overcome them and part of the way to overcome them was by engaging in somebody else's pain, understanding where they're going, where they are coming from, and how we can all heal together.[32] The arts is what I'm advocating for. I would like to see a mandatory four hours of arts instead of us working forty hours. I think we should work thirty-six and have four of art. I don't believe everybody got to be a child. I don't believe that everybody's environment allowed them to be a child, and their childhood could have been taken away by many different things: gangs, drugs, molestation. That's why art is there. That's why music is there. It's for that inner, most sacred part of you to find a place of happiness and unity with everybody else.

I remember when we finished revising the last page of *What It Iz*. I remember us flipping to the last page, we were back in the Chaffee school room. I remember feeling this accomplishment and gratitude.

Getting out and becoming a UCLA Inaugural Beyond the Bars LA Fellow and actually getting to see the play *What It Iz* at our conference was amazing.! I remember at CIW discussing whether or not Dorothy should have Chucks or Jordans on her feet to meet this day. . . .

BRYONN: [*laughs*]

WENDY: To see all those little details that nobody else in the room would have understood except for us was awesome.

JENNIFER: One of the [incarcerated] girls' sons had been shot and killed at Long Beach.[33]

WENDY: Yes, by police. And we all asked her if it would be okay if we could honor her son by putting his name into that. . . . I think those little intricacies that only we knew, because we helped revise it, was so personal and just so magnifying in the place. When I saw Jennifer there, I was so happy because the work that we had done together in many different avenues has been so gratifying.

BRYONN: And now it'll be immortalized again in this interview when it is published and folks read about it. I will tell you that all the actors in the cast—I explained to them what we talked about in each scene as they learned each scene. I got to say, you know, the conference had between 700 and 1,000 people show up. We had very different people or more every night for the show and even Rosario Dawson came.[34] She was moved.

JENNIFER: She treated me like I was a star.

WENDY: I remember her telling about the story; she was just like, "Oh my gosh! You know? Like I can't believe I am meeting you!"

BRYONN: Scott Budnick came. Rick Ross came. Melina Abdullah from Black Lives Matter LA came. Jason Dorsey, one of the writers of *What It Iz* from the East Coast, came, but having you out there was a highlight.[35]

WENDY: I think that was probably my favorite piece as far as personality or being personal with that. Here we have the man who actually put the *What It Iz* together, and I got to share with Jason out on the porch of the theater my "What It Iz" poem that I wrote, which of course was inspired by revising the *What It Iz* script. I just felt really honored.

BRYONN: Well, having you there was a real honor and a privilege for me.

4. SELF-LOVE AND ACCEPTANCE

BRYONN: We started with your first day at CIW. What was it like on your last?

JENNIFER: My last day was unreal. Like something out of a psychological thriller. I wasn't quite sure what was real and what wasn't: "Am I making this all up? Are they really going to let me out?" I barely slept the night before because, of course, I procrastinated and didn't have everything ready. I guess I never truly believed the day would come. I woke up super early so I could spend some uninterrupted time with my thoughts and emotions before my entire world shifted. Disbelief was overwhelming and overpowering just about everything. I talked to my family pretty early, and that's when the excitement kicked in. Finally! I get to be free and with my family again.

That changed quickly, though. My friends started coming by to say bye, and I thought my heart would break. I was sad I had to leave them all behind. Devastated they had to stay in such a dark and lonely place. On top of that, I thought, "Why do I get to leave here and be free when there are so many far more deserving women who need to go home?" and "What if I can't make it out there? What if I can't transition? What if I can't do this or that? What if I fail?" And the list goes on. I was on the twistiest, scary, emotional roller coaster I had ever willingly jumped on. I think that I was so afraid of being happy about finally getting out that I did whatever I could to feel anything but joy. I have always been secretly fearful of anything that brings a smile to my face, a pep in my step, a giggle to my lips, or a lightness to my heart. So afraid that it would all come crashing down somehow. That's just a part of what I felt that day. It was a vicious cycle of those wonderful things called emotions.

BRYONN: Californians for Safety and Justice found that there are more than 4,800 things that you cannot do once you come home if you have a felony on your record.[36] So, what were the greatest challenges still inside, but also coming home—between family relationships, health care, employment, housing, and education? What was the single biggest challenge for you at CIW and the single biggest challenge for you coming home?

JENNIFER: The greatest challenge since CIW was finding myself and my identity: who I am, what are my morals, what do I believe in, what makes me who I am, what things do I like, what do I want in a friend, what kind of friend do I want to be, what kind of worker or employee I would be, what kind of boss do I want to be? I didn't know anything about myself because I had completely been molded into what someone else wanted me to be, and that was really challenging for me and especially in an environment where I want to get close to people. How can I learn about myself if I don't interact with other people? When you're by yourself, you can try to learn something, but you can't.

For me, interacting with other people really opened my eyes to who I am and what I want in life, and that was really hard for me. It took quite a few years because I was struggling with the shame . . . I shouldn't get all of these things that I'm getting! I don't deserve this and deserve to have the friends that I have, the job I have. It's been the same challenge coming out—now I have to find myself all over again. I found my identity inside and I had a life for myself and a purpose and I really made the best out of my time in there.

WENDY: This is going to sound so simplistic, but I didn't have needs or wants. I chose to make good decisions and walked in a power greater than myself. I stopped trying to control everything. Everything just started to change. I literally hit my knees and told the Lord, "I'm going to witness for you and I'm going to serve others." I just kept doing that and I kept finding other people that were way worse off than I was. I lived with a happy heart. I would pray with people and let the way I lived my life be my testament. I was only at CIW prison for twenty months and I left with thirty-two certificates. I'm not saying that like I'm patting myself on the back. I'm saying it because I had to find a way out of my past traumas and pain, and I had. It was the motion of self-discovery. By helping others—that healing just transformed me, my life, and my heart without me even knowing it.

The obstacles on the outside? I'm going to say supervision has been an obstacle.[37] There have been times where I had a wonderful parole officer. She was so wonderful, and then she retired and we got this new parole officer, who had this idea about the things that I do with the Actors' Gang, being a UCLA Fellow, as well as me speaking in conferences. She just thought I was so big on myself, and so—and she had no idea who I was. That was a challenge, and then she used to talk to other parolees about me. "I'm fighting to get GPS on these ankle monitors because Wendy took advantage of it." And they came back and they would tell this story, and I'd said, "Yeah, she's talking about me."

BRYONN: What do you mean? What do you mean, she "took advantage of it"?

WENDY: She thought I was taking advantage of the ankle monitor because it didn't have GPS. She, in turn, told a group of fourteen women parolees that I had been taking advantage of the ankle monitor, so she was now fighting for GPS to be added. She had no choice but to give me clearance because I had talked to Captain Fields in Sacramento, who was in charge over all ankle monitors in California, about needing clearance to stay at UCLA for four days because of the conference that my fellowship had built. When he contacted her, he told her I was cleared—period—because it would be politically incorrect to not support me and the UCLA Beyond the Bars conference. I'd only been out for two months at that point, and I actually talked to him about Prop 57 and I told him, "Look, I'm not asking for any freebies or any, you know, 'get-out-of-jail-free card.' I'm not asking for any of that. I'm asking just for you guys to look into my case and see if I'm eligible." Well, they did. Albert Rivas, who was his right-hand man, he literally walked over on July First and put my case in their hands and had me, one of the first people, evaluated and I appreciate that totally. But we've had a relationship ever since. And so, when it came to our conference, the Beyond the Bars conference, I needed permission to go and stay. I wasn't allowed to do overnights because I was considered to still be in custody.

BRYONN: How would you describe Beyond the Bars LA and its impact?

WENDY: UCLA's inaugural Beyond the Bars LA [BTB LA] Fellowship and conference—I applied for it once I got out through you and the Justice Work Group, and I was chosen as one of those BTB LA Fellows. I'm in that fellowship and we built a conference. The theme was "The End of Mass Incarceration." And so that's my goal: to constantly advocate and to change policy and to do those things. But she [the new parole officer] became very bitter because I talked to him, Albert, and said, "Hey, I need to get to Captain Fields." The guy over everybody. I talked to him and said, "Mr. Fields, you know what I'm doing. I'm in UCLA. I need permission." He goes, "You know what, I'm going to e-mail her right now." So I basically went over her head and she didn't like that because he told her, "This is what you're going to do because it would be"—this is exactly the words that he used and that my staff at the program told me: he told us and your parole officer that "it would be politically incorrect to not allow you to participate," and she disliked that. But that's part of the struggle: when we rise to the occasion and we do those things that people would never expect of us, they think that we're trying to be, you know, big man on campus. No, I'm proud of where I am and I'm not going to allow you to break me down.

The other struggle that I would say that I had was housing. When my funding changed, I was homeless and you can remember, I called you desperate. "I'm homeless, I don't have any place to go, and I'm not going back . . . to my old life."[38] I'm in my car. I'm no longer at the program. It was very difficult. When I left the program, I was now off parole and on probation. . . . Being homeless and not having an address, they put an ankle monitor right back on me. According to probation, I was now a "high-risk" probationer because I was "homeless." They have the homeless show up every Tuesday behind the building. This came right out of the mouth of probation: "because we don't want all those homeless people standing on the street where everybody can see them." That's what I was told. I'm telling you, there's probably, when I was there, probably a hundred and that's not including the people that came when I wasn't there. But they don't want those homeless people standing on the street where everybody can see them. Now it's just ridiculous the way that they treat people. The program eventually found me a bed in their sober living [program] and my probation pays for it. However, probation mandated me to quit college.[39]

The struggle for me inside was not hard. Outside it got a little more challenging because of what, like Jennifer said, is that you've worked so hard to find this place of comfort within yourself, like being in my own skin and to like myself. It felt so good and so routine and all of a sudden you go out and you have nothing to do. The program I was in, there was no walking. We walked everywhere in prison. The prison facility was eleven acres. I went from walking everywhere to walking nowhere.

BRYONN: Did you have any issues finding housing?

JENNIFER: So many issues! I had set everything up—place to live, job, et cetera—about nine months before I paroled. Unfortunately, about four months before I was to leave, I was told I couldn't go where all my support was. I was sent to a different county, one where I had no one and no support. My brother tried for months before I got out to find me a place to live—a sober-living residential program, treatment program, transitional housing, anything—but to no avail. Most of the programs for women are aimed toward mothers to aid in family reunification. This is a beautiful and much needed service. Unfortunately, I was not accepted into those programs because I was not bringing my children with me.

More programs denied me because there was nothing in my file to say I had any kind of drug or alcohol problem, so I couldn't go to any treatment programs.[40] My brother talked with some places that said I needed to speak with them when I was released. When I did, there were no beds available. For the first week and a half, I stayed in a hotel that my family paid for. If I hadn't had their support, I would've been sleeping on the streets. My brother had contacted a sober living [program] before I was released, and they told him no because they didn't have any felons there.[41] On a whim, I contacted them to plead my case, and the woman agreed to let me live there. While all this was happening, I did not receive any help from my counselors at the prison or my parole officer after I got out.[42] It was essentially all up to me to find what few resources are available to women.[43]

BRYONN: Were you able to find work after you were released?

WENDY: I obtained part-time employment with the Actors' Gang theater troupe. I had been in their program while incarcerated. I am currently seeking full-time employment and have run into barriers because of my felony record.

BRYONN: Do you think the prison education programs helped?

JENNIFER: I believe the education programs did help. I was incarcerated for a little over ten years and really knew nothing about the workforce in the "free world." The programs at the prison taught me how to put together a decent résumé, answer tricky questions in an interview, et cetera. More than that, the education programs help build a better sense of self. I was able to create a real confidence inside of me, not some false confidence that I previously had lived off of for too long. With that confidence, I was emboldened to stick my neck out, to apply to jobs I thought were above me. I learned things about myself I never knew. I grew in immeasurable ways. I was also able to take the numerous rejections and move on from them, not get stifled and hopeless. Yes, it was discouraging, but I had to tell myself that it was not a reflection of my skills, talents, or even me as a human being. With all the knowledge I gained from the education programs, I could see the logic behind such decisions, painful as it was. Without those education programs, I am afraid to imagine where I would be at now, geographically, mentally, emotionally.

BRYONN: I'm really grateful for all that time and effort that you have committed to make sure that we get your stories out, so other folks can hear from your experiences, learn from your experiences, and I just want to offer you a chance to give any final thoughts or words on what you gained through the process and any words of wisdom or insight you would offer to other women or folks who are reading this interview in the days ahead.

WENDY: There's a movement right now where people are not having it anymore. They really are realizing the injustices that are happening behind bars. If you're inside, do something different: go find some arts, do something that you normally wouldn't do, because there are people there that want to help you. I'm forty-nine years old and I feel like I finally know what I want to be when I grow up. It took forty-nine years to get here, but I'm so proud of myself because I'm a survivor. I've made it through the worst of traumas, and I'm just proud to know the people I know and know that they're my family. I can come to any one of them. And having my daughter back in my life . . . my twins aren't ready yet, but that will come as long as I keep doing what I'm supposed to do. I don't have to prove anything to anybody, which is what I've always tried to do. I needed love and attention and I always had to prove myself, and now I don't because I know who I am. I think it's amazing. Because of all the things I have done and all the connections that I made, I have learned so much about myself and the direction I want my life to go in. I don't have to live a nine-to-five life running on the same track every day. I could make it what I want to make it. And if I say, "Oh, I totally want to do this!" and decide later I don't, that's okay. I do something else because I have all these different tools now that I didn't have before.

JENNIFER: And then another thing that I would say is, you just have to stay connected. I'm all the way out in San Diego, so it's hard. It's really hard at times, but staying connected to the people, the connections you made inside. Networking is the biggest thing that I could ever push on anyone. It's so important to network, and it doesn't have to be like job opportunities. It could just be like people who you connect with, like Wendy and I. We both were incarcerated together. We connect on many different levels. But I mean, it's just important to stay connected to people because you're not so alone in the world. When I'm connected with people who I've shared some experiences with or just talked about some things with, then it's okay and then that world doesn't seem so dark. I can just be okay with everything.

BRYONN: I love that as you're saying that, you're giving Wendy your telephone number on her cell phone. [*laughs*]

JENNIFER: I was thinking, actually, like, "Do I really have her phone number?"

BRYONN: And now there you are connected, and making the connection happen as you tell folks that you do it. You're actually good at being the change that you want to see in the world! Thank you both for making time for this. I just want to say I am truly blessed and honored. This dialogue has been so valuable, and I know it's going to be appreciated by so many folks. And I just want to let you both know that if you don't know already, I am on Team Wendy and Team Jennifer for the long haul, and I'm so grateful for this time. Thank you, and I look forward to many more conversations to come.

JENNIFER: Absolutely.

WENDY: That's the difference, right, for my life. Can I just say one more thing?

BRYONN: Of course! The mic is all yours.

WENDY: It does not have to be on record, but I know I said this before at the *What It Iz* talk-back. Jennifer said something in a circle of the Actor's Gang. She said, "You know, what I discovered is that I don't have to judge people and I don't have to stay away from them either; I can just love them right where they are." It was like an epiphany for me because that's how I felt, but I just hadn't put it in words yet. That day, I became connected to Jennifer. Look at us today.

LINER NOTES

Track #5's interview took place February 20, 2018, at University of California, Los Angeles. Originally published as "Women Beyond Bars: Jennifer Claypool and Wendy Staggs on Life after Lockdown," *UCLA Women's Law Journal* 25, no. 2 (2018). Research for the original article was contributed by Annie L, the Narratives of Freedom Collective, and the editorial staff of the *UCLA Women's Law Journal*.

1. The current facility was built in 1952 with 1,398 beds. Today, it incarcerates more than 1,800 women. Division of Internal Oversight and Research, Office of Research, *Weekly Report of Population as of Midnight October 10, 2018*, California Department of Corrections and Rehabilitation, www.cdcr.ca.gov /Reports_Research/Offender_Information_Services_Branch/WeeklyWed /TPOP1A/TPOP1Ad181010.pdf, https://perma.cc/BT6X-84EE; Don Chaddock, "Unlocking History: Original Tehachapi Women's Prison Was Novel in Approach," *Inside CDCR*, February 13, 2015, www.insidecdcr.ca.gov/2015/02/unlocking-history-ciw-tehachapi.

2. Elizabeth Swavola et al., *Overlooked: Women and Jails in an Era of Reform*, Vera Institute of Justice and Safety and Justice Challenge, 2016, 6, https://

storage.googleapis.com/vera-web-assets/downloads/Publications/overlooked-women-and-jails-report/legacy_downloads/overlooked-women-and-jails-report-updated.pdf; TRT World, "Who Is Benefitting from California's Cannabis 'Green Rush'?" *Route 66*, March 6, 2018, www.you-tube.com/watch?v=vBPCrSV9jp4& sns=em.

3. For an analysis of a study of sixty women regarding their experiences of violence and trauma, see Dana D. DeHart, "Pathways to Prison: Impact of Victimization in the Lives of Incarcerated Women," *Violence Against Women* 14 (2008): 1362. "[S]exual abuse is one of the strongest predictors of whether a girl will be charged again after release." Malika Saada Saar et al., *The Sexual Abuse to Prison Pipeline: The Girls' Story*, Human Rights Project for Girls, Georgetown Law Center on Poverty and Inequality, and Ms. Foundation for Women, 2015, 7–9, https://rights4girls.org/wp-content/uploads/r4g/2015/02/2015_COP_sex-ual-abuse_layout_web-1.pdf, https://perma.cc/AC32-SDRW.

4. Timothy Hughes and Doris James Wilson, *Reentry Trends in the US*, Bureau of Justice Statistics, 2018, www.bjs.gov/content/reentry/reentry.cfm, https://perma.cc/D3T8-F39K.

5. Debbie Mukamal et al., *Degrees of Freedom: Expanding College Opportunities for Currently and Formerly Incarcerated Californians*, Stanford Criminal Justice Center and Chief Justice Earl Warren Institute on Law and Social Policy, 2015, 1, www.law.berkeley.edu/files/DegreesofFreedom2015_FullReport.pdf.

6. "The denigration of, and backlash against, assertions of child sexual abuse results in part from the fact that sexual abuse, especially of female children, is a harm that exists in an epistemological vacuum and is surrounded by denial, resistance, ignorance, and fear." Lynne Henderson, "Without Narrative: Child Sexual Abuse," *Virginia Journal of Social Policy and Law* 4 (1997): 479, 498. For studies on survivors' reluctance to disclose child sexual abuse, see Kamala London et al., who in "Review of the Contemporary Literature on How Children Report Sexual Abuse to Others: Findings, Methodological Issues, and Implications for Forensic Interviewers," *Memory* 16 (2008): 29, 31, conclude, based on a review of retrospective accounts from adults disclosing child sexual abuse, that "55–69 percent of adults indicated that they never told anyone about the sexual abuse during childhood." For the many barriers that keep survivors of child sexual abuse from coming forward, see also Delphine Collin Vézina et al., "A Preliminary Mapping of Individual, Relational, and Social Factors that Impede Disclosure of Childhood Sexual Abuse," *Child Abuse and Neglect* 43 (2015): 123, 127–31.

7. Children who grow up in disadvantaged households or have early adverse life events often experience adverse results later in life such as stress, poor health, alcoholism, and drug use. Timothy W. Bjorkman, "A State in Shackles: The Effect of a Dysfunctional Childhood on Crime and Imprisonment," *South Dakota Law Review* 62 (2017): 211, 228, 239. Half of the imprisoned population reported drug or alcohol addiction problems. Sharon Dolovich, "Foreword: Incarceration

American-Style," *Harvard Law and Policy Review* 3 (2009): 237, 245. The tie between substance abuse and criminality among incarcerated women leads to many of these women turning to substance abuse as a way to "self-medicate depression ... or to avoid deeper traumas." Myrna S. Raeder, "Gender-Related Issues in a Post-Booker Federal Guidelines World," *McGeorge Law Review* 37 (2006): 691, 697–98.

8. Religious institutions—particularly the Catholic church—have a history of claims alleging sexual abuse. See, for example, O'Bryan v. Holy See, 556 *Federal Reporter* 3d 361 (6th Circuit 2009), denying a motion to dismiss punitive class-action claims for violation of human rights, negligence, and breach of fiduciary duty brought against the Roman Catholic clergy by alleged sexual abuse victims; and Martinelli v. Bridgeport Roman Catholic Diocesan Corp., 196 *Federal Reporter* 3d 409, 432 (2d Circuit 1999), denying the Catholic diocese's motion for judgment as a matter of law after a jury found breach of fiduciary duty of a child who alleged sexual abuse by a priest.

9. The school-to-prison pipeline is a nationwide trend where poor and minority students are funneled out of the education system and into the criminal justice system. India Geronimo, "Systemic Failure: The School-to-Prison Pipeline and Discrimination Against Poor Minority Students," *Journal of Law in Society Symposium* (Wayne State University Law School) 13 (March 25, 2011): 281. Zero-tolerance policies at schools are the main contributor to increasing a child's probability of entering the prison system. Rocio Rodríguez Ruíz, "Comment, School-to-Prison Pipeline: An Evaluation of Zero Tolerance Policies and Their Alternatives," *Houston Law Review* 54 (2017): 803.

10. Sheryl Pimlott Kubiak et al., "Differences Among Incarcerated Women with Assaultive Offenses: Isolated Versus Patterned Use of Violence," *Journal of Interpersonal Violence* 28 (2013): 2462. The overwhelming majority of women in prison are survivors of domestic violence. Court Services and Offender Supervision Agency, *Statistics on Women Offenders*, 2016, www.csosa.gov/newsmedia /factsheets/statistics-on-women-offenders-2016.pdf. Approximately 70–80 percent of incarcerated women experienced intimate partner violence. Melissa E. Dichter and Sue Osthoff, *Women's Experiences of Abuse as a Risk Factor for Incarceration: A Research Update*, National Online Research Center on Violence Against Women, 2015, 1.

11. "A longitudinal study of 3,006 women found that drug use increased the risk of intimate partner violence and intimate partner violence increased the risk of substance use." Larry Bennett and Patricia Bland, *Substance Abuse and Intimate Partner Violence*, National Online Research Center on Violence Against Women, 2008, 1. Many women have difficulty succeeding in domestic violence self-defense claims due to a requirement that they fear "imminent" attack. See, for example, State v. Norman, 4 *North Carolina Reports* 253, 254 (1989), which holds that the defendant, who was abused by her husband for more than twenty years and was

diagnosed with battered spouse syndrome, was not acting in self-defense because there was no fear of imminent death or great bodily harm when she shot him in his sleep.

12. Hillel Aron, "Why Are So Many Inmates Attempting Suicide at the California Institution for Women?" *LA Weekly*, July 20, 2016, www.laweekly.com/news/why -are-so-many-inmates-attempting-suicide-at-the-california-institution-for -women-7156615; Victoria Law, "Erika Rocha's Suicide Brings Attention to the Dire Need for Mental Health Care in Prison," *Rewire News*, May 20, 2016, https:// rewire.news/article/2016/05/20/erika-rochas-suicide-brings-attention-dire-need-mental-health-care-prison. CIW's high suicide rates prompted a statewide audit. California State Auditor, *California Department of Corrections and Rehabilitation: It Must Increase Its Efforts to Prevent and Respond to Inmate Suicides*, Report 2016-131, 1, www.auditor.ca.gov/pdfs/reports/2016-131.pdf.

13. The warden during Wendy Stagg's first incarceration was John Dovey, who assisted in bringing the Prison Pup Program to CIW, in which women trained dogs to become service animals. See Blanca E. Sanchez, "Pups Win Praise from CIW Prisoners," *Inland Valley Daily Bulletin*, September 19, 2002, LexisNexis Academic. During Wendy's second incarceration, the warden was Kimberly Hughes; CIW was suspected of having "systemic and pervasive problems" during this time period. See "Wardens at Two Women's Prisons Retire Amid Abuse, Suicide Claims," *Los Angeles Times*, August 4, 2016, www.latimes.com/local /lanow/la-me-wardens-20160804-snap-story.html, https://perma.cc/UA42-5X53. The suicide rate at CIW was eight times the national average for incarcerated women; State Senator Connie M. Leyva called for the state auditor to investigate. See California State Auditor, *It Must Increase Its Efforts*.

14. Under California law, a child may be placed in foster care if "the child's parent has been incarcerated . . . and cannot arrange for the care of the child." California Welfare and Instituional Code § 300(g). In "arrang[ing] for the care of the child," the mother is generally required to make the proposed caretaker a temporary legal guardian. See *In re* Athena P., 103 *California Appendix* 4th 617, 629–30 (2002), terminating an incarcerated mother's parental rights because, though she left her daughter in the care of the child's grandparents, she failed to make the child's grandparents temporary legal guardians. But see *In re* S.D., 99 *California Appendix* 4th 1068, 1078 (2002), refusing to terminate an incarcerated mother's parental rights because two of her sisters expressed willingness to care for her son during her incarceration, and the dependency court got involved before she could make further arrangements.

15. The proportion of incarcerated women who are pregnant could be as high as 10 percent. See Estalyn Marquis, "'Nothing Less Than the Dignity of Man': Women Prisoners, Reproductive Health, and Unequal Access to Justice Under the Eighth Amendment," *California Law Review* 106 (2018): 203, 210 n. 39, which estimates that 8 to 10 percent of women are pregnant when they enter prison, and on

average these women remain incarcerated for six to twelve months after giving birth. Of the roughly 200,000 women currently incarcerated in America, 6–10 percent are pregnant. Laura Dorwart, "Giving Birth in Jail Can Traumatize Women for Decades," *Vice*, January 16, 2018, https://tonic.vice.com/en_us/article /kznxav/giving-birth-in-jail-can-traumatize-women-for-decades, https://perma .cc/TC9S-PRR3.

16. Some mothers are denied the ability to nurse newborns, stay with newborns for any length of time, or introduce newborns to other family members, and outside of a small number of programs, incarcerated mothers are denied ongoing access to their infants. Deborah Ahrens, "Incarcerated Childbirth and Broader 'Birth Control': Autonomy, Regulation, and the State," *Monthly Law Review* 80, no. 1 (2015): 1–30.

17. Over half of incarcerated mothers never receive visitation rights while in prison; many are also unable to meet court-mandated family reunification requirements for visitation with their children and consequently lose parental rights. See Malika Saada Saar and Jill C. Morrison, *Mothers Behind Bars: A State-by-State Report Card of Federal Review on Conditions of Confinement for Pregnant and Parenting Women*, The Rebecca Project and National Women's Law Center, 2010, 7–13, which assesses state and federal laws on a variety of issues of concern for incarcerated women and mothers and indicates that only thirteen states offer any kind of prison program, most of which are limited in availability and duration.

18. Studies from California indicate that pregnant women in prison are particularly susceptible to developing mental health problems, and the anticipation and experience of being separated from their babies as well as the uncertainty surrounding their infant's well-being causes profound anguish among incarcerated mothers. Robin Levi et al., "Creating the 'Bad Mother': How the US Approach to Pregnancy in Prisons Violates the Right to Be a Mother," *UCLA Women's Law Journal* 18 (2010): 1.

19. Studies "suggested two- to threefold increased risk of major depressive disorder and . . . increased risk of elevated depressive symptoms and postpartum depression among women exposed to intimate partner violence relative to nonexposed women." Hind A. Beydoun et al., "Intimate Partner Violence Against Adult Women and Its Association with Major Depressive Disorder, Depressive Symptoms and Postpartum Depression: A Systematic Review and Meta-Analysis," *Social Science and Medicine* (2012): 959, http://doi.org/10.1016/j.socscimed.2012.04.025. Recent studies suggest that "although approximately 12 percent of white mothers in the United States will develop [postpartum depression (PPD)], nearly 38 percent of low-income mothers and mothers of color will develop PPD. Moreover, the majority of low-income mothers and mothers of color are neither formally diagnosed nor receive appropriate treatment." Robert H. Keefe et al., "The Challenges of Idealized Mothering: Marginalized Mothers Living with Postpartum," *Journal of Women and Social Work* 18 (2017): 221–22; Teri Pearlstein, Margaret

Howard, and Caron Zlotnick, Centers for Disease Control and Prevention, "Prevalence of Self-reported "Postpartum Depression," *American Journal of Obstetrics and Gynecology* 200, no. 4 (2014): 357–64, http://doi.org/10.1016 /j.ajog.2008.11.033.

20. Incarcerated mothers are more likely than incarcerated fathers to experience family dissolution, since mothers are more likely to be the sole caretaker for their children prior to incarceration. Philip M. Genty, "Procedural Due Process Rights of Incarcerated Parents in Termination of Parental Rights Proceedings: A Fifty State Analysis," *Journal of Family Law* 30 (1992): 757. Incarcerated women are likely to suffer higher rates of substance abuse, domestic violence, and domestic abuse that make it more difficult for them to comply with state standards for retaining parental rights; additionally, incarcerated women must overcome stereotypes about effective mothering that likely play into parental termination decisions. Deseriee A. Kennedy, "The Good Mother: Mothering, Feminism, and Incarceration," *William and Mary Journal of Women and Law* 18 (2012): 161.

21. While there is little research regarding whether or not prison jobs translate to postincarceration employment, some studies indicate that incarcerated people who work are less likely to recidivate. See Shawn Bushway, "Reentry and Prison Work Programs," paper presented at the Urban Institute Reentry Roundtable, May 19–20, 2003, www.urban.org/sites/default/files/publication/59406/410853-Re-entry-and-Prison-Work-Programs.PDF, https://perma.cc/9BFM-TU4J, which found the recidivism rate for incarcerated people who participated in work or treatment programs to be 20 percent less than that for nonparticipants. The daily wage for regular prison jobs ranged on average between 86 cents and $3.45 in 2003; in six states, these jobs were unpaid. Wendy Sawyer, *How Much Do Incarcerated People Earn in Each State?* Prison Policy Initiative, April 10, 2017, www.prisonpolicy.org/blog/2017/04/10/wages, https://perma.cc/4SS4-WTQA.

22. "[I]nmates experience little variety in the types of food and meals they receive and in how the meals are prepared. They possess little autonomy over when, where, and with whom they can eat, how long they can take for their meals, and even how they may be dressed when they eat." Avi Brisman, "Fair Fare? Food as Contested Terrain in US Prisons and Jails," *Georgia Journal on Poverty Law and Policy* 15 (2008): 49, 54. Evidence suggests that "correctional inmates are 6.4 times more likely to suffer from a food-related illness than the general population." Joe Fassler and Claire Brown, "Prison Food Is Making Inmates Disproportionately Sick," *The Atlantic*, December 27, 2017, www.theatlantic .com/health/archive/2017/12/prison-food-sickness-america/549179.

23. For the prevalence of trauma and retraumatization in prison, and models for trauma-informed care in the institutional setting, see Sharyn Adams et al., *Trauma-Informed and Evidence-Based Practices and Programs to Address Trauma in Correctional Settings*, Illinois Criminal Justice Information Authority, July 25, 2017, www.icjia.state.il.us/articles/trauma-informed-and-evidence-

based-practices-and-programs-to-address-trauma-in-correctional-settings, https://perma.cc/LE7K-T9KC. For a successful trauma-informed mental health program in a California women's prison, see, for example, Marisa Taylor, "A New Way to Treat Women's Mental Health in Prison," *Al Jazeera America*, July 31, 2015, http://america.aljazeera.com/multimedia/2015/7/women-in-prison-find-common-ground-in-trauma.html, https://perma.cc/4MSE-HA5K.

24. "In many California prisons, the system of medical record-keeping amounted to piles of documents strewn around spare rooms with no apparent organizational structure." Sara Mayeux, "The Unconstitutional Horrors of Prison Overcrowding," *Newsweek*, March 22, 2015, www.newsweek.com /unconstitutional-horrors-prison-overcrowding-315640, https://perma.cc /Q25D-8MBA. See also Moreland v. Virga, No. CIV S-10-2701-GGH, 2011 WL 476543 (Eastern District California February 4, 2011), dismissing a pro se plaintiff's claim that his due process rights had been violated because he was the victim of erroneous prison recordkeeping and that prison officials have failed to protect him by not incarcerating him under the correct name, thereby subjecting him to cruel and unusual punishment.

25. See, for example, Jessica Pishko, "'The System Failed Her': Behind a Suicide Spike at a California Women's Prison," *The Guardian*, May 10, 2016, www .theguardian.com/us-news/2016/may/10/suicide-california-womens-prison-mental-health.

26. "[I]ncarceration influences self-stigma, but education enhances a sense of empowerment and motivation to resist the negative effects of self-stigma. Reducing the stigmatization of formerly incarcerated individuals is important because if they view themselves positively, it can improve their reentry and life trajectory." Douglas N. Evans, Emily Pelletier, and Jason Szkola, "Education in Prison and the Self-Stigma: Empowerment Continuum," *Crime and Delinquency* 64 (2018): 255.

27. Participation in correctional education reduced recidivism rates within three years of release by approximately 13 percent. Lois M. Davis et al., *Evaluating the Effectiveness of Correctional Education*, RAND Corp. Report 33, Bureau of Justice Assistance, 2013, www.bja.gov/Publications/RAND_Correctional-Education-Meta-Analysis.pdf, https://perma.cc/VQY4-SNZQ.

28. For more information on UCLA's Prison Education Program, see https:// prisoneduprogram.ucla.edu/.

29. The Actors' Gang Prison Project provides workshops in California prisons in order "to unlock human potential in the interest of effective rehabilitation." The Prison Project's weekly and intensive workshops in prisons, weekly reentry program, and newly designed program for correctional officers have created a profound impact for people who are incarcerated and work in prisons, as well as their families. According to California Department of Corrections and Rehabilitation's preliminary analysis, the recidivism rate for people in prison who complete the program is 10.6 percent, as compared to California's recidivism rate of 61 percent.

"Prison Project," the Actors' Gang, accessed May 29, 2018, https://theactorsgang
.nationbuilder.com/theprisonproject. In addition, there is an 89 percent decrease
in disciplinary incidences for those who complete the course in prison. Robert J.
Benz, in "Incarceration and the Liberating Effect of the Arts," *Huffington Post*, July
20, 2017, www.huffingtonpost.com/entry/incarceration-and-the-liberating-
effects-of-the-arts_us_5945a4f3e4b024b7e0df4cb6, https://perma.cc/R5BA-
9VHY, cites Larry Brewster, "The Impact of Prison Arts Programs on Inmate
Attitudes and Behavior: A Quantitative Evaluation," *Justice Policy Journal* 11, no.
1 (2014): 1, https://perma.cc/7G4B-L97U.

30. The CIW Think Tank is a committee of women at the prison organized to
guide UCLA in the development of higher-educational opportunities. In collaboration with the UCLA School of Law International Human Rights Law Clinic, the
Think Tank and community partners used human-rights standards to analyze and
make policy recommendations to build a more just system. Through a survey of
incarcerated women, with the help of the UCLA clinic and UCLA Prison Education
Program, the Think Tank identified housing and employment as two urgen priorities for reentry. See CIW Think Tank and the UCLA School of Law International
Human Rights Law Clinic, *Women Beyond Bars: Reentry and Human Rights*
report, November 29, 2018, https://afam.ucla.edu/2018/11/29/women-beyond-
bars-reentry-and-human-rights.

31. *What It Iz*, a prison abolitionist hip hop theater remix inspired by the 1975
musical *The Wiz*, was adapted by women at CIW prison. A fusion of traditional
musical theater, hip hop, and spoken-word poetics, *What It Iz* follows a journey of
self-discovery from the birth of hip hop through the rise of the prison crisis.

32. Arts therapy programs benefit those incarcerated by enhancing life effectiveness skills, social skills, confidence, and motivation. Larry Brewster, "The Impact of
Prison Arts Programs on Inmate Attitudes and Behavior: A Quantitative Evaluation,"
Justice Policy Journal 11 (2014): 1. For a discussion of the rehabilitative benefits of
arts therapy programs, including the Actors' Gang, in California prisons, see Lyle
Zimskind, "Arts-in-Corrections Program Returns to California Prisons," KCET, June
24, 2014, www.kcet.org/shows/artbound/arts-in-corrections-program-returns-to-
california-prisons, https://perma.cc/6C52-TPG4.

33. Tyler Woods, age nineteen, was killed in his neighborhood by Long Beach
police officers in 2013. James Queally, "Long Beach to Pay Nearly $3 Million after
Shooting Unarmed Man 19 Times in 2013," *Los Angeles Times*, June 23, 2016,
www.latimes.com/local/lanow/la-me-ln-tyler-woods-long-beach-20160623-
snap-story.html. Following Woods's death, a district court awarded his family over
$1 million in damages, including punitive damages, after a jury's verdict that the
officers had used excessive force against him. See Woods v. Fagan, No. CV
14-08374 VAP (SPx), 2016 WL 4778896 (Central District California July 7,
2016). On appeal, the Ninth Circuit Court affirmed the district court's judgment
following the jury verdict, noting that "ample evidence supported Appellees' the-

ory that Woods posed no immediate threat to Appellants or the surrounding community; that Appellants therefore had sufficient time, both before and during the shooting, to deliberate over Woods's safety and the necessity of deadly force; and that they in fact did so." See Woods v. Fagan, 714 *Federal Appendix* 814, 815 (9th Circuit 2018). Long Beach also agreed to pay Woods's son, who was a baby when Woods was killed, $1.9 million. Queally, "Long Beach to Pay Nearly $3 Million."

34. Rosario Dawson, an actress (*Rent, Men in Black,* etc.) and activist, is a supporter and cofounding member of Sankofa, a nonprofit organization launched by Gina and Harry Belafonte to end youth incarceration using art and activism; see www.sankofa.org.

35. Scott Budnick, producer of *The Hangover* and *Just Mercy* and founder of the Anti-Recidivism Coalition, served as a panelist at the inaugural UCLA Beyond the Bars LA 2017: The End of Mass Incarceration conference. Rick Ross was sentenced to life imprisonment in 1996 under the three-strikes law after being convicted for purchasing more than a hundred kilograms of cocaine from a federal agent in a sting operation; a series in the *San Jose Mercury News* revealed a connection between one of Ross's cocaine sources, Danilo Blandón, and the CIA as part of the Iran-Contra affair. Ross eventually discovered a legal loophole that would lead to his release: his case was brought to a federal court of appeals, which found the three-strikes law had been erroneously applied and reduced his sentence to twenty years; he was released from Federal Correctional Institution, Texarkana, in 2009. Melina Abdullah, cofounder of Black Lives Matter LA, participated in an interview featured in track #4, "Critical Justice: Mass Incarceration, Mental Health, and Trauma"; she is the former chair of the Pan-African Studies Department at California State University, Los Angeles, and also served as a panelist at the Beyond the Bars 2017 conference. Jason Dorsey is a founding member of Blackout Arts Collective in New Haven, Connecticut, and a writer for *What It Iz*.

36. "In California there are more than 4,800 different restrictions placed on someone with a criminal record. More than half of these (58 percent) are employment-related, and 73 percent of the restrictions are lifetime bans." Californians for Safety and Justice, "How to Organize a Record Change Clinic: A Toolkit for Organizations Seeking to Provide Proposition 47 and Other Record Change Services," Safety and Justice.org, 2016, 5, https://safeandjust.org/wp-content/uploads/CSJ-Record Change-toolkit-F-ONLINE.pdf, https://perma.cc/7D93-9RJ6.

37. Parole supervision has been transformed ideologically from a social service to a law enforcement system that prioritizes surveillance over rehabilitation. Joan Petersilia, "Parole and Prisoner Reentry in the United States," *Crime and Justice* 26 (1999): 479, 508. The rise of a "new penology" is less focused on deterring individual misconduct and more focused on managing risk at the aggregate level. Malcolm M. Feeley and Jonathan Simon, "The New Penology: Notes on the Emerging Strategy of Corrections and Its Implications," *Criminology* 30 (1992): 449, 452.

38. Returning to associate with the same individuals that were a "bad influence" on their lives prior to being incarcerated can increase a former inmate's likelihood of recidivism. "Symposium, Notes from the Field: Challenges of Indigent Criminal Defense," *NYC Law Review* 12 (2008): 203.

39. Many people who have been incarcerated may also face restrictions on the ability to secure government funding for education; student ineligibility for government higher education funding is based on convictions for possession or sale of controlled substances. 20 U.S.C. § 1091 (r)(1) (2000). Various limits on access to grants, loans, work-study, and other forms of higher education funding are faced by those with prior convictions involving fraud. Deborah N. Archer and Kele S. Williams, "Making America 'The Land of Second Chances': Restoring Socioeconomic Rights for Ex-Offenders," *NYU Review of Law and Social Change* 30 (2006): 527, 533–44.

40. Invisible consequences of incarceration include that those incarcerated can be denied public housing, parental rights, welfare benefits, mobility to obtain jobs that require driving, and access to higher education. Jeremy Travis, "Invisible Punishment: An Instrument of Social Exclusion," in *Invisible Punishment: The Collateral Consequences of Mass Imprisonment*, edited by Marc Mauer and Meda Chesney-Lind, 1, 15–36 (New York: New Press, 2002). The relationship between housing insecurity and prisoner reentry is affected by mental illness, substance use, prior incarceration, and homelessness; protective "buffers" against housing insecurity and homelessness include earning and social supports. David J. Harding et al., "Homelessness and Housing Insecurity among Former Prisoners," *Russell Sage Foundation Journal of the Social Sciences* 1, no. 2 (2015): 44–79.

41. The increased reliance on criminal background information in the application process by private housing providers poses difficult obstacles for formerly incarcerated people trying to secure housing. Rebecca Oyama, "Note, Do Not (Re) Enter: The Rise of Criminal Background Tenant Screening as a Violation of the Fair Housing Act," *Michigan Journal of Race and Law* 15 (2009): 181–222. But, for "how the discriminatory effects and disparate treatment methods of proof apply in Fair Housing Act cases in which a housing provider justifies an adverse housing action—such as a refusal to rent or renew a lease—based on an individual's criminal history," see US Department of Housing and Urban Development, Office of General Counsel, *Guidance on Application of Fair Housing Act Standards to the Use of Criminal Records by Providers of Housing and Real Estate-Related Transactions*, 2016.

42. "[T]he sort of guidance or help that one might imagine a parole officer could supply too often was rendered impossible due to case overload and a lack of both will and resources to engage in any meaningful intervention in the lives of individuals released on parole. Thus, even under a traditional model, society has relied on the formerly incarcerated largely to manage their own reintegration." Anthony C. Thompson, "Navigating the Hidden Obstacles to Ex-Offender Reentry," *BC Law*

Review 45 (2004): 255–306; Jennifer E. Cobbina, "Reintegration Success and Failure: Factors Impacting Reintegration Among Incarcerated and Formerly Incarcerated Women," *Journal of Offender Rehabilitation* 49 (2010): 210, 227–28.

43. For discussion of reentry programs and the challenges that women face in reentry, see generally Sara Malley and Jennifer R. Scroggins, "Reentry and the (Unmet) Needs of Women," *Journal of Offender Rehabilitation* 49 (2010).

TRACK #6
FIGHT THE POWER

CHUCK D. + ALICIA V.

#6 Fear of a Black Movement

A Dialogue with Alicia Virani

I am the law and you are not
In fact, I'm God, I got a lot . . .
. . . keep them hands in the air
Better not breathe, you dare not dare
Don't say nothin', don't think nothin'
"Make America Great Again" the middle just love it
When he wanna talk, walk y'all straight to them ovens
Human beings of color, yeah we be sufferin'

—Chuck D

The legendary Public Enemy's "State of the Union" was released in protest against Donald Trump's 2020 reelection bid while calling attention to the killing of Black people at the hands of law enforcement. It is this kind of fearless truth speaking and rebel energy that the movement now requires. Hearing this new release urged me to revisit the dialogue I'd had with Chuck D and Alicia Virani, my colleague and collaborator on the Connecting Art and Law for Liberation (CALL) Festival, a convening we organized together with students and faculty at UCLA in 2019. Alicia and I discussed the power of connecting movement lawyering and advocacy with the arts, culture, and media.[1] As evidenced in the lyrics above and the discussion that follows, Chuck's uncompromising message is as relevant as ever to the global transformations happening now.

In 1985, Public Enemy emerged as a hip hop crew on Long Island, New York, and became a cultural and political force influencing generations of artists around the world to fight injustice. From LA's own N.W.A.[2] to Brooklyn and Florida's hip hop duo dead prez,[3] as well as groups around the world—from Calle 13 in Puerto Rico to Dam in Palestine. The *New York Times* recognized Public Enemy's albums as among the twenty-five most significant of the last century. The Library of Congress includes the 1990 classic *Fear of a Black Planet* on its 2004 list of fifty sound recordings worth preserving in the National Recording Registry.[4] In 2013, Public Enemy was inducted into the Rock and Roll Hall of Fame.[5] But these are just a handful of the countless examples of their impact.

Born and raised in Queens, New York, Chuck D, born Carleton Douglas Ridenhour, began his career in the 1980s with a series of critically and internationally acclaimed and commercially successful albums addressing issues of race, class, police brutality, white supremacy, capitalism, and inequality—using a combination of inspiration and information; with power, with passion, with intellect, Chuck has never shied away from sharing his view of the world with an urgency that makes us all want to stand up and declare our own outrage at injustice and oppression. A visual artist and best-selling author who runs his own record label, Spit Slam, his service includes leading roles as national spokesperson for Rock the Vote, the National Urban League, and the National Alliance of African-American Athletes. He truly embodies exactly what the CALL festival is about in one person: art, law, activism, and advocacy.

In the spring of 2019, Alicia and I worked with students, faculty, community partners, and university and corrections staff to organize the festival to link silos dividing social justice initiatives underway at UCLA—the most applied-to institution in the nation. This convening was ultimately envisioned as a much-needed effort to bring together a diverse range of participants including visionary artists, legal advocates, scholars, and students, from culture workers and incarcerated clients to progressive criminal justice attorneys, prison educators, and abolitionists. The inaugural festival, hosted by the UCLA Prison Education Program, the UCLA School of Law's Criminal Justice Program, and Prison Law and Policy Program, was a CALL to action to end mass incarceration by sharing innovative, cutting-edge collaborations at the intersection of art and law and by uniting communities through various artistic media while simultaneously developing and disseminating new advocacy strategies.[6] Alicia Virani, the Gilbert Foundation director of UCLA School of Law's Criminal Justice Program, and I were asked to guide this initiative, on campus as well as in two LA correctional facilities in collaboration with incarcerated youth.

On the final day of the festival, we introduced Chuck D as our keynote speaker. There was no way to deny how his booming pro-Black and anti-racist voice inspired and politicized me as a teenager, like so many millions worldwide. His art helped me to understand the urgency of the fight to bring greater power to the People and to see more fulfilling pathways for myself as an artist, activist, and scholar. Recognizing his undeniable global and intergenerational influence, it was more than an honor to welcome one of the most iconic political artists of our time and to dialogue with him on so many of the critical issues at the heart of justice movement building today. I grew up witnessing his work as an activist, author, digital music pioneer, leader, and cofounder of one of the most militant music groups of all time, so the opportunity to just sit and build with the legendary Public Enemy's Chuck D was the fulfillment of a lifelong dream.

.   .   .   .   .

CHUCK D: Thanks for having me here.

BRYONN BAIN: Thank you for joining us today. I first met you at Sankofa, when Harry Belafonte was starting his art, activism, and mass incarceration organization [Sankofa.org], and your energy was undeniable in that room. Thinking about that moment and how it connects to this one, I want to ask you what motivated you to use your career and your platform to move social justice forward, and specifically to fight mass incarceration? What has been the primary motivation behind using your work and your words to move in that direction?

CHUCK D: Well, thanks a lot, Bryonn—time, space, and proximity. I was born in 1960. So, it happened to be a crossroads of a time where we were coming out and even demanding more as a people off the heels of a generation that wasn't going to take it no more. Post World War Two. My parents were born in 1938, '39, respectively. They're from Harlem, New

York. And so they had seen everything, from the BS to the sweet, coming through there. And when it came down to the '60s, you had a generation where it was a convergence of a lot of different ideas. I think James Baldwin is from that period of time in the '30s, where they were like, "I'm going to challenge this bullshit with a narrative that y'all haven't heard before."[7] Because movements were stifled in the past, but the movement was still there.

Whether you want to talk about Reconstruction, whether you want to talk about the Black Renaissance[8] and, before that, up in the New York area, Marcus Garvey.[9] So, movements were always coming up, but they were stifled and extinguished to a certain degree because of racism, oppression, the system, and then also the passage of time. Can you really pass down what you know to fight off racism? Can you pass it down in time? A lot of times you hear people talking about "Damn! We should be better right now! We should know this!" No! The reason is, is that new generations come in and older generations die off. So that's important. To challenge institutions and eliminate institutional bullshit. So the arts are very clear about taking it on and having kind of like a veil to operate. Until the government realizes that they could smash that veil or they could co-opt it to do actually the opposite of what it set out to do.

I'm born in 1960. The first ten years of my life, I'm going through a period that really has never been seen—1960 to 1970—especially racially, in the United States. On my birth certificate I have "Negro."[10] By five or six years old, the civil rights movement happened. So-called civil rights, right? The rights for all human beings to be civil, consider themselves civilizing the United States, and also treated civil, right? So this is an act of law. And I'm five years old on the edges of going into kindergarten, right? At that time we called ourselves "Colored." Matter of fact, me and my sister and brother, we use to always watch the TV show called *The Newlywed Game* where a Black couple, once in a while, would come on and all the other couples were white. And we would always say, "I hope the Colored couple wins!" So we were clearly Colored.

Then that kind of ran adjacent with what was happening in South Africa, which at that time could have been like on another planet. Even if we ask, you know, USAers today (and the reason I don't just call them

Americans is because that's some audacious bullshit to claim all of America when you just the United States). But anyway, at that time we were . . . Colored. Then by the end of the '60s, we were Black. And not only were we Black, but Black was beautiful! And you have a lot of things that actually push that narrative, from the Black Panthers[11] to SNCC,[12] to Dr. Martin Luther King Jr., who everybody in the present tense tries to treat like just a "dreamer" and not a "doer." He's actually a radical and a revolutionary. You know?

All this in the first ten years of my life. Not just my first ten years, but also my peers and me all move from Queens, in 1969, to Long Island. Which basically was like a zone thing of [a] fifteen-minute drive anyway, right? We're gonna go to the country and then all of a sudden after twelve minutes we like, "Oh, here we are!" Right? No longer New York City. "Now we Nassau County!" But that was a town that also was the example of white flight.[13] We moved into a house, and a lot of time people kind of have this misnomer. Saying, "Oh, you grew up middle-class." But no, we happened to grow up with my mother and father, who happened to be double workers, so they had incomes from both sides. If you had single-parent income, then you couldn't move out the city. We had double. We hung on just for this. I was like, "If we're middle-class, [why is it] every time I look in the refrigerator we have no food?"

We happen to have a house based on white flight. We got the house from a white family that moved out, and when we moved into Roosevelt, it was 75 percent white in '68, it was 60 percent white in '69, 30 percent white in '70, 15 percent white in '71. And they were going to other schools anyway. They weren't going to Roosevelt High. Those are stories you might hear from this guy named Howard Stern. He tells the story of coming from Roosevelt during that time with white flight and his family hanging on in there.[14]

BRYONN: You felt like Public Enemy number one at that time?

CHUCK D: Howard Stern felt like Public Enemy number one! I was incubated by a Black town by the time I was eleven and twelve years old. Which is good and bad. What galvanized me was a sum of many parts. When we said we were Black and it was beautiful, that was the cultural narrative by the end of the '60s and let me tell you, it didn't start from culture. It was galvanized by culture: James Brown had made one song that even made white kids say, "Say it loud, I'm Black and I'm proud!"[15] They were like, "Look, how the hell are white kids up there saying, 'Say it loud, I'm Black and I'm proud'?"

That narrative—"say it loud, I'm Black and I'm proud"—made us Black at the end of the '60s. But in my personal conversation with Kwame Ture, aka Stokely Carmichael, he said, "Yeah, he made that song, but trust me: the movement of artists and culture came out of the movement of real people doing real things!" He said, "We were on James Brown's ass every day! Damn right he came up with it at the end of the '60s because we was on his ass in the middle of the '60s!" And so, the movement did not start from the culture. The movement started from the people, who then said the culture had to reflect that. Art is short for artificial. It's not real. It is not real. It is a facsimile of real life. It's a reflection of real life and it can galvanize it.[16]

ALICIA VIRANI: These cultural narratives that you mention—they were so powerful, but they also kind of died out, and then it takes years for them to emerge again. What intervened in these narratives?

CHUCK D: J. Edgar Hoover, who was still in the government at that time, he said this is the fucking problem. This is the first ten years of my life. And you have Black Panthers, you hear Nation of Islam. Every campus had radical leaders. Whether they were black, white, green, or purple, they were very forward in trying to say, "We gon' get away from the status quo!"

They put pressure on the so-called white kids. The reason I say *so-called* white kids is because this is the racial narrative that they pimped the United States of America out on—one drop bullshit. That don't apply nowhere else in the world, but it applies in other different ways. And at the time, they—white kids—were radical in trying to make change. They [the US government] put pressure on them, like, "Well, you gon' be radical, but broke and dead with them niggas." That's why a lot of them moved on out of that and said, "You know what, I'll become less of a radical because I do want a house, and my kids are hungry, so I will say, Mom and Dad, I love you again." Aka Patty Hearst.[17]

ALICIA: This conversation about history and the roots of movements I think is really important and something we aren't necessarily engaging in and talking about enough around the criminal justice system. The history of the struggle against the creation of the system and the destruction of lives that this system is causing. Your music has tracked that trajectory of the problems with the criminal justice system. What would you say is the most pressing issue regarding how things have changed with the criminal justice system? And what can we all do as artists and activists and lawyers in this room to attack these issues?

CHUCK D: Art must always follow astute people. Astute people do research. They're diligent. Not saying that what they have may always be the right information, but it ain't freestylin' off the top of your head based on how you fucking feel. Government is not a joy ride. It needs people that dot the i's and cross the t's. It's thankless when it comes down to government say, "Well, how do you house the people? How do you feed the people? And how do you govern the people?" So when something does go amok and you just watching it, thinking people gonna take care of it, the people need protection. Right now, I'm ill equipped, seriously, at my age and stage as triple OG[18], right, to really have a comment, . . . about what happened to Nipsey Hussle in the 'hood.[19] I'm not equipped to give that answer right now, because I could be a little bit vigilante-ish and that is not necessarily the right conversation to have. When the government is responsible down into the cracks, you know what I'm saying? But you got to come up with some kind of real solutions. Be practical as a motherfucker! You got to understand. You got to be practical. Somebody robbed your mom, you have to figure that out, you know? You can't think, "I'm about to get this mothafucka back!" on a vendetta. Nope. You not that cat. You ain't living that life. Somebody's got to come to your service and aid. And it's got to be some situation in your community that governs itself.

The Black community has never been able to govern itself. It's been on plantations since 1865. You know, a plantation state is when you don't have control of economics. Your economics, your education, or your enforcement, or your environment. That means you're asking for help and you're asking for someone to do all those things for you. We're not governing ourselves. We're always being policed—like it's an overseer looking over you and now it's in all facets of life.[20]

And that's why you want to rely on astute people. We don't need hip academics: "That's a fly motherfucking academic nigga!" We don't need that.

When it comes down to the prison industrial complex, which is the machine, how do we go from a hundred thousand Black men in 1970 to the numbers that we have now?[21] I've done some of the research, but we seriously need to not look down on educators and academics. We gonna listen to Rihanna today? Sometimes it disturbs me when I look on the news programs and you see four talking heads up there all screaming at each other, and every single one of these people are equipped and educated, but they don't have the time to get along. To get out the narrative. So they have to actually come like an entertainer and spit out the sound bites. And so you got generations who are just like hogs in a trough. Just gobbling up sound bites and reacting to the problem.[22]

Meanwhile, all this bullshit that's going on now in this government and these systems going on because they know, in this time and place in the century, that all they had to do is throw three books of words at people and they will be distracted and say, "That shit is too deep for me." And you gonna leave it up to somebody else to do the battles, and the people that you put up in the war are outnumbered. And then they stressed out. You goddamn right they smoking blunts at seven fucking o'clock p.m.— after their hard-ass, thankless job that nobody really gives a damn about. So we need people to say, "You know, I'm trying to be a lawyer and I'm tired of you disrespecting my tenure, my résumé, just because you think that your life is about fun and games and popcorn." At the end of that spectrum, somebody will put your whole family in fucking jail . . .

BRYONN: That's a very accurate statement. It's necessary to rely on astute people to guide the direction of the culture. Looking at where we are now, do you feel the impact of social media has influenced us to go in the opposite direction?

CHUCK D: Twitter is the only social media I do. I have a rule: if you're over fifty years old, just concentrate on one. I do Twitter. My daughter runs the Instagram. She runs the Snapchat. She does everything. She handles all that. Matter of fact, I'm very astute technically, but with her, I increasingly play dumb and play my age. As an old head, you will not win against a millennial talking about the future. Now, a young person won't win talking to an old head about the past. But in the present, both of y'all better pay fucking attention.

BRYONN: How do you see where we are right now?

CHUCK D: Where we're at right now? When people ask me, Exactly what should we do? You don't need a sound bite. The best to ever do it, in a sound bite way, being concise, intelligent, and also speaking to a broad audience, was President Barack Obama. When President Obama came into office and people were kind of like throwing confetti and getting their dance on, I looked at it like an hourglass: we got four years to get some shit together.[23] We got four years, or maybe we have eight. But now, get yo' shit together, 'cause it's going to be an even bigger mess. We lucky we got eight!

Intelligence is very important. Now we know some intelligence is just like, "Well, fuck it! I want to challenge it, but I want to be rich too!" I want these things. I don't want, like, Lil Nas X[24] to have more shit than me. And all he did was a half country song. And I went to law school for thirty years, man! And this dude is driving the Bugatti and I still got my Toyota Corolla, you know? I grew up with the arts, and the arts happen to be my vehicle to be able to take everything that we do, whether it was visually or audibly, and knock it into a sound bite. But that's entertainment, people. For entertainment, you going to have to fill your words up with something. Or you ain't gotta fill it up with anything. But the entertainment value is to knock whatever's in life and truncate it, into a sound bite or visionary thing, where you say, "Oh, I get that piece of visionary art. I get that." And it's a painting that tells a thousand or a million words. And especially in the days of Instagram, now, a picture could tell a million words. So, that's entertainment. It shouldn't be a national initiative for people that run systems to actually be flying and entertaining as they do it. It's a lot of boring work, but there's people that come up and say, "I'm meant to do that."

BRYONN: One of the greatest movies of all time, 1989, *Do the Right Thing*, Spike Lee,[25] your music was featured prominently throughout the movie, and I remember being a kid, with my family coming from Trinidad to Flatbush, that movie meant everything. You know what I'm saying? Just to see the neighborhood and everything. There's a particular scene where Radio Raheem, one of the key figures in the film, shows his knuckle rings. On one hand he has "LOVE" and on the other hand he has "HATE," and he gives this brilliant soliloquy about this central tension. About this being what life is about. The freedom fighter and comandante of the Cuban Revolution, Che Guevara, famously wrote, "The true revolutionary is guided by feelings of love."[26] We're so often blamed for hating this group and hating that group. No, we hate oppression and injustice. We're trying to overthrow that because we love our people.

And at the same time, I have to bring to the conversation, the deep anger, the deep rage—Prophets of Rage, right?[27] We think about, you know, this festival for the first two days took folks into two different correctional facilities to see young folks, our children, our babies, locked up in shackles and chains like we just came off the slave ship. We still on the plantation. And that's a lot of trauma that they're experiencing on a daily basis, and there are folks who went in experiencing that trauma. You come out, you got to be angry; if you ain't, then you ain't breathing. You have no nerves in your body if you're not feeling angry, upset about that. And you, Chuck D, have in your career done a brilliant job of channeling the anger that you and our communities been feeling into this incredibly productive outlet. Into being a voice for folks who have felt voiceless and to creating an international consciousness about the anger and that pain. So I just want to ask you to share your thoughts on how we can think about that anger, that pain, that rage that we feel when we look at the conditions that our communities are in?

CHUCK D: Well, when we met, Bryonn, for the first time, at Mr. Harry Belafonte's[28] Sankofa meeting, he was very clear in saying that his inspiration was Paul Robeson.[29] So when we have a conversation with Belafonte, we having a conversation with Paul Robeson and his influences of coming into that leg—or I should say, that digital chord that's connecting us, man. It's just that older people transition on and younger ones like us happen to be able to pick up the mantle and then we have to inspire people. . . . You know? You—and the arts and

academia and stuff like that. Me—in the academia and the arts or whatever, and say, "Well, what other person can carry this on?" And I felt that
that was the purpose for me to say, "Yeah, it can't be about *me*. It has to
be about *we* . . ."

And it's good to be able to approach things with some solutions. To
tell people things like, "Look, it's gotta be a total effort. If you can't
change your head and change your mind, how you gonna change your
block? If you can't change your block, how you gonna change your town?
If you can't change your town, how you gonna change, you know, the
state or the region you live in?" You know? So this whole, "I wanna
change the world." That's a little bit of a big sentence, "change the world."
Especially if you ain't been to the world. So how you gonna change the
world?

The isolated box of the United States of America is a prison cell for
Black people if we don't connect to the diaspora.[30] It's a prison cell for
Black and Brown, people of color—if we don't connect to the diaspora
of the rest of the planet. It's just one country out of 215. So what we
doing to change the world? Let's start to get people to change their
minds. Let's get people to try and change your block. These things are
instrumental for communities to look at and say, How do we find and
make each one of these small parts better as a sum of a bigger part?
And try to come up with, once again, a conversation, a narrative other
people can follow.

But also, you got to know your enemy. Your enemies don't want that.
And your enemies are situational people, human beings, who are
embedded into systems that benefit them at the expense of others. The
prison industrial complex.[31] "Oh yeah, we need the prisons, we need the
prisons . . . because of crime." They're not even getting into the detail of
what it is. All this talk . . . I don't like the separation of human beings,
number one. And I don't like the separation of black and brown in this
country because there's things happening right on the line.

BRYONN: How can we continue to harness what was established in the
past and keep moving forward?

CHUCK D: So this is what I'm saying. In the systems—I'm saying something really important here. These are generations that are accustomed

to getting things thrown at them like that. And when it comes down to policy and real shit like voting—you know, the narrative about voting. We can't have the *street narrative* about voting. We understand where it comes from because voting, in the street, is like, "We don't care about that!" Okay, but who is the judge that locked yo' ass up? Who voted this dude in? You know? Voting in this country is as essential as washing yo' ass in the morning. Now, you ain't gotta wash. Look, man, there is no crime in not washing yo' ass or brushing your teeth. You can just go, "Yo, man, I just woke up and I'm just up." But you can't run around saying, "Shit stinks" either. So it's just something that you gotta do.

And don't get caught up into the ESPN version of the presidential election. See, you know, you gotta figure out, voting starts with your understanding. Like, who owns this block? Who named this damn block? Why is Slauson, Slauson? Why is Crenshaw, Crenshaw?[32] You see, this whole thing of street cred being pushed into the—once again, I'ma use that word—*narrative* in America where people feel that I gotta have some street cred to communicate. Don't give too much credit to the goddamned street. People are on the street. "Who's running the streets?" gotta be the question. Who is zoning the streets? Who is coming up with the rules for the streets, the law for the streets that you're on? Just being in it don't mean a damn thing. You're going to be in it, or live in it, or survive in it and die in it. Being on the street ain't enough. You don't want to be on the street. What the people want is, How do I live on the street? How do I have ownership on the street? How do I build some of these buildings on the street that my family or I could pass on down? Not *be* on the goddamned street. You don't want a check from the God damned street.

So, this whole thing about the street cred is already pushed to so many people to steer them away from being educated. So this whole hip street-cred shit, I go and dismember it. Now, I don't want to dismember people and their feelings and their attachment to the reflection of art because it gives them a GPS of what's going on and gives them a language to understand.

But do not diminish your education. That's what we need. A long answer to your short question. That's what we need when we come down to asking questions about what we should do now. You cannot disengage from people that put in the work to do research and come up with studies. Not to say they just came up with the research and the studies. What we gonna do with it comes from a community effort. You know? There is a difference between doers and thinkers. Usually, thinkers are introverted. They're going to think and stay in their little cubicle. Even though now, it's even a different zone right now. You also gotta pay attention to the context of the time and the year and the space. Now, the introverted thinker who stays in the basement, now they can be a keyboard thug too. You know what I'm saying? You see them on social media, "Yo, when I get there, I'ma blast the whole fuckin' gymnasium!" and shit like that. And in reality, they're sitting in their basement with wires in their head and, you know, in front of their laptop or their phone or whatever.

So, now we have to pay attention since everybody's connected. You know, lining up with real people, doing real things. And understand, you gotta take the heat because there's gonna be criticism all the time, especially because people are connected. So they might not like this or like that, or like this song or all that, but somebody's gotta be able to interpret that. And literacy in society is very important. Literacy in the law is important, and not everybody's going to be feeling that. You know, if you know LeBron James's latest ten games stats and you don't know the stats that's affecting your block, and you thirty-eight years old, then somebody else gotta do it, and you can't cry about it for not knowing. You know?

ALICIA: You describe the cyclical and interconnected nature of organizing and change so well. We need to understand and know what is going on locally and build relationships in our own communities. At the same time, you mention the importance of not staying so US-centric and connecting movements across space and time. How have you been able to connect with the world and the diaspora in your art and activism?

CHUCK D: So, Public Enemy, in all my travels to 112 countries, I just didn't go to say, "Okay, so we can get to the hotel and order food?" I was very cognizant of where I was going, where I was at, who I was speaking to, how to align different struggles and stories with stories that we have in the United States of America. Growing up in a patch of the Northeast, in a place called New York, and going around, going to Brazil and knowing that they were split up into eight different racial categories. And I'm saying, "Wow!" Going in telling them, "Y'all all Black!"

And they would say, "We not all Black because blah blah blah!" And then going with the power of rap music, because they would go there, and then they'd be like, "Oh yeah, we get it now!" And Public Enemy has started cultural revolutions by rap music in all these places. Now, okay, don't hang your hat on it. Because culture moves and culture turns into something else. Another phase comes in. But during our time, we laid it down. And those seeds sprouted into gigantic trees that also had fruit, bore more fruit, and brought seeds of their own.

ALICIA: How do you make sure people understand, and don't distort, the power of the messages in your music?

CHUCK D: We're in a disinformation age; most people are not "Net-literate." They're not digitally literate. So, the people are used to being told, as opposed to going and being forensic into what's coming at them. Not everybody has that ability. We're not trained in this country to have that ability, but in other places in the world they have that ability. You just can't throw shit at them and they gon' catch it, like, "Yeah, we believe that." No, they're gonna be angry. We're conditioned and got two generations already on the bricks right now. Are they conditioned? They conditioned from the womb damn near. So those conditions is different [from] when I was coming up in the '60s and '70s.

BRYONN: From COINTELPRO[33] to the drug war, there's a long history of infiltration and sabotage of Black movements.

CHUCK D: . . . I'll give you a case in point. The first wave of narcotics that they really zoomed in on was during the '40s in Harlem. But it was just too much of a togetherness going on. And it went through the jazz artists, because they knew people followed jazz.[34] So they went and got all the jazz cats, you know, on smacking stuff, like, back in the day. So then they made it hip to be fucked up on drugs.

BRYONN: Early Malcolm.

CHUCK D: Early Malcolm, right. If you want to be like a jazz cat, boom, you got to get some heroin. All this shit was premeditated. Next movements that come up, they figure out, "You know, we can't have these people come together. Throw them something that'll get them distorted, arguing with each other, separated, and then it will manifest upon itself."

So these movements have been disrupted for a whole bunch of different reasons.

And when I was growing up, right, I kind of knew stories from 1943. I'm born in 1960, that's what, seventeen years before me. Well, just think about that right now. What's seventeen years before us right now? It's even still over the 2,000-year mark, right. When you talk about Public Enemy . . . it's like, man, it's like the Renaissance period. I mean, really, seriously. It's, like, I was born in 1960. It would be like talking about Countee Cullen[35], you know, Marcus Garvey. You know what I'm saying? And by the '60s, you already had movements in the '50s that people locked into so you had to listen to the movements of the '40s in the '50s, instead of going way back to Marcus Garvey. So this is why, sometimes, it's like "Public Enemy's gonna speak." And you talking to somebody who's like seventeen years old, right? It's like, man, they need upgraded, updated, relevant situations on a regular to the point that they're tired of hearing it.

You know, education is, to me, the thing that also saves you from the enforcement. It makes you look at the environment different, you know? And of course, damn sure makes you understand economics, right? Education, if it was revamped with culture, and not just national culture, because this is like Hostess Twinkie shit here.[36]

AUDIENCE QUESTION #1: You're not talking about the Department of Education, are you?

CHUCK D: I'm talking about all education and especially public education. I'm talking about public education, as far as, just to be short-term with it, a kid going to the, like, fifth grade. If they don't have the arts integrated into the school systems,[37] they will never learn what's going to come within the next thirty years. Let me tell you, this is the strength of the arts, right. I'm not in public policy or government policy. . . . My research is in the arts and as artists, worldwide and in and of this country. I teach the arts. Through the arts, you can weave everything through it, but it's sort of like . . . water.[38]

There's a reason why the education of Blacks and the arts is powerful. Because as a disenfranchised or separated people, all you had was the expression of code. And code was everything. But code is almost like, you know, that look, like . . . you can't put that in, you can't write that down, like, you walk by somebody, right? It can start a fight. It can get your ass kicked, or it can be like, yo, it's props. There's no way you can write that down.

And in this country's so-called white-institutionalized system narrative, there's all kinds of, they're trying to figure it out in research, down to a point where Justin Timberlake will have the final say-so on all this shit, right? But it ain't Michael Jackson's dance and shit. It's all this other shit that goes with it. These nuances that you could never ever get because they verbally can't get transferred on how much they mean.

ALICIA: It's significant that you address the "white-institutionalized system narrative" as we sit here in this law school—a place that epitomizes the *white-institutionalized system narrative*. The racially coded language in the case law books we use here emphasizes your point about how words can communicate an entire system of oppression.

CHUCK D: That's why I'm going down to Brazil. I can't speak the language, right? I can't speak the language, and I damn sure don't know how to speak English, right? You know we speak American here . . . USAers, right? Go down there. There's nuances there in that situation that you can only feel and you cannot even interpret it. And these are the things that have to kind of like get illuminated when you're in a school system. And you got to teach culture. And not in a manipulative way. Not for a way where it's an advantage for corporations and a disadvantage for people. You know? The problem is, with culture in this country—it's sold. It's marketed. And the pressure is on for culture to sell. Culture has to be given. It can't be, at the end of the day, "who's going to have a say-so on culture is going to be Apple music." Going back in the day, "it's going to be Sony."

And this is the conversation that's current, that's under the United States of America. So this is why Black culture was so important, because, don't say nothing, all the other cultures were appropriated. . . . You go down to Mexico . . . "that part of the Americas," our people have pyramids down there, right? And they introduced instruments that came from Europe for a various bunch of reasons, which is in mariachi today. Culture brings all these human beings together for our similarities and knocks aside the differences.

This is why it has to be given fairly in school systems from zero to twelve. You have a lot of people wide open . . . wouldn't let a corporation have the final say-so. When a corporation has a say-so on a culture, especially now, they could steer you anywhere. They could take you anywhere. They'd be like, "Yeah, oh alright, we'll get this person to represent this and they'll believe that tomorrow, they'll believe this tomorrow." Now culture is not just only audible, but it is visual. It's also in style and it's also a story, and if they're steering these four areas of culture, they can take the masses and turn the masses into them asses, they just move the "m" over. See, I'm a wordsmith. Some of y'all will get this tomorrow.

BRYONN: What role do you see scholars and researchers playing in movements for justice?

CHUCK D: Let me tell you, gun culture has silenced intelligencia for the last fifty years. COINTELPRO is in perpetuity in this country. It wasn't a style. It's always in effect. It's number one on the hit charts. Number one on the hit charts as far as the system is concerned. It's not an individual, it's a system. It's a—an organism of its own. It's Godzilla. And if you don't attack institutions with an army of intellectuals, artists, policy makers, people in the neighborhood, you know, you gotta get them on a page that attacks this thing that works.

ALICIA: What about the role of artists now in attacking those institutions?

CHUCK D: I'm going to give you a little bit of what I know. I'm going to always continue to make art. If you want to go into my catalog, you'll see exactly what I mean. Yes, a big part of my life is in words that I've written. A big part of my life is in the arts that I've done, but that ain't my life. That ain't my life. I ain't operating every minute of the day like, "I gotta write a song outta this and then see if this goes number one so I can be on American Music Awards." Nah, man, but I think my area is the arts and I think the arts could actually be taught better. . . . I think the arts could actually illuminate and steer people in the right direction and give people proper props. See, it's up to the artists and entertainers to give real people props, not the other way around. We have to reflect the people and give the people props, you know? That's why people like Johnny Cash[39] will write a song about a person he knew that was actually cooking in the diner and the struggle they had. That's Johnny Cash talking about a person in regular life. It's not always about the other way: "This is me." What I'm going through, when I'm flying like this and that, and people are looking up to that. It's so important for artists to bring people up instead of people looking at artists and pushing them further up.

BRYONN: Thank you, brother Chuck. What's the future looking like for you?

CHUCK D: If you want to check out two things I'm doing with my career that I have the most fun with—other than my daughter always running me and telling me exactly how we should do it, and she's totally right and I love her and she is my other half of the brain as far as going forward into this 2020 decade. I have a lot of fun orchestrating rap station radio, internet radio. Matter of fact, it's the internet for rap music and hip hop. We have ten station channels. You can get it free on your phones. It's a groundbreaking app because it highlights all the hip hop music news, information on ten station channels and we have an all-women station channel called She Radio.

Because a lot of people just say, "Ahh, man, it's just Nicki Minaj and Cardi B."[40] You know, there are more women doing rap music and hip hop and producing, making music, tracks, orchestrating than ever before. So we accomplished that. We've accomplished Hip Hop Guides, which is artists with fifteen-year careers. For international, Planet Earth, Planet Rap, which is everywhere else in the world. There are hip hop artists putting it down, Man. Different languages, you know, especially super spitters that are able to do two or three languages . . . especially in this region where people look down on our Brown brothers and sisters because they can speak two languages, maybe three. So, it's about the world.

We reflect the world hip hop. Matter of fact, we also tell people, "You send us your album, your music, we'll put that in flotation too with an evaluation." We evaluate it and treat it like NPR. So that's on one. It's called Rap Station. Just go to Rap Station 365. Just pull it down. It's on Google and also iTunes and we ushered in that whole thing. So, when people say they know about hip hop and rap music, I'm like, I been doing this show for, like, ten years in a row. It's on Pacifica stations. Rap Station really is the place to be. We serve also as a minor-league operation for information. For LL Cool J's Sirius XM "Rock the Bells." So, we're totally into this, like ESPN would be into basketball right now. We doing this. Another thing is running a record label and another thing is running my mouth.

LINER NOTES

Track #6 is published courtesy of Chuck D and Alicia Virani. Special thanks to researchers Brisa Smith-Flores and Andre Chapman of the Narratives of Freedom (NOF) Collective, a participatory oral history initiative examining the effects of racialized hyperincarceration on families.

1. See *NYU Clinical Law Review*'s Symposium Edition, "Rebellious Lawyering at Twenty-Five" (Spring 2017), for essays on innovations and reflections on rebellious and movement lawyering.

2. N.W.A. (Niggaz Wit Attitudes) was a rap group that formed in the late 1980s, criticized by the mainstream media as leaders of the "gangsta rap" movement. The core group included Eazy-E (born Eric Wright), Dr. Dre (born Andre Young), and Ice Cube (born O'Shea Jackson), with MC Ren and DJ Yella. N.W.A. is best known for their unapologetic lyrics, including those from "Fuck the Police" and "Straight Outta Compton." J. Kautz, "N.W.A," *Encyclopedia Britannica*, May 3, 2018, https://www.britannica.com/topic/NWA.

3. Inspired by revolutionaries from Marcus Garvey and Malcolm X to Public Enemy, dead prez is a hip hop duo made up of MCs stic.man and M-1. Formed in 1996, with roots in Florida and New York, they are known for militant politics, lyrics focused on justice, self-determination, and Pan-Africanism. Their debut album, 2000's *Let's Get Free*, is a movement classic that features activist Omali Yeshitela and "Animal in Man," a reimagining of George Orwell's *Animal Farm*. The instrumental version of their song "Hip Hop" is featured by Dave Chappelle as the opening music for every episode of his hit Comedy Central show. See www.allmusic .com/artist/dead-prez-mn0000811234/biography, accessed August 23, 2021.

4. "Librarian of Congress Names 50 Recordings to the 2004 National Recording Registry," Library of Congress, April 5, 2005, www.loc.gov/item/prn-05-087 /librarian-names-50-recordings-to-the-2004-registry/2005-04-05. Chuck D's album is discussed in Alex Henderson, "Public Enemy—Fear of a Black Planet," in *All Music Guide: The Definitive Guide to Popular Music*, 4th ed., edited by Vladimir Bogdanov, Chris Woodstra, and Stephen Thomas Erlewine (San Francisco: Backbeat Books/All Media Guide, 2001).

5. Public Enemy is the fourth hip hop group to make it into the Rock and Roll Hall of Fame. Group member Chuck D predicts that in years ahead, more hip hop talent will be recognized and join Public Enemy in the Hall of Fame. "Public Enemy," Rock and Roll Hall of Fame, 2013, www.rockhall.com/inductees/public-enemy.

6. "About CALL—CALL to Action: UCLA April 12–14, 2019," CALL to Action | UCLA, accessed August 11, 2020, www.calltoactionucla.com/about.

7. James Baldwin, essayist, playwright, novelist, and voice of the American civil rights movement, was born in 1924, in Harlem, New York. Known for his essays on the Black experience in America and his sharp critique of racism in America, in 1953 Baldwin published his first book, *Go Tell It on the Mountain* (New York: Knopf). Other notable works include *Giovanni's Room, Notes of a Native Son*, and *The Fire Next Time*.

8. From 1918 until 1937, the Harlem Renaissance brought notice to the great works of Black art, inspired and influenced future generations of artists and intellectuals, and instilled in African Americans across the country a new spirit of self-determination and pride, a new social consciousness, and a new commitment to political activism. This movement served as a foundation for the civil rights movement of the 1950s and 1960s. "A New African American Identity: The Harlem Renaissance," National Museum of African American History and Culture, March 14, 2018, https://nmaahc.si.edu/blog-post/new-african-american-identity-harlem-renaissance.

9. Pan-African leader Marcus Garvey founded the Universal Negro Improvement Association, which attracted more than 4 million members in 1920. "Marcus Garvey," Biography.com, June 24, 2020, www.biography.com/activist/marcus-garvey.

10. The 2017 documentary *I Am Not Your Negro* is based on James Baldwin's unpublished manuscript "Remember This House." Directed and produced by Raoul Peck, Rémi Grellety, and Hébert Peck and narrated by Samuel L. Jackson, the award-winning film includes footage of Harry Belafonte, Marlon Brando, and others. https://en.wikipedia.org/wiki/I_Am_Not_Your_Negro.

11. The Black Panther Party was founded in 1966 by Huey P. Newton and Bobby Seale; during a speech, Bobby Seale stated, "The Black Panther Party was not a gang. They grew out of a young black intelligentsia on college campuses." Alicia Di Rado, "Ex-Black Panthers Criticize Negative Depictions of Party: History: Bobby Seale, Eldridge Cleaver Tell Cal State Fullerton Audience about Militancy, Civil Rights Work," *Los Angeles Times*, February 23, 1995, www.latimes.com/archives/la-xpm-1995-02-23-me-35350-story.html. In his autobiography, Huey P. Newton went on to state, "Black men and women who refuse to live under oppression are dangerous to white society because they become symbols of hope to their brothers and sisters, inspiring them to follow their example," highlighting the shift to a narrative focused on Black pride. Newton, *Revolutionary Suicide* (New York: Harcourt Brace Jovanovich, 1973), 184–85.

12. The Student Nonviolent Coordinating Committee (SNCC) was a civil rights group founded in 1960 at Shaw University in North Carolina by Black college students. In 1966, Stokely Carmichael, later known as Kwame Ture, became the chairman of SNCC and brought the slogan "Black Power" to the media during his speech at the conclusion of a solitary Walk Against Fear from Memphis, Tennessee, to Jackson, Mississippi. "We been saying 'freedom' for six years," Carmichael said. "What we are going to start saying now is 'Black Power.'" "Stokely Carmichael," History.com, December 18, 2009, www.history.com/topics/black-history/stokely-carmichael. He continued this narrative in his book *Black Power: The Politics of Liberation*, coauthored with political scientist Charles V. Hamilton: "It is a call for Black people in this country to unite, to recognize their heritage, to build a sense of community. It is a call for Black people to begin to define their own goals, to lead their own organizations and support those organization. It is a call to reject racist institutions and values of this society." Carmichael and Hamilton, *Black Power* (New York: Penguin Random House, 1967, repub. 1992).

13. An example of a government agency that contributed to this pattern is "the Federal Housing Administration, which financed mass production builders of subdivisions starting in the '30s and then going on to the '40s and '50s." At "places like Levittown [New York] for example, and Nassau County in New York, and in every metropolitan area in the country, the Federal Housing Administration gave builders like Levitt concessionary loans through banks because they guaranteed loans at lower interest rates for banks that the developers could use to build these subdivisions on the condition that no homes in those subdivisions be sold to African-Americans." Richard Rosthstein and Terry Gross, "Historian Says Don't 'Sanitize' How Our Government Created Ghettos," National Public Radio, May 14, 2015, www.npr.org/2015/05/14/406699264/historian-says-dont-sanitize-how-our-government-created-the-ghettos.

14. Howard Stern, an American author and television and radio personality best known for the *Howard Stern Show*, recalls a much different high school experience at Roosevelt than Chuck D's: "My mother sent me into an all Black school every day to get my ass whooped. The [English class] was dangerous, that was an all Black class. . . ." Zicofirol, "Howard high school horror stories PART1 (Very Funny).wmv," excerpt of *Howard Stern Show*, October 19, 2009, YouTube video posted December 26, 2009, www.youtube.com/watch?v=X1Na3vzbpeI.

15. The events that were transpiring in real life galvanized and inspired the artistic expression of the individuals during this time. The birth of the civil rights movement, Black Power, and Black pride that began to exist shifted the narrative, which is reflected in the funk song James Brown performed in 1968, "I'm Black and I'm Proud": "Some people say we've got a lot of malice. Some say it's a lot of nerve. But I say we won't quit moving until we get what we deserve." Since art was a reflection of real life, artistic expressions drew from the movements already in motion and only added strength to those movements. "Say It Loud—I'm Black and

I'm Proud" held the number-one spot on the R&B singles chart for six weeks and peaked at number ten on the Billboard Hot 100. The song became an anthem for the Black Power movement. Brown, "Say It Loud—I'm Black and I'm Proud," two-part single, 1968, later included on *A Soulful Christmas*, 1968, and *Say It Loud—I'm Black and I'm Proud*, 1969, Vox Studios, Los Angeles.

16. In 2002 Bakari Kitwana wrote, "Today, the influence of these traditional purveyors of Black culture have largely diminished in the face of powerful and pervasive technological advances and corporate growth. Now media and entertainment such as pop music, film, and fashion are among the major forces transmitting culture to this generation of Black Americans." Kitwana, *The Hip Hop Generation: Young Blacks and the Crisis in African American Culture* (New York: Basic Civitas), 7.

17. Patty Hearst, the granddaughter of newspaper magnate William Randolph Hearst, was nineteen years old when she was kidnapped by the Symbionese Liberation Army. The kidnapping stunned the country and made front-page national news. "Soon after her disappearance, the SLA began releasing audiotapes demanding millions of dollars in food donations in exchange for her release. At the same time, they apparently began abusing and brainwashing Patty, hoping to turn this young heiress from the highest reaches of society into a poster child for their coming revolution. That seemed to work. On April 3, the SLA released a tape with Hearst saying she'd joined their fight to free the oppressed and had even taken a new name. A dozen days later, she was spotted on bank surveillance cameras wielding an assault weapon during an SLA bank robbery, barking orders to bystanders and providing cover to her confederates. The FBI launched one of the most massive, agent-intensive searches in its history to find Hearst and stop the SLA. She was finally captured in San Francisco on September 18, 1975, and charged with bank robbery and other crimes. Despite claims of brainwashing, the jury found her guilty, and she was sentenced to seven years in prison. Hearst served two years before President Carter commuted her sentence. She was later pardoned." FBI, "Patty Hearst," May 18, 2016, www.fbi.gov/history/famous-cases/patty-hearst.

18. According to Steve Champion and former South Central Los Angeles gang member Anthony Ross in 2006, the term *original gangster* first started being used in the early 1970s by the LA-based Original Gangster Crips. The term was derived from the gang's name and initially signified "we're the first." Crips members would use the OG abbreviation as a shorthand when writing which part of the gang they belonged to (e.g., Original Eastside Crip or OG Eastside). It entered more mainstream vernacular in the 1980s and '90s through commercialized rap, most notably Ice-T's single "O.G. Original Gangster" on the album of the same name, which reached number seven on the Billboard rap charts in 1991. See "What Does OG Mean?" Dictionary.com, accessed August 23, 2021, www.dictionary.com/e/slang/og/.

19. Ermias Asghedom, an Eritrean American better known as Nipsey Hussle, was a two-time Grammy Award–winning rapper, as well as an entrepreneur, community activist, and father of two. His focus was on Black empowerment and community development as he helped develop Destination Crenshaw, a 1.3-mile-long outdoor art and culture experience celebrating Black Los Angeles. He also invested in Vector90, a coworking space in South Central Los Angeles for entrepreneurs and creatives as well as a place for youth to take classes in science, technology, engineering, and mathematics (STEM). Hussle channeled a violent past into community activism and philanthropy that will define his legacy as much as will his music. His death in 2019 severely impacted the entire Los Angeles hip hop and Black communities, as celebrities such as JAY-Z and Barack Obama offered condolences. Scott Stump, "Who Was Nipsey Hussle?" *Today*, April 1, 2019, www .today.com/news/who-was-nipsey-hussle-5-things-know-about-rapper-t151302.

20. Black communities in the US that have attempted to govern themselves without white intervention have been met with extreme violence or policing used to intimidate. The Greenwood district of Tulsa, Oklahoma, for example, known as Black Wall Street in the decade prior to 1920, was home to Black millionaires and countless Black business owners, doctors, pharmacists, and banks. In June 1921, due to enormous racial tension, events transpired that led to a white mob murdering more than three hundred Black men, women, and children; buildings were destroyed and burned down; and Black Wall Street was erased. "1921 Tulsa Race Massacre," Tulsa Historical Society and Museum, accessed August 11, 2020, www .tulsahistory.org/exhibit/1921-tulsa-race-massacre. From the Black Codes adopted in the 1860s to Jim Crow laws codified to limit the movement of black bodies in the late nineteenth and early twentieth centuries, Black people have always been overpoliced in America. Paul Butler, in his book *Chokehold*, describes this process: "A chokehold is a process of coercing submission that is self-reinforcing. A chokehold justifies additional pressure on the body because the body does not come into compliance, but the body cannot come into compliance because of the vise grip that is on it. This is the black experience in the United States. This is how the process of law and order pushes African American men into the criminal justice system. . . . The Chokehold is a way of understanding how American inequality is imposed." Butler, *Chokehold: Policing Black Men* (New York: New Press, 2018), 5. See also David Fremon, *The Jim Crow Laws and Racism in American History* (Berkeley Heights, NJ: Enslow Publishing, 2000).

21. "Approximately a half million people are in prison or jail for a drug offense today, compared to an estimated 41,100 in 1980—an increase of 1,100 percent. Drug arrests have tripled since 1980. As a result, more than 31 million people have been arrested for drug offenses since the drug war has begun. Nothing has contributed more to the systematic mass incarceration of people of color in the United States than the War on Drugs." Michelle Alexander, *The New Jim Crow: Mass Incarceration in the Age of Colorblindness* (New York: New Press, 2020), 59.

John Ehrlichman, President Richard Nixon's counsel and Assistant for Domestic Affairs, admitted they "couldn't make it illegal to be either against the war or black, but by getting the public to associate hippies with marijuana, and blacks with heroin, and then criminalizing both heavily, . . . we could disrupt those communities. We could arrest their leaders, raid their homes, break up their meetings, and vilify them night after night on the evening news." Tom LoBianco, "Report: Aide Says Nixon's War on Drugs Targeted Blacks, Hippies," CNN, updated March 24, 2016, www.cnn.com/2016/03/23/politics/john-ehrlichman-richard-nixon-drug-war-blacks-hippie/index.html. This tactic facilitated the two-thirds rise in federal inmate population and more than half the rise in state prisons of drug convictions between 1985 and 2000.

22. A recent example of this phenomenon of sound bites being accepted without critical analysis is the support received by the #8CantWait campaign. The hashtag #8CantWait went viral in the days after the killing of George Floyd by the Minneapolis Police Department, which sparked massive uprisings in response to the murders of not only Floyd but also Tony McDade, Breonna Taylor, and Ahmaud Arbrey, among many others. The #8CantWait campaign, which gained support from the public as well as government officials, is a project of Campaign Zero, a project of the nonprofit WeTheProtesters that encourages policy makers to focus on solutions with the strongest evidence of effectiveness at reducing police violence. Campaign Zero promotes eight changes in use-of-force policies in police departments, including bans on choke holds and shooting at moving vehicles and requiring officers to intervene if other officers are using excessive force. The campaign, which alleged these eight use-of-force policies, if adopted, would reduce police killings 72 percent, continually updates its platform in response to the findings and insights of researchers and organizers nationwide—based on a range of new research studies, including those on community representation in policing and body cameras. Campaign Zero reports there is little to no evidence of these methods effectively reducing police violence. The campaign supports analysis of policing practices across the country, research to identify effective solutions to end police violence, technical assistance to organizers leading police accountability campaigns, and the development of model legislation and advocacy to end police violence nationwide. See www.campaignzero.org/#vision, accessed August 23, 2021.

Though Campaign Zero is popular nationwide, no empirical relationship has been provided to date between the adoption of these policies and reductions in police killings. Yet police departments around the country have already adopted many of these proposals. George Floyd was still callously murdered while pleading for his life. Calls to defund the police by the Movement for Black Lives are now the rallying cry pushing back against the #8CantWait reforms, seeing them as counterproductive, because, often, adopting policies related to training increases law enforcement budgets. The public outcry against Campaign Zero caused one of its cofounders to resign and the organization to make several public apologies about the ways in which their reformative advocacy was harmful to the defund movement. The sound bite still impacted policy before there was time to investigate claims they made about their proposed reforms. See, for example, Cherell Brown and Philip V. McHarris, "#8cantwait Is Based on Faulty Data Science," *Medium*, June 5, https://medium.com/@8cantwait.faulty/8cantwait-is-based-on-faulty-data-science-a4e0b85fae40; and Matthew Yglesias, "8 Cant Wait, Explained," *Vox*, June 5, 2020, www.vox.com/2020/6/5/21280402/8-cant-wait-explained-policing-reforms. Since then, #8CantWait has maintained its initial focus on the eight use-of-force policy changes but has shifted to include harm reduction, community safety, and abolition on its website, https://8cantwait.org.

23. Chuck D's point echoes that of progressives who recognize a lack of preparation and strategy to pressure then-newly elected President Barack Obama to pass long-overdue policies like comprehensive immigration reform or federal criminal justice reform. On the contrary, Obama's power to be more progressive was constricted by racist resistance both in Congress and the public. Ta-Nehisi Coates's aptly named article "Fear of a Black President" (a riff on Public Enemy's album *Fear of a Black Planet*) grapples with feeling so much potential and promise from a critical understanding of race and racism displayed by Obama in his own memoirs versus the ways in which he was disappointed by President Obama's almost complete silence on issues of race during his presidency. Coates, "Fear of a Black President," *The Atlantic*, September 2012, www.theatlantic.com/magazine/archive/2012/09/fear-of-a-black-president/309064.

24. Lil Nas X is a two-time Grammy Award–winning twenty-year-old American singer, songwriter, and rapper who has reached fame due to his critically acclaimed song "Old Town Road," which is the longest-running number-one song in history. According to Billboard.com, "In the Billboard Hot 100 dated August 3, it became official: Lil Nas X's 'Old Town Road,' featuring B. R. Cyrus, became the longest-leading number-one single in Hot 100 history, with an unprecedented seventeen weeks on top. Two weeks later, the song—which first took the top spot on the chart dated April 13—had ruled for a stunning nineteen weeks total." A. Unterberger, "Nineteen Weeks of 'Old Town Road': A Week-by-Week Look Back at Lil Nas X's Historic Run at Number One on the Hot 100," *Billboard*, April 14, 2020, www.billboard.com/articles/columns/chart-beat/8524232/lil-nas-x-old-town-road-week-by-week-number-one.

25. *Do the Right Thing*, written, directed, and produced by Spike Lee, thrust Public Enemy into the mainstream, as "Fight the Power" became an anthem for marginalized Black youth. Tambay Obenson, "*Do the Right Thing*: Why Spike Lee's Masterpiece Remains Essential Cinema Thirty Years Later," *IndieWire*, June 29, 2019, www.indiewire.com/2019/06/do-the-right-thing-spike-lee-30-anniversary-1202154208. Public Enemy wrote and recorded the soundtrack for *Do the Right Thing*; "Fight the Power" grew to be the movie's most popular song. "Fight the Power" draws on influence from the Isley Brothers mixed with the

individuality embodied by Public Enemy to encompass "Black style and power. Blending funk, soul, and rap, the song explodes with textures, from its delirious thicket of rhythms to its manic scratches to Chuck D's furious poise." S. Kearse et al., "Why *Do the Right Thing* and 'Fight the Power' Are Eternal," *Pitchfork*, June 11, 2020, https://pitchfork.com/thepitch/why-do-the-right-thing-and-fight-the-power-are-eternal.

26. Ernesto "Che" Guevara, "Man and Socialism in Cuba," in *Venceremos! The Speeches and Writings of Ernesto Che Guevara*, edited by J. Gerassi (New York: Macmillan, 1968), 398.

27. For three years, Chuck D was in supergroup Prophets of Rage, a rap rock group formed in 2016 consisting of three members of Rage Against the Machine and Audioslave (bassist and backing vocalist Tim Commerford, guitarist Tom Morello, and drummer Brad Wilk), two members of Public Enemy (DJ Lord and rapper Chuck D), and rapper B-Real of Cypress Hill. The group disbanded in 2019 following the reuniting of Rage Against the Machine. During its three-year existence, Prophets of Rage released one EP and one full-length studio album. See https://prophetsofrage.com.

28. Jamaican American actor, singer, and activist Harry Belafonte has achieved lasting fame as a civil rights activist (see track #1, The Blueprint: The Radical Solidarity of Dolores Huerta and Harry Belafonte), for such songs as "The Banana Boat Song (Day-O)," and for his film and humanitarian work.

29. Paul Robeson, a star athlete and performer, is remembered for his performances on stage and film, for his written works, and for his political activism. Robeson spoke out against racism, became a world activist, and gained an international following. In 1958 Robeson wrote his autobiography, *Here I Stand*. In 1995 he was inducted posthumously into the College Football Hall of Fame. On stage and screen, his unique voice earned him universal artistic acclaim, but when he raised it in support of civil rights and social justice, his voice often aroused violent controversy. "Singer, Actor, Athlete, Activist Paul Robeson Dies," History.com, accessed August 23, 2021, www.history.com/this-day-in-history/singer-actor-athlete-activist-paul-robeson-dies; "Paul Robeson," Biography.com, accessed August 23, 2021, www.biography.com/musician/paul-robeson); also see Gerald Horne, *Paul Robeson: The Artist as Revolutionary* (London: Pluto Press, 2016).

30. A diaspora is the dispersion of any group of people from their homeland. Chuck D argues that connecting with the African diaspora can have a larger impact when fighting against systems of oppression. See C. L. R. James, *A History of Pan-African Revolt* (Oakland, CA: Charles H. Kerr Library, 2012).

31. The *prison industrial complex* (PIC) is a term used to describe "the overlapping interests of government and industry that use surveillance, policing, and imprisonment as solutions to economic, social, and political problems. Through its reach and impact, the PIC helps and maintains the authority of people who get their power through racial, economic, and other privileges. There are many ways

this power is collected and maintained through the PIC, including creating mass media images that keep alive stereotypes of people of color, poor people, queer people, immigrants, youth, and other oppressed communities as criminal, delinquent, or deviant." Critical Resistance, "What Is the PIC? What Is Abolition?" 2020, http://criticalresistance.org/about/not-so-common-language.

32. In the 1970s, Crenshaw, Leimert Park, and neighboring areas together formed one of the largest African American communities in the western United States. The Crenshaw Boulevard commercial corridor has had many different cultural backgrounds throughout the years, but it is still "the heart of African American commerce in Los Angeles." Today, Crenshaw still has one of the largest Black communities west of the Mississippi. Recently in the face of impending gentrification in the area, the Black community has come together to promote local Black ownership. In particular, ground broke in March 2020 on Destination Crenshaw (see note 19), a 1.3-mile open-air museum of Black history and culture that also provides communal public spaces and serves "as an economic incubator for residents and legacy businesses." Zena Howard, "1.3 Miles of Art and Culture Celebrating Black LA," Destination Crenshaw, March 24, 2020, https://destinationcrenshaw.la/; also see Erin Aubry Kaplan, "Black Empowerment Outside the Headlines," *New York Times*, November 8, 2020, www.nytimes.com/2020/11/08/opinion/crenshaw-la-black-redevelopment.html.

33. From 1956 to 1971, the FBI ran the Counter-Intelligence Program (COINTELPRO) intending "to expose, disrupt, misdirect, discredit, or otherwise neutralize the activities of civil rights groups" by engaging in invasive surveillance tactics such as wiretapping, blackmailing, spreading disinformation, raiding offices and homes, fabricating evidence and committing perjury at trials, vandalizing, and exposing targets to violence and death. Though COINTELPRO ended, the FBI's desire to destroy Black activism has not. COINTELPRO operated under the guise of investigating radical Black extremism and violent Black nationalism or separatism. The FBI continued to target "Black separatism" long after COINTELPRO was dissolved in scandal in 1971. In 2017 the FBI coined the term *Black identity extremism* (BIE) in direct response to increased Black activism and the growing Black Lives Matter movement following the killing of Michael Brown. By 2019 the threat previously described as BIE was grouped with white supremacy extremism (WSE) as two forms of the same kind of violence—racially motivated violent extremism. These allegedly equivalent tendencies were treated as a threat to national security and used to justify a major program of surveillance, investigation, and infiltration. Yet there is no similarly vigorous arrangement to interrogate the underpinnings of the likes of Dylan Roof and Timothy McVeigh—white men whose violence in defense of whiteness-as-ideology led to attacks on "dissenting and nonwhite Americans." The attacks of Roof and McVeigh killed more people than any "BIE" has throughout the past century. Kimberlé Williams Crenshaw, "Fear of a Black Uprising," *New Republic*, August 13, 2020, https://

newrepublic.com/article/158725/fear-black-uprising-confronting-racist-policing.

34. In Jill Jones's book *Hep-cats, Narcs, and Pipe Dreams*, she states, "The post-war heroin was peddled much as the prewar heroin had been, in the hangouts of poor and working-class neighborhoods . . . and as many of these neighborhoods became black . . . a new generation . . . began experimenting with and becoming addicted to drugs. . . . Many heroin addicts believe no one can be knowledgeable or 'hip' unless he is an addict." Jones, *Hep-cats, Narcs, and Pipe Dreams: A History of America's Romance with Illegal Drugs* (Baltimore: Johns Hopkins University Press, 1996), 137–38.

35. Countee Cullen (1903–1946) was recognized as an award-winning poet by the time he was in high school. During the Harlem Renaissance, Cullen became known for his poetry, fiction, and plays. His works *Copper Sun* and *The Ballad of the Brown Girl* (both 1927) made him a leading light of the Harlem Renaissance and in 1935, he became the first Black writer in the twentieth century to translate and publish Euripides's *Medea*. "Countee Cullen," Biography.com, April 12, 2019, www.biography.com/writer/countee-cullen.

36. Carla Alpert, "Twinkies Aren't Made the Way They Used to Be," Well Humans, October 3, 2019, https://wellhumans.com/functional-medicine/2017-11-25-twinkies-arent-made-the-way-they-used-to-be.

37. Founded in 1960, Americans for the Arts is the nation's leading nonprofit organization for advancing the arts and arts education. Their research has found that low-income students who are highly engaged in the arts are twice as likely to graduate college as their peers with no arts education. See www.americansfort hearts.org, accessed August 23, 2021.

38. Chuck D is refering to Bruce Lee: "Empty your mind. Be formless. Shapeless, like water. Now you put water into a cup, it becomes the cup. You put water in a bottle, it becomes a bottle. You put it into a teapot, it becomes the teapot. Water can flow or it can crash. Be water, my friend." Terry Lee McBride, "Bruce Lee: Be as Water, My Friend," YouTube, August 14, 2013, www.youtube.com/watch?v=cJMwBwFj5nQ.

39. "Johnny Cash is one of the most important, influential, and respected art-ists in the history of recorded music. From his monumental live prison albums to his extraordinary series of commentaries on the American spirit and the human condition, to a mesmerizing canon of gospel recordings, to his remarkable and unprecedented late-life artistic triumphs of will and wisdom, his impact on our culture is profound and continuing." "Biography," JohnnyCash.com, March 25, 2019, www.johnnycash.com/about/biography.

40. Onika Tanya Maraj, professionally known as Nicki Minaj, was born in Saint James, Trinidad, and moved with her family to Queens, New York, at the age of five. Growing up, she witnessed the difficulties her mother endured, which influ-enced her to strive for self-determination and become a symbol of female empow-

erment and unapologetic sexual freedom. To reach her goals, she developed personas for herself that helped land her as the first female solo artist to have seven
singles on the Billboard 100 charts at the same time. "Nicki Minaj," Biography.
com, July 20, 2020, www.biography.com/musician/nicki-minaj. Cardi B was born
as Belcalis Almanzar in 1992 in the Bronx, New York, where she was raised. She
is best known for her single "Bodak Yellow," released in 2017, and she received a
Grammy for her debut album *Invasion of Privacy*. Cardi B's first introduction to
the limelight came as she candidly discussed life as a stripper. "Cardi B," Biography.
com, August 12, 2020, www.biography.com/musician/cardi-b.

TRACK #7
LIVE FROM JUVI

ALOE + MAYA + ROSIE

#7 Live from Juvi

THE ARTIVISM OF MAYA JUPITER AND ALOE BLACC

A Dialogue with Rosa M. Rios

New slave labor, poor kids lose
Walk around the neighborhood and see cops cruise
Hunting looking for a new suspect
Lock them in the cell to collect the next check
Three strike rule means kids out of school
Straight down the pipeline for a lifetime

—Maya Jupiter

The United States continues to imprison more people than any nation in recorded history. Because it also incarcerates more young people than any other country in the world,[1] it is critical for us to engage this issue with youth who are surviving behind bars. Like countless children nationwide, youth incarcerated in Los Angeles were unable to connect with their parents and family members as soon as the coronavirus pandemic caused a global lockdown. While educational programs and family visits came to a halt in March 2020, one year later infections and deaths in juvenile correctional facilities continued to climb without adequate city, county, state, and federal resources to protect the lives of minors behind bars.[2]

In April 2019, the UCLA Prison Education Program organized with a coalition of artists, scholars, students, activists, advocates, and those formerly incarcerated and directly impacted by the criminal legal system to deepen our collective analysis and strengthen justice movement networks. At this convening, we explored how solidarity across disciplines, communities, universities, and those confined to carceral spaces can create

191

change. Throughout the weekend, dialogues and actions were simultaneously hosted on the university campus, at Central Juvenile Hall in East Los Angeles, and Barry J. Nidorf Juvenile Hall (BJN) in Sylmar, LA's northernmost neighborhood.

In collaboration with Rosa M. Rios (aka Rosie), who directed the UCLA Prison Education Program with me at the time, I facilitated the first half of the following dialogue at BJN Juvenile Hall to enable the youth incarcerated there to participate. Our featured artists and activists—*artivists*—included award-winning singer and musician Aloe Blacc ("Wake Me Up") and radical feminist MC Maya Jupiter ("Global Village"). We facilitated the second half at the Fowler Museum in Los Angeles later that evening, with UCLA participants and community partners, co-organized by the UCLA Prison Law and Policy Program, cosponsored by the UCLA Department of World Arts and Cultures/Dance and the UCLA Department of African American Studies. Hailed as "the Chicana from down under," Maya Jupiter's artivism began in her early twenties in her hometown of Sydney, Australia. Aloe Blacc, a California-raised child of Panamanian immigrants, began his music career influenced by socially conscious artists like KRS-One. Now raising a family together in Los Angeles, Maya and Aloe have cofounded Artivist Entertainment with Quetzal Flores, Alberto Lopez, and Veronica Gonzalez to provide support and produce events with artists using their work to promote positive social transformation.

.   .   .   .   .

BRYONN BAIN: I want to start off jumping right into it and asking you, What motivates you to use your platform to shine light on issues of justice? Especially on the issue of mass incarceration?—which I know you have talked about a lot in recent years.

MAYA JUPITER: It's really just a human rights issue. I mean, the fact that the United States incarcerates 25 percent of the world's [prison] population . . .

ALOE BLACC: . . . the US only has 5 percent of the world's population.[3]

MAYA: Exactly. This was and is, just as we all know, disproportionately Black and Brown youth and people who are incarcerated. For me, that just screams that we have an issue and a dysfunction and the system is not working the way it should be working. It shouldn't look like that, and so for me, it is a human rights issue. It is slavery. That's how I see it. I see it as modern-day slavery, and I would like to be a part of ending slavery.[4]

ALOE: For me, it's about everybody having an opportunity. Everybody having a chance. Not everybody got that from the jump. I'm saying that some people are born into situations. They don't roll over, and so the system is built to be punitive for certain actions and activities. There is no reconciliation for, "What if I was born in this situation?[5] I didn't get the opportunities or chances to even know that there was something different." How do we compensate for that? How do we give opportunity for that? This is where I always think "that is what I'd like to get involved in." Finding other ways to create opportunity where there was none.

ROSIE RIOS: This festival is Connecting Art and Law for Liberation. How do you see artists and lawyers working together to create change in the justice system?

MAYA: I've witnessed Alessandro Conceição [facilitating] Theater of the Oppressed[6]—which is an incredible method. A practice that I have been practicing for the last, almost twenty years, both in Australia and here is the collective songwriting. It's about being in community. It's usually done in a circle because a cipher is an ancestral practice, but it is something that many tribes have done, and everyone contributes and everyone's idea is respected. It is also testimony. It's telling your story. It's listening. It's sharing, and through that you end up writing a song together. You are writing words and together you create this piece of art collectively, and it really is about the process of that. Through the talking and the sharing and the honing down of ideas, it might also be a way to apply that to changing laws and seeing what laws need to be created and erased. And film as well.

ALOE: Yeah, film is also another way. It really helps bring a visual to a lot of people at one time where they can watch and empathize with a story and get active. When lawmakers and lawyers help write and make the laws of legislators—when they need massive action and buy-in from the community and voters—film can absolutely help with the bigger scale.

BRYONN: In the context of this festival, as we think about how we can make art and law end mass incarceration, who brings art together with activism to impact the world?

MAYA: Locally, I'll say it's Ernesto Yerena.[7] He's one of my favorite street poster artists. He really talks about a lot of Indigenous issues. And on that global scale, people like John Lennon, who was really politically active. And Bob Marley.

ALOE: Yeah, one of my favorites is Bob Marley because he would put together songs that the whole world was singing, like the song "Buffalo Soldier, Dreadlock Rasta." You have the whole world singing that song the way he's talking about actual Black Americans who were fighting in the Civil War.[8] He was basically shouting out and calling out, saying, "I'm shouting out my ancestry, my history, and telling Black Americans you don't even know about your history like that."

Stevie Wonder is another one. He is a legendary musician and artist and was able to get the government to create Martin Luther King Jr. Day. They didn't want to do it. They didn't want to shout out the king for a day and he wrote a song, a song that helped to market and promote.

BRYONN: People of color make up the majority of the prison population in the US.[9] What is it like coming here from Australia?

MAYA: Well, there are a lot of similarities because we had a white Australian policy up until 1973.[10]

ALOE: Break it down even more to see how widespread the concept of people of color and incarceration in Australia is across the world.

MAYA: Australia did not allow nonwhite people to migrate to Australia until the end of the white Australia policy in 1973. My family migrated in 1980. What happened then was, they realized they didn't have workers. The population was only 10 million people so they needed to open up their borders. So my family jumped on that opportunity. I was born in Mexico. My father is Mexican. My mom is Turkish, and they were already applying to Canada, but Australia answered first, basically, so that's why we ended up down there. We had no family there growing up. Eventually, my mom's sister moved over about twenty years later.

Australia committed genocide on its Indigenous peoples. Australia is made up of many nations with hundreds of different languages spoken, dialects all across the continent that pretty much were wiped out. The same thing that happened here.[11] They took children from their families and placed them in missions. They are now referred to as the Stolen Generation. This was the removal of Aboriginal children . . .[12]

The Aboriginal people are the "Blackfellas" of Australia, as they call themselves now. You can see similarities with the United States. There have been 437 Aboriginal deaths in [police and prison] custody since 1997. Aboriginal and Torres Strait Islanders make up 28 percent of the prison population, but only 3 percent of the general population. So you can see the similarities between what's happening there and what's happening with our Black and Brown people here.

The history here is, you have the Spaniards who were here before the English. The Spaniards colonized Indigenous people of this land of the West Coast. A lot of Mexicans say this is Aztlan. This is our country. Yes and no, because we were here before the English, but we were a part of that colonization of the Tongva people. This is Tongva land and the Chumash were on the coast. There's so many layers, but in terms of incarceration, yes, we have the same problem [in Australia]. It's not as high, though.[13]

BRYONN: What other similarities do you see today between the prison industrial complex here in the United States and systemic injustice in other parts of the world?

MAYA: . . . there's this other horrible stuff that's happening in Perth [Australia] where Aboriginal women are some of the most highly incarcerated people anywhere in the world.[14] It's happening in Western Australia because they introduced this stupid law where if you get a parking ticket, a parking fine like a misdemeanor, rather than pay your fine, you can do a weekend in jail.[15] So people that don't have any money, they see it as an opportunity: "I'll just go there for a weekend and I'll pay my debt." So what's happening is, it has incarcerated a lot of Indigenous folk who are getting into the system, and that's the worst thing. It's also psychologically damaging because you're normalizing the prison. In 2014, a twenty-two-year-old Aboriginal woman, Ms. Hu, died in police custody for being in jail for unpaid fines.

ROSIE: Our festival's theme was "A CALL to Action." What is the one thing that people should take from this as an action step?

ALOE: A simple call to action is: love is the answer. It's so easy for someone to look at a fifteen-year-old "murderer" and say that you don't have the right. It's hard to look at that fifteen-year-old child and ask, "Who did this to you?" And that is the thing that we have to recognize. It's the compassion to forgive and to restore. Love is the answer. That is the simple action.

LINER NOTES

Track #7 is based on an article developed in collaboration with the Narratives of Freedom (NOF) Collective, a participatory oral history initiative examining the effects of racialized hyperincarceration on families. Lead researcher and Graduate Fellow Brisa Smith Flores and the NOF Collective made valuable contributions to the research and development of this track. Published courtesy of Maya Jupiter, Aloe Blacc, and Rosa M. Rios.

1. American Civil Liberties Union (ACLU), "Youth Incarceration," accessed August 24, 2021, www.aclu.org/issues/juvenile-justice/youth-incarceration. While rates of incarcerated youth continue to drop, the US still incarcerates more young people than any place in the world—not only in the criminal justice system, but also in Immigration and Customs Enforcement detention centers. Shani Saxon, "The US Has the World's Highest Child Incarceration Rates," *Color Lines*, November 19, 2019, www.colorlines.com/articles/us-has-worlds-highest-child-incarceration-rates.

2. Josh Rovner, "COVID-19 in Juvenile Facilities," Sentencing Project, May 18, 2021, www.sentencingproject.org/publications/covid-19-in-juvenile-facilities.

3. ACLU, "Mass Incarceration," accessed October 26, 2019, www.aclu.org /issues/smart-justice/mass-incarceration.

4. See Michelle Alexander, *The New Jim Crow: Mass Incarceration in the Age of Colorblindness* (New York: New Press, 2010), 31. As described by Alexander, while the Thirteenth Amendment abolished the formal institution of slavery in the US, it continued to allow for free-labor indentured servitude to persist as a form of punishment for incarcerated populations. This issue is compounded when the racial demographics of prisons in the US are taken into account, as Black people make up the majority of the incarcerated population. Black communities are policed more frequently and Black individuals often experience generally harsher sentences for infractions than their white counterparts. As a result, Black popula-

tions are more vulnerable in the US to incarceration and free-labor or low-wage labor conditions. Also see Ava DuVernay, *13th*, documentary film released October 7, 2016, on Netflix; released April 17, 2020, for free viewing on YouTube, www.youtube.com/watch?v=krfcq5pF8u8.

5. Mary Caprioli, "Primed for Violence: The Role of Gender Inequality in Predicting Internal Conflict," *International Studies Quarterly* 4, no. 9 (2005): 161–78, www.amherst.edu/media/view/233359/original. "We need to examine the underlying cultural norms that legitimize violence and facilitate a call to arms. Intrastate conflict is more likely in those societies whose cultural norms support violence as a legitimate means toward addressing grievances. Such conditions are inherent to structural inequality, leading to structural violence." Judith Armataa, *Ending Child Sexual Abuse: A Transformative Justice Handbook* (Minneapolis: University of Minnesota Press, 2018), 37–44.

6. Zhaleh Almaee and Marc Weinblatt, "Anti-Oppression Work with Playback and Theatre of the Oppressed," in *Playback for Social Impact: Stories and Practical Tips*, edited by Anne Ellinger and Christopher Ellinger (Port Townsend, WA: Belmarlin Press, 2020), posted May 13, 2021, by Mandala Center for Change, www.mandalaforchange.com/resources/articles/anti-oppression-work-with-playback-and-theatre-of-the-oppressed.

7. Born in El Centro, California, a midsize farming town bordering Mexicali, in 2008 Ernesto Yerena Montejano created the "Hecho Con Ganas" publishing project to produce politically and socially conscious images in limited-edition silkscreen prints. "Fueled by his cross-national upbringing, his art practice reflects observations of interactions between the Mexican communities living on either side of the US-Mexico border." His work shares the narratives of conflicting identities he feels are "kindred to what many Chicanos of these communities experience." Ernesto identifies as Chicano and as Native/Indigenous to this continent, which is reflected in the way his work "depicts his frustration with the oppression . . . of dignity and rights. Through his brazen imagery, [he] brings political concerns to light with . . . cultural icons, rebels, and everyday people voicing their stance against oppression." Ernesto Yerena Montejano, "Hecho Con Ganas—About," accessed August 24, 2021, www.hechoconganas.com/bio.

8. Krewasky A. Salter and Lonnie G. Bunch III, "Buffalo Soldiers," National Museum of African American History and Culture, accessed August 24, 2021, https://nmaahc.si.edu/explore/manylenses/buffalosoldiers. They were called "buffalos" not because they rode on buffalos but, as some accounts hold, because their hair was so knotty and dreaded like a buffalo's, and they were fierce and noble fighters like buffalos.

9. Wendy Sawyer, "US Incarceration Rates by Race and Ethnicity, 2010," graph, Prison Policy Initiative, accessed August 24, 2021, www.prisonpolicy.org/graphs/raceinc.html.

10. "White Australia Policy," *Encyclopedia Britannica*, November 24, 2020, www.britannica.com/event/White-Australia-Policy.

11. See Edwin Schupman (Muscogee), "Native Words, Native Warriors," chapter 3, Boarding Schools, National Museum of the American Indian, Smithsonian Institution, accessed August 24, 2021, https://americanindian.si.edu/nk360 /code-talkers/collection-gallery. Native American children, in the late 1900s, were forced to attend government- and church-operated boarding schools where they were prohibited from speaking their language, had their hair cut, and had to give up their traditional clothing. Children were separated from their families for long periods of time. See also Benjamin Madley, *An American Genocide: The United States and the California Indian Catastrophe, 1846–1873* (New Haven, CT: Yale University Press, 2016).

12. See Australian Human Rights Commission, "Bringing Them Home: Report of the National Inquiry into the Separation of Aboriginal and Torres Strait Islander Children from Their Families," April 1997, https://humanrights.gov.au/our-work/bringing-them-home-report-1997. Aboriginal and Torres Strait Islander people were taken from their families as children to be raised in institutions or fostered or adoped by white families.

13. See Australian Bureau of Statistics, "Corrective Services Australia," March 6, 2021, www.abs.gov.au/ausstats/abs@.nsf/mf/4512.0?OpenDocument.

14. See Greg Jericho, "No, Australia Is Not the US; Our Shocking Racial Injustice Is All Our Own," *The Guardian*, June 7, 2020, www.theguardian.com /business/grogonomics/2020/jun/07/no-australia-is-not-the-us-our-shocking-racial-injustice-is-all-our-own.

15. This practice is similar to modern-day debtors' prisons in the US—jailing of working-class people who cannot afford to pay legal debts. See ACLU, "Ending Modern-Day Debtors Prisons," accessed August 24, 2021, www.aclu.org/issues /smart-justice/sentencing-reform/ending-modern-day-debtors-prisons.

TRACK #8
TRAP CLASSICS

B. BAIN/BLACKOUT

#8 Trap Classics

WHO'S CAPITALIZING ON CANNABIS AND INCARCERATION?

It's back-to-school time for America's children, and while drug and alcohol abuse cuts across all generations, it is especially damaging to the young people on whom our future depends. . . . Drugs are menacing our society. They're threatening our values and undercutting our institutions. They're killing our children.

—Ronald Reagan, September 14, 1986

President Ronald Reagan pledged to fight the proliferation of drugs and crime and protect the next generation, but there was a brutal irony underlying these promises. The sobering outcome of America's drug war has been a *tenfold rise* in incarceration for drug-related crimes.[1] His promise was broken for a generation of youth from working and poor communities—people of color, all of those most aggressively targeted and whose lives were ultimately devastated by the War on Drugs. Of course, Reagan's drug-war declaration followed a similar one made by a predecessor whose infamous exit all but eclipsed his noteworthy contribution to the legacy of mass incarceration. On June 17, 1971, President Richard Nixon declared drug addiction "public enemy number one" and insisted that "to fight and defeat this enemy . . . it is necessary to wage a new, all-out offensive."[2] And so the 1970s' War on Drugs began—a decade and a half before Ronald Reagan's remix.

My work is rooted in experiences of incarceration regularly justified by this paramilitary campaign. In my own life, I never had any trouble with the law, until I went to law school. Just months before I graduated from Harvard Law, journalist Mike Wallace interviewed me on *60 Minutes* about how my brother, my cousin, and I were unjustly incarcerated by the New York Police Department. Twenty million people tuned in as I retold my story, previously published in the *Village Voice* article "Walking While Black."[3] That was the only offense we committed. I sued the NYPD and went on to write, produce, and perform a show inspired by these experiences, *Lyrics from Lockdown,* at prisons and universities nationwide and in theaters around the world.

Today I live in Los Angeles, the City of Angels, reportedly the incarceration capital of the world.[4] And women are the fastest-growing population behind bars: from 1970 to 2015, the number of women in prison grew from 7,000 to 110,000—a fourteenfold increase, many for drug-related crimes.[5] As of 2018, after nearly eight million Californians voted for a referendum known as Proposition 64, LA also became the largest legal marijuana market in the nation.[6] Prop 64 not only legalized the sale and use of marijuana for adults, but it also opened the door to "social equity" programs aimed at channeling resources from the booming billion-dollar cannabis industry back to communities struggling to recover from the drug war.[7] As I write this, I am traveling in LA to dialogue with a diverse group of influential Angelenos to investigate just how the war on drugs and the legalization of marijuana are impacting different individuals and communities. The following are highlights from these critical conversations.

1. DRUG WAR SURVIVORS VS. BENEFICIARIES?

> Legalization of marijuana has taken place in California, and there's a tax on there that will benefit the community. But I think back to all the people that languished in prisons and were criminalized for this marijuana that's legal now. Urban communities were under a hell of an attack through the war on drugs. And that attack, I believe, just devastated the women in our communities and drove them by the thousands into prisons across this nation. Now we're realizing what happened. We're beginning to repair the damage that happened through the war on drugs. I think about how people capitalize on the incarceration of folks from

marijuana. Now that it's legal, while we'll get some resources, who is capitalizing off the marijuana industry now? Is it the same people who provided services and capitalized off the incarceration of folks? I guess we'll take the tax dollars and resources and try to make the most of it in our communities, but these other questions really linger in my mind.

—Susan Burton, February 12, 2018[8]

Drug war survivor Susan Burton raises valid questions about what resources will come from Proposition 64 to working poor Black and Brown communities. Her concerns are reminiscent of a passage my class on Malcolm X just read in an LA juvenile hall: Frantz Fanon's *The Wretched of the Earth* reminds us, "When the head of a wealthy state declares with his hand on his heart that he must come to the aid of the poor underdeveloped peoples, we do not tremble with gratitude . . . we say to ourselves: 'It's just a reparation which will be paid to us. It is our due.'"[9] To get a closer look at who was primed and prepared to cash in on the so-called California Green Rush,[10] I went to downtown LA to check out MedMen—the emerging cannabis giant, already valued at well over a billion dollars.

Daniel Yi, MedMen's vice president of corporate communications, showed me around the store. In its raw form, marijuana can be sticky and smelly, but it was easy to see how MedMen has been sanitizing it, using iPad screens displaying its properties, quantities, and prices and providing sleek user-friendly packaging. It combined the tablet-centered, tech vibe prevalent at the Apple Store with the urban organic-grocer chic of a Whole Foods. MedMen even has products for pets. This "one-stop shop" for all things THC is a far cry from the hole-in-the-wall weed spot or street-corner weed guy making hand-to-hand transactions. This new gold standard for ganja product sales seems designed to obliterate the competition.

.   .   .   .   .

DANIEL YI: One of the things that is happening in the US as marijuana becomes more and more mainstream: five, ten years ago, you would not dream of coming into the cannabis space. Now there are MBAs from Harvard, there are people who are coming out of culinary school, and designers, or accessory designers, technology designers, IT experts, right? They're coming in like, "Oh wait, this is a growth industry!" This has got to be one of the most innovative spaces.

BRYONN BAIN: It is astounding to see how fast the industry is growing and how quickly corporate America is cashing in. How do we make sense of the folks who have been caught up in the drug war over the last several decades? The Black and Brown communities that have been targeted and incarcerated? How do we make sense of the fact that we now have the opportunity for other folks to profit from it . . . when we have folks languishing in prisons as a punitive measure that the government is taking? How do you make sense of that?

DANIEL: It doesn't make sense. It doesn't make sense that we have sent generations of young men, for the most part young men of color, to serve ludicrous prison sentences. The war on drugs, specifically when it comes to marijuana, doesn't make any sense. And I think people are realizing that.

BRYONN: I got to push a little further. What about hiring folks who have had drug-related convictions? Are you hiring folks who have those kinds of records?

DANIEL: Obviously, we welcome those conversations. Here at MedMen, when we do our hiring practices, we hire from local communities. We hire a diverse workforce. Do we give professional preferential treatment to somebody who has a drug conviction? Not necessarily. But you know we're in the marijuana business, so if you come to us and even if you haven't had it expunged, of course it would be ludicrous for us to say, "You know, you have a marijuana conviction: we can't hire you."

2. DRUG WAR TARGETS?

Alfred, Expungement Seeker

The stark reality, for many people who have marijuana felony convictions on their records, is that they have not been able to get a job after getting out of prison. Californians for Safety and Justice reports there are 4,800 things you cannot do when you are convicted of a felony in the state of California.[11] Since organizations like Drug Policy Alliance led the way to bring Proposition 64 into existence, those with marijuana-related convictions have had the opportunity to have the convictions on their record expunged. At an expungement clinic in South Central, a middle-aged Latino man offered to share his story, but not his last name.

. . . . .

BRYONN: Why are you here today, Alfred?

ALFRED: I'm trying to get my record expunged because I've been trying to get a job. It's been hard trying to get a job. There aren't enough of these programs out there.

BRYONN: How long have you been trying to clean your record?

ALFRED: For the last thirty years.

BRYONN: The past thirty years?

ALFRED: I got in trouble at twenty-five years old.

BRYONN: You're fifty-five years old?

ALFRED: Yeah, fifty-five.

BRYONN: Okay, since you were twenty-five, you've had this record following you around?

ALFRED: Yeah, when I was a bad boy.

BRYONN: Back in the day?

ALFRED: Back in the day, but I'm trying to do good now.

BRYONN: What is the benefit of having your record expunged?

ALFRED: To get the jobs you need and you want, and some housing programs. They deny you because of your background.

3. DRUG WAR SOLDIERS?

Virgil Grant, Cannabis Entrepreneur

Today, marijuana is legal for use in nine states and Washington, DC. In nineteen states, it is legal solely for medical use. Thirteen other states have decriminalized it, which means possession of small amounts no longer carries prison time as a criminal penalty.[12] Despite the fact that most of the United States no longer locks people up for possessing marijuana, the Trump administration pushed a "zero tolerance" approach at the federal level.[13]

Virgil Grant is a cannabis entrepreneur and one of the pioneers of a grassroots movement for social equity in the cannabis industry. His cannabis collective, California Minority Alliance, informs and empowers people of color who want to open marijuana dispensaries with a particular focus on helping those who have served time in prison on marijuana convictions. Virgil travels throughout the country to advocate and lobby for social equity programs. We hit the streets of Compton to get his perspective on how the drug war has impacted his hometown. Virgil knew every cannabis dispensary recently raided by the police.

We stopped to take a look at the location where he operated one of his six licensed medical marijuana dispensaries. That was, until the federal government raided his business in 2008. They sent him to prison on charges that included drug conspiracy and money laundering. Two years after his release, what was used to send him to prison is now legal in the state of California. Wealthy venture capitalists have entered the industry and made hundreds of millions of dollars. Virgil has diligently rebuilt his modest business and is developing it into what he hopes will become the nation's leading homegrown green empire, with his brand, California Cannabis.

·   ·   ·   ·   ·

BRYONN BAIN: How have you remained resilient for so many years while fighting for the right to be a cannabis entrepreneur?

VIRGIL GRANT: I'm someone who doesn't take no for an answer. That's kind of how I describe myself . . . the things I've gone through, and I'm still here. And I'm still doing what I love doing!

BRYONN: You went to prison from 2008 to 2014? Six years?

VIRGIL: I did six years.

BRYONN: You did six years for something the state is now taxing and making profits from?

VIRGIL: I'm a soldier of the cause. You know? I do what I do. Some people say, "Oh, I believe in this marijuana thing, and I'm an advocate!" Are you really, though? What are you willing to give? What are you willing to do for this?

BRYONN: We now have these white-owned companies downtown, like MedMen, that have tens of millions of dollars going into these operations. How do you make sense of that?

VIRGIL: That is unexplainable, but they just did what the heck they wanted to do. And they locked another Black man up. "Sorry about his luck. Too bad. Oh well." And another white man steps in his shoes, in his place, and takes it to a whole other level. So when people talk about my criminal history or my past, so to speak, of me going to prison, not once, not twice, but three times—that's my *résumé*. I fight for the underdog. You know? I always felt I was the underdog. Always.

4. DRUG REFORM SKEPTICS?

Michael Fisher, Pastor

Founded in 1954, Greater Zion Church Family is the oldest Black church in Compton, known previously—before white flight[14]—as the Little Zion Missionary Baptist Church. Pastor Michael Fisher took the helm of this dynamic congregation from his father and continues a long tradition of community engagement. In the wake of marijuana legalization, Pastor Fisher is also unapologetically outspoken in his opposition to the opening of cannabis dispensaries in his native Compton.

·   ·   ·   ·   ·

BRYONN BAIN: What impact will legalizing cannabis have on Compton?

PASTOR MICHAEL FISHER: Drugs in our communities have been the destruction of so many of our daughters and our sons, but it has also been unfortunately a great avenue for the government to funnel and fund and increase the mass incarceration movement. How does an industry make money off of you basically being stoned? I'm not talking about the medicinal part of it. I'm saying the commercial and recreational use of marijuana is just for you to be stoned out of your mind. How is that going to benefit our children? This is going to generate money. This is going to put the top one percentile in an even better position. They are not getting ready to give that to the people they're trying to still oppress and keep locked out of the system.

BRYONN: How is legalization shifting power, politics, and even community demographics?

PASTOR FISHER: This is the reason why we've seen more people in the city of Compton. We see more people who are not Black in our city council meetings than I've ever seen before! Because they're coming here to bring this here. Legalize it, and then all of a sudden, all the big shots show up, and they want to shut down the competition.

BRYONN: Who do you expect will be most directly affected by this reversal of white flight?

PASTOR FISHER: Pooky and them—who's been selling weed out of the trunk for years! That's where the criminalization is going to come in, because "we got to do something with them who already have their hands in the streets! We need those consumers. So we change the law. We criminalize it for him. We put him in jail. We take his customers!" That's what's really going to happen. And everybody sees it coming!

5. DRUG WAR CASUALTIES?

Will Robinson, Formerly Incarcerated Entrepreneur

Despite persistent disparities in race and class with "tough on crime" drug war tactics—first introduced by the Nixon administration and later expanded by Reagan[15]—views of marijuana in the US have shifted. Six in ten Americans support marijuana legalization, nearly double the support seen eighteen years ago. For many who spent years of their lives behind bars, like Will Robinson, it's the war on drugs—not marijuana—that has done the most damage.

·   ·   ·   ·   ·

BRYONN BAIN: Since coming home from prison, where are you in the process of transitioning?

WILL ROBINSON: Over the last six months, I've been reestablishing myself back into my community, my family, and just life. You know? Life after serving nearly thirteen years in federal prison. I owned a mailing parcel shipping business. I was indicted for shipping marijuana that wasn't mine. It was the customers who shipped through my business. And when the federal agents came to my business and told me they had apprehended a customer who booked a shipment, and they wanted to use my business as a sting operation to catch his partners, I didn't want to have anything to do with it. I didn't want to get my family in any harm's way. So when I didn't cooperate as they said, they put everything on me.

BRYONN: Did they go fishing around in your background to justify their extreme charges?

WILL: I was thirty-nine years old with zero criminal history. Couldn't tell you anything about selling drugs, other than what I've seen in movies. Along the way, you know, my marriage didn't survive. My kids—we lost our home, my kids were displaced, living with different family members. I lost my mother. [*pausing to wipe away tears*] I'm sorry . . . I haven't revisited that in a while, I'm sorry.

BRYONN: You're not the one who needs to apologize. And you're not alone in what you're going through. It's clear these unjust policies stole more from you than can ever be fully repaid.

WILL: During my thirteen years of prison, I've seen so many young Black and Latino kids come in, getting sentenced to ten, twelve, fifteen years. Most of them, the amount of drugs that they were selling wasn't even enough to pay rent on a one-bedroom apartment. Drugs are bad, but the sentence—tearing up of families is just senseless to me. It's barbaric. And it's still happening every day.

6. DRUG WAR ABOLITION

Los Angeles, the City of Angels. Dubbed by historian Kelly Lytle Hernández the "City of Inmates," because it has held the world record as the city confining the most human beings in cages.[16] LA is a significant intersection where drug legalization meets incarceration. Who has suffered? Who will benefit? How do we heal from this trauma? These are questions to which we must demand answers. This is a chance for us to rethink justice—not as incapacitation, retribution, or punishment, but as a pathway toward restoring more humane and healthy conditions in our communities. Rather than patch together piecemeal reforms, a wholesale *transformation* of dehumanizing systems maintaining injustice and inequity is long overdue.

LINER NOTES

Track #8 is published courtesy of TRT World, based on revised and annotated excerpts of interviews produced for *Route 66*, episode 10, "Drugs," regarding cannabis and incarceration in California. The interviews took place in Los Angeles between February 12 and 19, 2018.

Epigraph: Excerpted from Ronald Reagan, "Address to the Nation on the Campaign against Drug Abuse," Ronald Reagan Presidential Library and Museum, September 14, 1986, www.reaganlibrary.gov/research/speeches/091486a.

1. The number of people in prisons and jails for drug offenses has increased from 40,900 individuals in 1980 to 443,200 in 2018, a more than tenfold increase. The Sentencing Project, "Trends in U.S. Corrections," updated May 17, 2021, www.sentencingproject.org/publications/trends-in-u-s-corrections.

2. Chris Barber, "Public Enemy Number One: A Pragmatic Approach to America's Drug Problem," Richard Nixon Foundation, June 29, 2016, www.nixonfoundation.org/2016/06/26404.

3. Bryonn Bain, "Walking While Black," *Village Voice*, October 18, 2005, www.villagevoice.com/2005/10/18/walking-while-black-2.

4. Jessica Wolf, "How Los Angeles Became the Capital of Incarceration," *UCLA Newsroom*, May 10, 2017, https://newsroom.ucla.edu/stories/how-los-angeles-became-the-capital-of-incarceration.

5. Wendy Sawyer, "Table 1: Women's Prison and Jail Population Estimates and Incarceration Rates, 1922–2015," *The Gender Divide: Tracking Women's State Prison Growth*, Prison Policy Initiative, January 9, 2018, www.prisonpolicy.org /reports/women_overtime_table_1.html.

6. Proposition 64—the Control, Regulate and Tax Adult Use of Marijuana Act—became law in 2016. Proposition 64 "permits adults twenty-one years of age and over to possess and grow specified amounts of marijuana for recreational use." "The Control, Regulate and Tax Adult Use of Marijuana Act: Proposition 64," California Commission on Peace Officer Standards and Training, November 8, 2016, https://post.ca.gov/proposition-64-the-control-regulate-and-tax-adult-use-of-marijuana-act.

7. East Los Angeles was one of the communities hit by the crack cocaine epidemic that began consuming countless Black and Brown lives in the 1980s. Instead of treating addiction to crack as a public health issue, harsh prison sentences were meted out under racially disproportionate sentencing guidelines, commonly known as the 100 to 1 disparity. Why the name? Because while crack and powder cocaine are chemically identical, possession of 5 grams of crack cocaine carry the same prison term as possession of 500 grams of powder cocaine. These inequities exposed a racial fault line in the war on drugs. Most crack users were Black. Most powder cocaine users were white. Joseph J. Palamar, Shelby Davies, Danielle C. Ompad, Charles M. Cleland, and Michael Weitzman, *Powder Cocaine and Crack Use in the United States: An Examination of Risk for Arrest and Socioeconomic Disparities in Use*, National Institute of Health, National Library of Medicine, Drug and Alcohol Dependency, April 1, 2015, http://doi .org/10.1016/j.drugalcdep.2015.01.029. African American communities have also suffered the most from marijuana prosecutions. In Los Angeles alone, African Americans comprise less than 10 percent of the population, yet they comprise 40 percent of marijuana arrests between 2000 and 2017. According to LA Police Department data, South Central LA is ground zero for marijuana arrests. "Editorial: Can Los Angeles Repair the Damage Done by the War on Marijuana?," *Los Angeles Times*, November 4, 2017, www.latimes.com/opinion/editorials/la-ed-social-equity-marijuana-20171104-story.html.

8. See also Susan Burton and Cari Lynn, *Becoming Ms. Burton: From Prison to Recovery to Leading the Fight for Incarcerated Women* (New York: New Press, 2017), and "Susan Burton: Creating a Crucial Path Forward After Prison," *Scheerpost*, June 4, 2020, https://scheerpost.com/2020/06/04/susan-burton-creating-a-crucial-path-forward-after-prison.

9. Frantz Fanon, Jean-Paul Sartre, and Homi K. Bhabha, *The Wretched of the Earth*, trans. Richard Philcox (New York: Grove Press, 2004).

10. The term *green rush* is used to describe the growing marijuana industry in the US and Canada, alluding to the profit-making potential of this industry.

11. Jeremiah Mosteller, "Why Prison Reform Matters in America," Charles Koch Institute, June 22, 2018, www.charleskochinstitute.org/issue-areas/criminal-justice-policing-reform/why-prison-reform-matters.

12. For an interactive map on the laws regarding marijuana in all states in the US, see "Map of Marijuana Legality by State," Drug Intervention Services of America (DISA) Global Solutions, accessed August 24, 2021, https://disa.com/map-of-marijuana-legality-by-state.

13. Under the Trump administration, the Department of Justice led by Attorney General Jeff Sessions "rescinded an Obama-era policy that discouraged federal prosecutors in most cases from bringing charges wherever the drug is legal under state laws." Instead, the department signaled a desire to resume crackdowns on the use and sales of marijuana, including in states that have fully legalized marijuana. Charlie Savage and Jack Healy, "Trump Administration Takes Step That Could Threaten Marijuana Legalization Movement," *New York Times*, January 4, 2018, www.nytimes.com/2018/01/04/us/politics/marijuana-legalization-justice-department-prosecutions.html.

14. White flight is mostly often used to refer to the post–civil rights era large-scale migration of white people from cities to suburbs, mainly going away from areas that become more racially diverse. Between 1960 and 1980 in Los Angeles, white families, particularly those with school-aged children, considering school desegregation a threat, moved out of the public education system in the city and into suburbs or private schools. Jack Schneider, "Escape from Los Angeles: White Flight from Los Angeles and Its Schools, 1960–1980," *Journal of Urban History* 34, no. 6 (2008): 995–1012.

15. *Tough on crime* is also referred to as *law and order* or *war on crime*. It demands strict criminal penalties for crimes and has contributed to mass incarceration. Both Nixon and Reagan were leading proponents for being tough on crime. Emily Dufton, "The War on Drugs: How President Nixon Tied Addiction to Crime," *The Atlantic*, March 26, 2012, www.theatlantic.com/health/archive/2012/03/the-war-on-drugs-how-president-nixon-tied-addiction-to-crime/254319. Reagan signed the Anti-Drug Abuse Act of 1986 into law, resulting in mandatory minimum sentences for drug-related crime. The harsh sentences disproportionately affected Black Americans. Arit John, "A Timeline of the Rise and Fall of 'Tough on Crime' Drug Sentencing," *The Atlantic*, April 22, 2014, www.theatlantic.com/politics/archive/2014/04/a-timeline-of-the-rise-and-fall-of-tough-on-crime-drug-sentencing/360983.

16. "No city in the world incarcerates more people than Los Angeles . . . the City of Angels is, in fact, the City of Inmates, the carceral capital of the world." Kelly Lytle Hernández, *City of Inmates: Conquest, Rebellion, and the Rise of Human*

Caging in Los Angeles, 1771–1965 (Chapel Hill: University of North Carolina Press, 2017). See also Vera Institute of Justice, *Los Angeles County Jail Overcrowding Reduction Report*, Los Angeles Countywide Criminal Justice Coordination Committee, October 26, 2011, 1, www.vera.org/publications/los-angeles-county-jail-overcrowding-reduction-project-final-report.

#9 Sing Sing Blues

REFLECTIONS OF A STREET COP TURNED WARDEN

In the summer of 2015, my then thirteen-year-old son reluctantly began the summer bridge program for rising freshmen at University High School in Los Angeles. Before we signed him up, Indigo and I were both told "Uni High," as Angelenos call it, is one of the most diverse schools in the city. With reports of a track record of high-achieving Black and Brown youth, this predominately Latinx public school came highly recommended by several educators and colleagues in the area. Nevertheless, Indigo's reluctance was born of his disdain for moving away from family and friends in Brooklyn and his desire to be anywhere in the world but school during his eagerly anticipated summer vacation. As I picked him up and asked how the second day was, his response alarmed me more than most of the challenges I have faced to date as the young father of a child the color of chocolate: "The teacher said, 'Don't be late for school and don't miss class. If you do, the police will come to your house and take you to juvenile hall.'"

Say what?

Press rewind: More than a decade and a half earlier . . . I'm in a workshop led by a grassroots prison activist organization—Prison Moratorium Project—in the Brooklyn we knew and loved in the 1990s.[1] I hear a hauntingly similar report: "They have been building prisons in New York State based on fourth-grade test scores." From elementary-school children in New York to high-school freshmen in California, public schools from coast to coast —rather than preparing our nine-year-olds and ninth graders to be better, to become their best selves, to be astronauts or animators, astrophysicists or human rights activists, were preparing our next generation to be sent up the proverbial river, as my son and I learned from Uni High.

Fast forward: The summer of 2016 . . . I have the opportunity to interview the warden of Sing Sing prison—the ex-supercop turned superintendent, Michael Capra. The man with the parking spot directly in front of the maximum-security facility constructed thirty miles north of New York City on the east bank of the Hudson River.[2]

Pause: Unlike other interviews I have conducted, the topics and questions I would discuss with the warden were developed with the help of several men in the hip hop and spoken word workshop I am teaching at the prison. This team of brilliant minds inside who urged me to ask the questions that follow included Jermaine, Lawrence, Ivan, Jonadrian, Laron, Dennis, Kenyatta, Tyrone, Chris, Sedwick, Markey, J.J., and the poet laureate, Simeon, aka Sundiata. At first I was surprised by how many of these men respected the top cop in the big house for championing the range of arts and educational programs offered in the prison. This was a paradox for me—a source of personal conflict: On the one hand, I would rather see these brothers home instead of living confined to iron cages. At the same time, I saw the transformative potential and immeasurable value in recognizing their humanity through these opportunities for spiritual growth, personal development, and political education. Beyond my class, most of these students were involved in everything from pursuing college degrees with the Hudson Link initiative founded by formerly incarcerated advocate Sean Pica, TED talks directed by Academy Award winner Jonathan Demme (*The Silence of the Lambs*) and featuring actor Tommy "Tiny" Lister (aka "Debo" from Ice Cube's cult classic film *Friday*), theatrical productions with Rehabilitation Through the Arts, and even music lessons and concerts in collaboration with the legendary Carnegie Hall.

Sing Sing is the closest maximum-security prison to New York City.[3] Its roots reach back into the generation before chattel slavery was legally abolished amid a civil war so violent it claimed the lives of more Americans than both world wars combined: reportedly as many as 750,000. Both that conflict and the legacy of racial violence before, through, and after Reconstruction and into the civil rights movement, remind us of the broader political and economic realities of race and class, law and labor. The tension between forces of social control and movements for social justice remains alive and broiling in the radioactive pressure cooker that is one of the most famous—and infamous—spaces on the world's carceral landscape.

Over the last decade, the epidemic of viral video footage has turned state-sanctioned violence into a recurring phenomenon for millions, but left Black and Brown communities mourning and outraged with outpourings of "We told you so!" But what happens when the top cop calls out the violence caught on video in the big house? Does it matter when the law enforcement officer accused of abuse is Black and the victim of the violence is white? I sat with the warden of Sing Sing prison, on the heels of a trial unlike any he remembers, as he wrestled with these questions and shared his take on a case he testified in—against one of his own prison guards.

Play:

. . . . .

BRYONN BAIN: In the 1600s the Mohegans, Native peoples indigenous to this area we now refer to as New York, called this land Sinck Sinck— which meant "Stone by Stone." They also called their leader the Sachem.[4] I think it is important to recognize that in light of your title as superintendent, whereas in most prisons across the country, the person in the top position is called the warden. What is the difference?

SUPT. MICHAEL CAPRA: It is the same. It is basically a title. The term *warden* is commonly used in other states. *Warden* was used in New York State but over the years it was changed to *superintendent.* . . . The definition of *superintendent* is "chief administrative officer of a correctional facility." As in most things, perception carries a lot of weight with the general public.

BRYONN: The questions I'm going to throw at you today came from men who have been in leadership roles in many of the programs at the prison. We have been talking about these issues for weeks, so I'm just going to jump right into them now. To start off, on a personal note: who was Michael Capra *before* Sing Sing? And how are you the same or different today?

SUPT. CAPRA: Well, I think it's a lifetime of experiences. It starts with your upbringing, your family life, your faith base, and success—certainly a realization that I'm not here because of me. I'm here because the good Lord has put me here. I started this job thinking this would be a temporary situation until I was old enough to join the NYPD. I never intended to make this my career. I started this job as a corrections officer in 1981 and slowly climbed the ladder to my current position.

BRYONN: There is an ongoing conversation, especially within Black communities but increasingly in every community, around Black Lives Matter. How do we fundamentally change systems of policing, law enforcement, and "corrections" to focus resources on the *humanity* of people who have historically been dehumanized? In particular, let's focus on the recent incident with a corrections officer who was caught on video beating an inmate to the ground. How do you handle the responsibility to be fair and balanced when mediating charges of officer abuse of force in dealing with men in the population at Sing Sing?

SUPT. CAPRA: It is very trying. However, my decision isn't difficult at all. As the top cop in your facility, you have got to be confident in who you are and know what the right thing is. What is the expectation of law enforcement? Don't people expect more from us, to do the right thing? In the case that you are speaking of, it is very rare, if ever, as a superintendent to testify in criminal proceedings against one of your own officers.[5] I am the designated subject-matter expert for the southern part of New York for DOCCS [Department of Corrections and Community Supervision] and was directed by my principles to testify in this case.

BRYONN: Did that go over well?

SUPT. CAPRA: No, it did not. Does that still affect staff? Yeah. I still have to make the right decisions. The first day that person returned, he was told to come directly up to my office. We had a discussion and I reinforced that my position had not wavered: "You are back. That is good.

You are not a bad person. You had a bad day." He agreed and shook my hand and thanked me. We are going to move forward because that is what we do.

BRYONN: What impact does that have on your day-to-day work and the culture inside?

SUPT. CAPRA: It does not make you the popular guy all the time, and you have to accept that. Some staff believe that the facts do not matter. They look at you differently. Like whether you are on "our side" or not on "our side." But the bigger picture has to be, What was the right thing to begin with? You need to understand what the current culture is and decide if you have made a positive change in the future culture—what is acceptable and what is not. Then you have to take another step back and say, Leadership is what staff is looking for—consistency in having the reputation [for] for doing the right thing is very important.

BRYONN: Some advocates of criminal justice reform argue that training is the key to transforming the culture of law enforcement. I'm not convinced that's the only major change necessary, but I was surprised to learn that in the UK it is not uncommon for COs to receive hundreds of hours of social work and conflict resolution training. For police and prison guards in the US, I've been told hundreds of hours of firearms training is customary. Beyond that, the other nationwide norm I've learned of is the "Cooper Standard." What exactly is the Cooper Standard?

SUPT. CAPRA: A minimal physical fitness requirement for most law enforcement organizations. Depending on your age and sex, you are required to run 1.5 miles in a specific amount of time, do so many push-ups, so many situps, and a specific type of stretch. This is a prerequisite to enter many academies. There are also levels of that one needs to enter some of the law enforcement academies. Now, I don't think that a degree makes the person, but I believe that a combination of things attracts the right type of person for this type of job. We need to look at the acceptable norms of law enforcement today, because of technology, cell phones, body cams, people recording cops on the street during physical force situations that the whole world gets to judge. We also see what their norms are. What's the accepted level of what was right from wrong? We are charged to keep order and are trained to use force when necessary. This is the toughest job on the planet. Some of the best law enforcement people in the world work behind the walls of the prison system.

BRYONN: How did your previous work prepare you for challenges you face today?

SUPT. CAPRA: I started as an officer and learned my trade and developed my leadership abilities. As a sergeant you may have fifty officers working directly under you. You learn a lot from experience. I was also a commissioner of police in a small police agency. I started off there as a police officer and worked my way up there also. On one occasion I had to fire one of my own cops. I knew ahead of time this guy was a bad apple. When I first took over, I brought him in and said, "I know you did this, this, and this, and if you do that while I am in charge . . . He didn't listen and had to be discharged. But that process for me, there, was all my decision. The state has other divisions that handle discipline and the appropriate fines, suspension, or termination. I recommend action and then other divisions investigate. Other divisions decide what they are going to get, then there are union contracts that stipulate the discipline process; many times there is a third-party arbitrator who makes the final decision.

BRYONN: What impact does it have when an incident is recorded on video?

SUPT. CAPRA: If you see an incident on videotape, and it seems very clear what happened, you would think there would be no question. Well, it sometimes becomes what the public thinks about the incident, what was portrayed by each side, because then it becomes this whole public perception.[6] We had an incident, and the inmate was in prison for a horrific act. This was a jury trial. This was a case that was not about the facts. No one cared about the responsibility of law enforcement. It was who had the better attorney.

BRYONN: How exactly did that have an impact on the trial?

SUPT. CAPRA: In this case, the high-priced attorney convinced the jury how bad this inmate was, which was irrelevant to the case. So anything short of flogging the inmate would have been acceptable to the jurors because he is a "bad guy," which had nothing to do with this case. But it is the human element—when you play to that human element, and if you are a better actor than the next guy, you will win.[7] My officers put their lives on the line every day to protect others and maintain order throughout the facility. They have been assaulted, thrown on, and verbally abused on a regular basis. They are professionals. No one wants the bad apple in the bunch to represent them.

BRYONN: That's heavy . . .

SUPT. CAPRA: It is heavy, but when you put it into the context of we are human beings on this planet and we are judged by certain things, when it is all over, it is really all about your belief system. I believe . . . strongly, not necessarily in just being a "good person," but doing the right thing by others. Leadership is a major component. Being sensitive at times and steadfast at others. Sometimes you have to come down hard on people: kind of like a parent and a child. Sometimes your child needs to be punished.[8] Sometimes they need a hug. Knowing when to—and when not to—is the secret. You know, if you look at things in that simplistic way and understand your responsibility, and your response to that scenario, whether you should come on strong or you should back off, means the world of difference on how you succeed in changing the culture in a positive way. It is a delicate balance.

LINER NOTES

Track #9's interview was conducted on August 5, 2016, at the Sing Sing Correctional Facility in Ossining, New York. The interview was edited with support from lead research associate Joanna Itzel Navarro. Published courtesy of Michael Capra.

1. A grassroots Brooklyn-based abolitionist organization, Prison Moratorium Project questions whether the prison system is indeed the right form of punishment for crime and aims to reimagine alternatives to prisons; see www .nomoreprisons.org. See also Adrienne Brown, "An Interview with Activists at the Prison Moratorium Project," *Grist*, June 22, 2005, https://grist.org/article /brown-prison.

2. After two years of workshopping poetry with some of the brilliant bards at Sing Sing, I learned that the iconic colloquialism for sending someone to prison— "up the river"—emerged from the history of this fortress of iron and stone

constructed next to the water. And the movement of that body of water, visibly running free from within the prison, is as ironic as a symbol of freedom as the prison is iconic as a symbol of captivity. That 315-mile stretch of the Hudson River flowing from its origins in the Adirondack Mountains of upstate New York flows through the Hudson Valley into the Atlantic Ocean. It serves as the political boundary between the states of New Jersey and New York, and its flow is influenced from as far north as Troy, New York. That river is named after the British Henry Hudson, who sailed for the Dutch East India Company back in the early 1600s, when the world's first multinational corporation dubbed it the North River.

3. Sing Sing was built in 1826—four decades before General Ulysses S. Grant was celebrated for winning a war but within just five years of the rebellion-inspiring sermons of Nathaniel "Nat" Turner. As of this writing, the prison formerly known as the Ossining Correctional Facility is just a few years from its bicentennial. It has seen nearly two centuries of confinement for approximately 1,700 men per year, and the execution of 614 men—before the US Supreme Court found in the 1972 case *Furman v. Georgia* that the death penalty was unconstitutional as it was then applied. After the Supreme Court ruled in the 1976 case *Gregg v. Georgia* that the death penalty is constitutional under certain circumstances, executions in several states began again in 1977. Constitutional Rights Foundation, "A History of the Death Penalty," 2012, www.crf-usa.org/images/pdf /HistoryoftheDeathPenaltyinAmerica.pdf.

4. John Thomas Scharf, *History of Westchester County: New York, Including Morrisania, Kings Bridge, and West Farms, Which Have Been Annexed to New York City*, vol. 2 (Westminster: L. E. Preston and Co., 1886).

5. Based on the National Inmate Survey conducted by the US Justice Department's Bureau of Justice Statistics, Human Rights Watch reported in 2015 that in New York between 2010 and 2015, 120 abuse cases were brought against guards, 80 abuse cases were settled with disciplinary action (no dismissal), 30 guards were up for dismissal, and only 8 were officially dismissed. Jamie Fellner, Alison Parker, Shantha Rau Barriga, Joe Saunders, Dinah PoKempner, Samantha Reiser, W. Paul Smith, Kathy Mills, and Fitzroy Hepkins, "Callous and Cruel: Use of Force Against Inmates with Disabilities in US Jails and Prisons," Human Rights Watch, May 12, 2015, www.hrw.org/report/2015/05/12/callous-and-cruel/use-force-against-inmates-mental-disabilities-us-jails-and#.

6. "The widespread availability of video of police shootings—from bystanders' smartphones as well as from police body and dashboard cameras—has been a primary factor in the rising number of indictments of officers." In a national study, prosecutors cited video evidence in felony cases filed against officers over the previous year twice as often as in prosecutions over the previous decade. Kimberly Kindy, Marc Fisher, Julie Tate, and Jennifer Jenkins, "A Year of Reckoning: Police Fatally Shoot Nearly 1,000," *Washington Post*, December 26, 2015,

www.washingtonpost.com/sf/investigative/2015/12/26/a-year-of-reckoning-police-fatally-shoot-nearly-1000.

7. Calaff v. Capra, Superintendent, Sing Sing Correctional Facility, US District Court for the Southern District of New York, Case #1:2015cv07868, October 5, 2015, https://dockets.justia.com/docket/new-york/nysdce/1:2015cv07868/448297.

8. Heta Häyry, "A Critique of the Paternalistic Theories of Correction," *Canadian Journal of Law and Jurisprudence* 4, no. 1 (June 9, 2015), www.cambridge.org/core/journals/canadian-journal-of-law-and-jurisprudence/article/abs/critique-of-the-paternalistic-theories-of-correction/2C27A531F730DA8913C07A318A8B7BF3; S. Chapman, "Prisoner's Dilemma," *New Republic*, March 8, 1980, 20–23; Office of Justice Programs, US Department of Justice, National Criminal Justice Reference Service #66367, www.ojp.gov/ncjrs/virtual-library/abstracts/prisoners-dilemma.

TRACK #10
HOMECOMING

C.M.S.

COMMUNITY
CAPACITY
DEVELOPMENT

#10 Homecoming

RETURNING FROM FEDERAL PRISON IN A
PANDEMIC

A Dialogue with Cheyenne Michael Simpson

As a movement sweeps the nation demanding justice for those the
American legal system has never protected, a battle rages over the policing, imprisonment, and execution of black bodies in the US. Beyond the
bars and badges endowed with the power to take lives with impunity,
more than half a million people are released from jails and prisons every
year without the support necessary to survive in the "free" world.[1] Men,
women, and children in human cages, serving sentences that stretch from
days to decades, exit the gates of correctional facilities and are expected to
adjust to an environment they have been completely removed from and
forced to abandon after surviving an entirely different reality with its own
rituals, regulations, and rules of engagement. After living in concrete
boxes where we are told when to get up and go to sleep, where to shower
and shit, how to walk and wear clothes—and being counted by a number
rather than called by our own name—we are expected to return to our
homes, communities, and society at large and reconnect with the world
we left behind, even as parole and police officers keep us under continuing
surveillance, and we are threatened daily by institutions structured to
send us back into captivity. Pharoah, it seems, is still doing all he can to
avoid letting my people go.

Having a sense of the challenges facing us after incarceration, I sat down with my brother, Cheyenne Michael Simpson, just three months after he returned home from federal prison. In an effort to document the path of his transition and help process his experience of arrest, incarceration, and release, we met to discuss the key incidents and issues in his head and heart to reflect critically on them while still very fresh and easy for him to share.

. . . . .

BRYONN BAIN: It's a blessing to have you home. How you feeling?

CHEYENNE MICHAEL SIMPSON: Thank you. I'm happy to be here, Man.

BRYONN: It's July 19, 2020—you came home when?

CHEYENNE: April 22.

BRYONN: And that was after how much time inside? How long was your sentence?

CHEYENNE: Ninety months [seven and a half years], but I served about five years.

BRYONN: What has it been like to come home after being sentenced to ninety months and serving about five years inside?

CHEYENNE: Well, to finally get out of prison and get home, just to have the family and the love I received, and all the help to get me on my feet, and to transition back into society, it's a blessing. A lot of people don't get what I get right now. So, you know, that's making it easier for me.

BRYONN: You would have been in a halfway house had you not come home to Muma's home?

CHEYENNE: Yeah, once you leave prison, they send you to a halfway house.[2] But since we had the problem with COVID, the halfway houses were sending us home. If we had an address and a phone number or landline, they would send you home just so nobody would get sick, because New York was a little bad.

BRYONN: What were the living conditions like in the halfway house for the time you were there? You were there for a couple of days?

CHEYENNE: Yeah, I was there for seven days . . . before they okayed my home address and phone number.

BRYONN: And what were the living conditions like?

CHEYENNE: I mean, the food was pretty good, but the fact that there's a disease going on . . . they had all of us in a room. You know, twenty bunk beds in one big room. Everybody on top of each other. They were trying to spread us out. But, you know, it's hard with so many inmates coming home. And the fact that the Bronx halfway house closed down . . . so, all the weight was put on Brooklyn. Everybody was cluttered. But after seven days, they got me out of there because I had my home address and my phone.

BRYONN: So there are twenty men to a room in the Brooklyn halfway house?

CHEYENNE: Yeah.

BRYONN: What about your experience in the last couple of weeks when you were still in the Feds? I know that because of COVID-19, the global pandemic, they did some things that they may have not done normally. What was your experience like? How long were you in solitary confinement? What was that experience like for you?

CHEYENNE: Alright, so I went like this. You know when you get close to go home, your counselor calls you and you sign for your halfway house date? That's usually two to three months before the release date. So my first date was April 16. So two to three months, I'm waiting for that date, preparing for that date, getting ready, family on the phone. We making plans: "Come pick me up"; "Give me this to wear." Everybody's excited. Then a week before my date, they called me in there, and they snatched my date. They tell me, "You can't go home." I'm like, "What?" That was a shocking thing 'cause I know I got to get on the phone, tell my girl, my kids, my family—like, "They're not letting me go home."

So the man tells me, "We're going to take your date, but you're going to go home two weeks late. We need to send you to solitary confinement because of the virus." They wanted to quarantine me before I went home. Now prior to that, they already had us locked down for a month. No movement on the compound. So we've been locked down already. So you have to understand, it can be stressful, frustrating. It wasn't a game, especially mentally. And to know solitary confinement—the SHU[3]—I avoided that my whole bid because I know it's not easy to do. But for me to go home, they said that's what I had to do.

BRYONN: So when you're in solitary, how big is the space that you're in?

CHEYENNE: Five by nine.

BRYONN: Five by nine?

CHEYENNE: Like you got your shower, your toilet, and you got two bunk beds so you got somebody in there with you.

BRYONN: And do you ever come out of that?

CHEYENNE: You don't come out of there for nothing.

BRYONN: Not even for an hour of recreation?

CHEYENNE: They suspended all that for the quarantine people. Nobody could leave that five by nine—for fourteen days.

BRYONN: And four weeks before that month, you were in lockdown but you had one hour?

CHEYENNE: No, we were just in our dorm. They locked us down in our dorm. We couldn't go outside at all. Okay, see? We had really six weeks of lockdown.

BRYONN: Well, let's talk about the last ninety days. That's six weeks, about the last forty-five days or so. But the last ninety days, the last three months of your time inside, what was that like, knowing that your release date is on the horizon? What were your interactions like? How is that time different for you from the time before?

CHEYENNE: You know, you start getting anxious. Time starts to slow down. Days get longer because you know you're about to leave. You start working out more because you want to look the best you can. You start using all your minutes [for outside phone calls] because you're talking to everybody, letting them know you coming home. And you're just preparing to come back to society. But it does slow down and gets a little rougher as you get closer.

BRYONN: Was there any kind of relationships with folks inside, folks who maybe were coming out sooner or folks who are coming out after a much longer time? Did any of your relationships with those folks change? Anybody envious of you being released soon or try to make you do things to make you stay in longer? Anything like that a part of what happened?

CHEYENNE: Well, not for me. Thank God [my] paperwork was right in the New York car. . . .

BRYONN: What do you mean by the New York "*car*"? Can you explain what that means?

CHEYENNE: A New York car. I was in Maryland, so I was out of state. The people from New York that was there with me, we all stuck together [as a unit in the prison known as the "New York car"]. But your paperwork had to be right. That means you're not snitching. You need your docket sheet. You know? Everything to tell that you wasn't snitching. So, once you hand that in and everybody okay, just like a family gathers. You know? We stick together and make sure everybody good. So I was alright. And you know, people be happy for you, like, "My man is going home!" You know? 'Cause they know they're next. Some people count their time by "so-and-so goes home": "When he goes home, then I go home!" So it kind of helps other people get through their time.

BRYONN: I got to ask you about the paperwork situation for the New York car. So let's say someone does not have the right paperwork. First of all, who is reviewing the paperwork to determine if somebody could be in the New York Car versus the Maryland car, versus the Virginia car? Who looks over that paperwork?

CHEYENNE: Everybody has a person from each state, each car, that they trust to look over the paperwork. Basically, somebody [who is incarcerated in the prison] that works in a law library or who knows law, so they can read the codes and do the paperwork properly. But it's not something that is fabricated on the compound, because that person can get in trouble.

BRYONN: If somebody is discovered to be a snitch what happens to those people?

CHEYENNE: Well, those people get found out. The dude who check them in gets them off the compound. Sends them to the SHU. They usually send them to another compound or just don't mess with them. They don't rock with us. They are on their own.

BRYONN: The prison staff, like the warden, the corrections officers . . . they will move them?

CHEYENNE: When somebody gets checked in [when they first arrive at the prison], they know. I mean, nobody goes and tells them, but they know the routine, usually. . . . If somebody just be like, "Alright, I just got here. I'm checking in . . . got my stuff packed." They know they're not safe on the compound [because they are on their own without anybody who has their back].

BRYONN: But the New York car looks out for their own? Your other brothers in the New York car were looking out for each other?

CHEYENNE: Yes, sir.

BRYONN: Okay. I want to talk about the different facilities you were in and get a sense from you of what was different or unique or special about your experience at these different facilities, starting off with the last facility. And let's talk about the Cumberland, Maryland, Federal Camp. What was that experience like? What was different or unique about the experience there?

CHEYENNE: Well, Cumberland, that was like a little blessing to get to because it's a camp. And I came from the low[-security prison]. The low is more classified [than a camp]. Once your classification drops and comes to a lower-classification jail, that would be a camp. But I've got to go to Cumberland, Maryland. It was clean. We had a lot of freedom. You know the drug program was there. It wasn't as rough as other places. So you got that year off a little easier. And, you know, a little more freedom. And it was clean. The food was alright. Compared to the low, [where] you're locked down a lot.

BRYONN: Is that where the "hooch" is?

CHEYENNE: [laughs] Yeah, they have hooch everywhere. That's a part of jail.

BRYONN: How do you describe what hooch is?

CHEYENNE: The hooch is like an alcohol. It's like a wine that we put together. We get whatever we can: fruit, sugar, whatever is available for us to make it with, and some people just enjoy their weekends with it. Or some people make it as a business. But there's the hooch, and then there's a white lightning. So there're two different kinds. One is more expensive than the other. And one is cleaner than the other.

BRYONN: Which one is more expensive?

CHEYENNE: The white lightning.

BRYONN: What's special about the white lighting?

CHEYENNE: Hooch, you just leave for seven days. Let it rot. Let it get to where it needs to get to. And you can drink it like that—nasty. The white lightning, they take it from the hooch—clean the hooch, put a stinger in it, boil it, steam it, and let it clean. It looks like vodka you buy at a store. And it's much stronger.

BRYONN: What's the stinger?

CHEYENNE: A stinger? It's like a thing that heats up hot water for us. We make it out of an electric cord . . . basically, how we cook in the low. You know, I fried stuff and it helps out a lot.

BRYONN: So Cumberland, Maryland was a better experience than some of the other facilities you were in?

CHEYENNE: Yeah, it was more free.

BRYONN: More free? More open? You lived in dorms instead of cells?

CHEYENNE: Yeah, we had a dorm. And each wing had, like, thirtysome people on each wing and had four people to a cube. And there's two floors, four wings.

BRYONN: What were the range of sentences of other folks you know who are in Cumberland?

CHEYENNE: When you can go to a camp, soon as you'd like, there's people there like six months, a year, three years, ten years. Dudes with eighteen years in. Dudes with twenty-five years in, because as you go to the federal system, you start off in the pen[itentiary]. Go to a medium[-security prison]. You go to a low[-security prison]. And you go to the camp. That's how your classification drops. But you go to a camp no matter what. That's the transition of you going home.

BRYONN: Do people talk openly about their charges? Did everybody kind of know what everybody did? Was it kept quiet?

CHEYENNE: It's basically kept quiet. But, you know, your car usually knows.

BRYONN: Okay, let's talk about the facility you were in before that—Fort Dix in New Jersey. What stands out in your memory as being significant about that experience?

CHEYENNE: Fort Dix is like the projects. Anybody ever been in there knows it's just wild over there. And, you know, it's more secure than a camp. It's a low. But in your dorms there's so many things going on. So many people from around the world. So many cars and politics. And everybody know already: the cigarettes, the phones, the hooch, the deuce. Everything is moving crazy.

BRYONN: What the deuce?

CHEYENNE: Deuce is like a drug that they smoke in a cigarette.

BRYONN: Is that K-2?

CHEYENNE: Yeah.

BRYONN: Weren't there a lot of deaths related to K-2 in in New Jersey at that time?

CHEYENNE: Yeah, there was some. I think like a couple of deaths. But a lot of people hallucinate and were losing their mind, causing a lot of havoc, making the cops go crazy, making the whole facility go crazy.

BRYONN: How was K-2 smuggled in? What was the science behind how folks got it through all those levels of security and inside the prison?

CHEYENNE: Well, I think now they figured it out. So I'm just gonna say it, but they would make a chemical at home and spray it onto paper and then send a letter in. Like, I wrote you a letter, and it would be on the letter. And then they chop the letter up and sell it in strips. And people put it in a cigarette.

BRYONN: There were a lot of hallucinations from folks getting sick off of that synthetic weed?

CHEYENNE: Yup.

BRYONN: Let's go back before that: MDC Brooklyn, the largest federal detention center in the country. I've been to Metropolitan Detention Center in Brooklyn to perform and facilitate workshops I organized with Beyond the Bars. What was your experience like there?

CHEYENNE: Brooklyn was like a transit for me because I wasn't there that long, but a month . . . locked in a cell, just locked in. It was terrible.[4] But the fact that you're already sentenced. You see? I already got sentenced when I was there, so I was just waiting to go to the real jail; that would be Fort Dix. For the movement you get a job, do programs. But Brooklyn is more like a lockdown facility. There ain't a lot to do there.

BRYONN: And they had some deaths there. I think last winter. It got really cold, and folks did not have heat. Were you there before that?

CHEYENNE: I was there before that, but there was a situation when I was there because they were treating people poorly. The facility was ran poorly. Like, you look out the window sometimes and see people rioting and stuff. It was just a bad experience there, being locked in and then seeing all the people not being treated right . . . at least more stress.

BRYONN: People were outside protesting against the horrible conditions inside? Anything stand out to you that gives an idea of what the bad conditions were? Was it the food? Or the health care?

CHEYENNE: It would be like the heat, the water. You know, no proper bedding, the water.

BRYONN: What was wrong with the water?

CHEYENNE: They said, "Don't drink the water."

BRYONN: Okay, because it was toxic?

CHEYENNE: Yeah, it was actually.

BRYONN: From Fort Dix, you were there three years?

CHEYENNE: I was. Three years.

BRYONN: And then Cumberland, Maryland?

CHEYENNE: I was there for two years.

BRYONN: Alright, so last but not least, before all these was Valhalla (Westchester County Jail). Which is where exactly?

CHEYENNE: Valhalla is in [five miles from] White Plains.

BRYONN: North of New York City. What was the experience like in Valhalla? And how long were you there?

CHEYENNE: I was there for fifteen months. That was probably my worst experience, because that was the beginning. That was, like, they just rip me off the street. They just took everything from me. My body and my mind wasn't prepared for jail yet. So when they put me in there, there was a shocking. They just ripped me from a family, my kids, everything, my whole life, and just put you in a whole different life that you didn't know, you had to learn about. And you have to figure out. Valhalla is cells. So you're locked down. You get a rec[reation] deck. And that's the screen with one basketball court, two small TVs, a Spanish and an English. Food is terrible. Everybody's fighting. It's just, everybody's stressed because they're waiting to be sentenced. And it's just a rough time there.

BRYONN: You were in a cell with somebody else?

CHEYENNE: Out there, you're by yourself.

BRYONN: You're by yourself, then you get out for how much time a day?

CHEYENNE: In fact, usually two or three hours out. They lock you back in for another two or three hours.

BRYONN: How are the meals served?

CHEYENNE: A meal . . . somebody will bring a big tray to the dorm and hand it out.

BRYONN: So there's a mess hall?

CHEYENNE: No, you eat in your dorm.

BRYONN: So you don't have mess halls, chow halls, and other facilities?

CHEYENNE: Yeah, Fort Dix and Cumberland.

BRYONN: So you interact with other people?

CHEYENNE: Yeah.

BRYONN: Who had the best food? Who had the worst food?

CHEYENNE: Cumberland had the best food. Fort Dix was alright, but could have been better.

BRYONN: Valhalla was the worst?

CHEYENNE: Yeah.

BRYONN: What kind of stuff did they feed you in Valhalla?

CHEYENNE: You know, Thursdays is chicken. . . . It's like the best day of the week when they feed you, like, burgers, tacos. They make up all kinds of stuff on the menu.

BRYONN: Let's talk about the days before that. Leading up to Valhalla. Let's talk about the raid. Alright, so what was that experience? Walk us through from when the raid began to when you were charged. Take us through that story.

CHEYENNE: You know, I really went to jail for my phone. So one day I just woke up, started my day, started seeing people. And at the beginning of the day, I just . . . I felt funny. And I saw these cars following me. And then next thing you know, I stopped to see somebody. And they try to jump out on me. So I took off. Took them on a little chase. They hit me, knock me off the road, arrested me.

BRYONN: You're driving?

CHEYENNE: Yeah.

BRYONN: What were you driving?

CHEYENNE: I was driving a Lincoln MKS.

BRYONN: You know what they were driving behind you?

CHEYENNE: They had a Caravan, a Trailblazer, and another van.

BRYONN: There were three vehicles behind you?

CHEYENNE: Yeah, black, burgundy, and I forgot the other one. But once they got me out, it wasn't a big deal. 'Cause I'm like, they probably seen me make a sale, but then I started thinking, "Damn, it's too many of them. They had to have this planned, but I'm still good. I've got my people. They're gonna come get me." So they handcuff me, arrest me, bring me to the thing, put me in a room, starts questioning me. Boom. "We know this." "We know that." "We had your phone tap." This and that. "We're gonna give you fifteen minutes to make a decision." "You want to cooperate with us, or we gonna go arrest your whole family right now?" And I was like, "What?" He was like, "We know everything." "Well, I just need my lawyer." He was like, "I'm gonna give you one more chance." I was like, "I just need my lawyer." He grabbed me and put me in a cell. About a day later, I heard the door crack, and here came everybody. They had everybody handcuffed.

BRYONN: Who was everybody?

CHEYENNE: My girl, my baby's mother. My nephew. My baby mother's brother, two of my dudes. It was just like the whole clique I ran with. They had them all.

BRYONN: Did you ever get to speak to a lawyer before that?

CHEYENNE: Naw, I didn't speak to a lawyer till after they arrested everybody. Put us in a holding cell and they brought us from Middletown to White Plains. When I got to White Plains, I got to see a lawyer.

BRYONN: Which police department was questioning you?

CHEYENNE: This is Troop F, Middletown, New York State Troopers.

BRYONN: So the Middletown state troopers will question you without an attorney being present. You requested an attorney to be present, and they did not give you an attorney?

CHEYENNE: Naw.

BRYONN: And they questioned you and insisted that you cooperate without ever having a lawyer present?

CHEYENNE: Yes.

BRYONN: How many?

CHEYENNE: Seven.

BRYONN: After the seven people are brought into the cell with you, what happens next?

CHEYENNE: They start transferring us to White Plains.

BRYONN: Everybody's gone?

CHEYENNE: Everybody's gone.

BRYONN: So everybody ends up in Valhalla together?

CHEYENNE: Yeah.

BRYONN: At what point do negotiations start that result in some people getting to leave? How does that happen?

CHEYENNE: Well, soon. As soon as the marshals brought us to White Plains, they put us in a holding cell. And they started calling us. Boom. "You want to make your phone call?" "Call so-and-so if you got a lawyer. If not, one will be appointed." So they started doing that; some people had lawyers, some people didn't.

But as for me. I didn't have a lawyer. So they appointed one to me. So she told me straight off the bat, "You're the head of the indictment. They are hitting you with kingpin statute,[5] like you're the leader of this, so you might as well sit still." But then, you know, they gave my baby mother bail. They gave my girl bail. And in the feds, bail can be just a couple people put in signatures that if you do run, they'll pay or they'll be responsible for you. So we didn't have to put it out right away for them. So I was blessed to let them go home. And then they sent me to Valhalla.

BRYONN: And what were the actual charges?

CHEYENNE: Conspiracy to sell ten kilos.

BRYONN: Did they have any physical evidence?

CHEYENNE: See, that's where it gets crazy. That's why I thought, while I was getting my review, I'm going through my paperwork, and I'm like, "Conspiracy to sell 10 kilos? Man, I didn't sell no 10 kilos!" But they have this thing called "ghost drugs." So they have your phone tapped, and every sale, they have you recorded. Everything they assume you're talking about that they think is drugs, they add it all up. Really, in the raid . . . when they did raid the houses and stuff, all they really found was 365 grams of coke and 150 grams of crack. So that ain't no 10 kilos. But they put that, [and] whatever was on the phone, and it all added up to 10 kilos. So they give you the real drug, and they give you this thing called "ghost drugs."

BRYONN: So "ghost drugs" are basically how much drugs they *think* you were talking about, even though they're not actual drugs that anybody ever found? How do they determine whether or not something you were saying on a phone or a tapped conversation was drugs? Or was there something else you were talking about that may have just sounded like drugs? How did they determine that difference?

CHEYENNE: I guess the cops have somebody that listens to the phone calls, and they determine, like, "Oh, he's talking about this here." And that's what they do. The feds is dirty. All around the board.

BRYONN: Did it ever come up that they could be mistaken? Like, if you're saying, "Oh wow, looks like it's gonna be a white Christmas!" Maybe that's actually you talking about a white Christmas and not about cocaine?

CHEYENNE: I'm sure, that would sound nice, but you know, they're trying to get their conviction. And the simple fact they got their eyes on you . . . they want you. So they can do whatever they got to do to get you, and plus they spent money on this investigation . . .

BRYONN: How long were they tapping your phone for?

CHEYENNE: They said six months.

BRYONN: Six months? So when you came before a judge, finally, did you hear their arguments? Did you get a chance to hear what they were saying?

CHEYENNE: Yup, they were saying, "Mr. Simpson is a mole!" 'Cause, you know, I appealed my bail hearing so I can get bail because the first one they denied me. So they gave me an appeal for it. And that's when [our brother] K came with the house, $250,000. And Muma came with another $407,000 for the house, so we thought we'd appeal it, and I'm gonna go home. The district attorney stood up and was like, "He's a mole in the neighborhood. If he leaves now, we will not be able to find him. Mr. Simpson grew up here. He knows the ins and outs. He doesn't need a passport!" Because that was my fight. "Y'all got my passport. Y'all got everything for me to stay here. I got children. I got this, I got that." Trying to give him everything to let me out on this bail. But they were like, I didn't need to flee. I can hide right here where I'm at. And I was just saying, "I'm connected [to this place]. I have this [family]." They just fought in the best way.

BRYONN: Did you have any response to what they said?

CHEYENNE: See, when I got to the feds, it was like they took everything. They hid everything. From the phone being tapped, they knew where everything was. So they kind of had me. They took the work, the bread. They had everything. Plus they had my whole clique. So it was hard to be like, "Alright, go pay for this lawyer. Get me this lawyer. Do this, and do that." So I had to go with the one they appointed me . . . I really had the bread right in there to pay for one. And he came to me and told me straight up, "They got a 99 percent conviction. They are winning. I think we should just take the cop-out, and then, you know, go do your time, because they got you."

So you know, I just rolled with the punches and tried to get the best thing—to get my mandatory ten [years] dropped to mandatory five, because he started out with the ten to forty. And I was just trying to tell him to work that down for me. I mean, I know I got to do time, but get the time low. And then I just tried to get as much help for him from my brothers, you and K, and everybody look over my paperwork, whoever you know at Columbia [University], Harvard, your friends gave us pointers. And K too. We tried to make his job easier and let him know, "If you not gonna do your job right, we gonna see it!" So we tried to work in the best we could.

BRYONN: I remember talking to your lawyer at that time. I remember having a conversation with him. I read through your case file, trying to figure out whatever we possibly could to try to get your time down as much as possible. . . . But to be clear about what happened was, they had six months of surveillance recordings, and they basically were arguing that they could get between ten to forty years under this conspiracy and "kingpin" charge. And ultimately, that was cut down to from ten-to-forty to five-to-ten?

CHEYENNE: Yeah.

BRYONN: And then you ended up serving five and a half?

CHEYENNE: They sentenced me to ninety months. I had done the drug program and took a year off. Then during the course of my incarceration,

BOP[6] gave us extra good time that they were stealing and then people fought for it, so they gave it to us, and with my good time, I ended up doing about five and a half.

BRYONN: How many programs did you do while you were inside?

CHEYENNE: For every year, they want you to do at least three or four programs. So I did three programs a year: church, RDAP,[7] you know, whatever I needed to do stay busy.

BRYONN: What program was most helpful for you?

CHEYENNE: The CDL Program.[8]

BRYONN: What is the CDL about?

CHEYENNE: CDL is like for driving trucks. It's a special license. I mean, they make money, and it's a good start in society when you do get released, because they don't hold nothing against you if you got a felony or not. And like, you know, got no boss when you're in a truck. Got your music, little headphones in your cell phone. You know? It's a good way to get your life moving when you get home.

BRYONN: Let's talk a little bit about life before the raid happened. Because I know you had some entrepreneurial ideas that you were trying to get off the ground. We talked about what your plan was, how you were working to get out of hustling into something that was going to be more legit and less risky.

CHEYENNE: Yes. So you know, everybody starts off hustling. It's a good gig. But as you get older, you start seeing this kind of end one day, and it's not gonna end nicely. It's gon' end bad. So you start trying to prepare for a better and safer future, especially when you have children. So I started doing a little music with [our brother] K. That was working out a little bit. Then I wanted to get into business, so I started doing a yogurt store—self-serve [frozen] yogurt store. And everything was coming in place. Everything was working. It was all under construction. I had the store already, had the machines. We were just doing construction and getting ready to open. And then a week before we were supposed to open, that's when they grabbed me.

BRYONN: What was it about this particular business that seemed like it was promising?

CHEYENNE: See, I did my homework on this place called Hookla. And I've seen them open up stores around the world. And it worked, low maintenance. The store basically runs itself. And it's like an ice cream parlor, but all year-round. . . . You come inside. They pick the toppings, whatever yogurt. But the fact that kids can pull the knob, fill his own little cup up, and throw on the toppings, and it's as low maintenance. It's not like a business you got to be at all day. I can put my daughter in there and she could run it—make fifteen dollars an hour, and I could still give her a job. And I could still have my little bit of freedom and make money while I do my other business. So I could try to open up another one in a different town or a different city. That's how I looked at.

BRYONN: While you were inside for the five and a half years, were there conversations ever with folks who asked you about your business ideas or business plans that you wanted to actually pursue when you came home? Did that ever come up?

CHEYENNE: Sometimes. You know, inmates, we locked up, so we have a lot of free time. And a lot of people build together, especially if you're in a car and your paperwork is good. You've been building relationships with people from all over New York. You know what I'm saying? And it's always good to talk about home, takes the homesickness away. But yeah, everybody had their stories. You know, jail is a place with lots of stories. I used to tell people about my little yogurt store, my music, and stuff like that.

BRYONN: But the prisons didn't have any programs designed to help you figure out how to get that going when you came home?

CHEYENNE: I took a class called Money Smarts. And I mean, you figure, most of the programs are ran by inmates. They don't really have . . . like right now, the BOP, they got everything on a budget. Their money is low. They're not trying to put nothing into programs like that. . . . You just go in there, and you don't even got to go. You can sign in and leave, basically. But I was to sit next to this little Jewish dude. He used to teach the class. He was from Brooklyn. So I used to sit with him. And he use to talk about, "Do this Money Smart thing. Always make a savings, bank account, stocks," stuff like that.

BRYONN: Financial literacy?

CHEYENNE: Yeah.

BRYONN: I went to England. They have the Brixton prison in London. They got a five-star restaurant in the prison run by the guys in the prison.

CHEYENNE: What?

BRYONN: They learn how to run a whole business. I'm just wondering if you would have anything like that while you're inside. It would have given you the inner workings. You know? You could have seen the inner workings of a business while you're inside to prepare to come out and start your own. That's the kind of thing I feel like might be worth, you know, trying to bring here. . . . I think we should close most of the prisons and figure out how to invest in the folks in our communities. But while folks are still inside, give them what they need so when they come home they can be on their feet again. Let's talk about your daughter and your son.

CHEYENNE: Your niece and nephew.

BRYONN: You know it! What was their life like before you went in?

CHEYENNE: My firstborn, Cheyenne, she's twenty-one now. When I left, she was fifteen or sixteen. I got locked up like three days before her birthday. And my son, Dakota, he just turned sixteen. I left when he was ten. But thanks to God, and you know, the time I spent with them, the things I try to teach them, their mom being there for them. My girlfriend, L. A., all the family. They stayed on the right path. My daughter, she graduated high school. She goes to college now for physical therapy. Orange County Community College. She's in the third year. My son, he's sixteen. He plays lacrosse. I'm still mad he left football and went to lacrosse! . . . as long as he's doing something.

BRYONN: [*laughs*]

CHEYENNE: He got his permit. He already got his car in high school. He's doing alright. And I'm just happy my daughter didn't get pregnant and go off with the wrong guy or get caught up in the wrong stuff. And my son, he didn't run, run with a gang or get in the streets or, you know. . . . He just stayed in school playing sports and on the right path. So I'm blessed for that.

BRYONN: So what is your message to them now? When you think about all you've seen, all you've gone through, right? You remember being their age or being, like, twenty-one, sixteen, or what age they were when you went inside? When they were ten and sixteen? How do you help them to understand? How you went down this path that took you away from them for five years? And how important is it for them to *not* go down that path?

CHEYENNE: Like, we talked about all the time, because they were a little older, so they got to really see what happened. And plus their house was raided. Their mother was taken. Their father was taken. For a minute, they didn't know if we were coming home or not. Thank God their mother got to come home, but the hurt and the pain, and then me not being there, and then the financial state they had to go through. And then the things I embedded in them before it all happened. And the struggle their mom had to go through. I think they know, and plus, the way we talk. I know they know that, to stay out of the streets and not sell drugs. Fast money is not the way. Always embedded what I learned from Muma—that school is the right path. No matter what, graduate from high school, go to college, get a degree, and then find a nice career.

BRYONN: What do you think would have helped you to go down a different path, right? I mean, you talked a little bit about how so many of us get involved in hustling because there's so limited opportunities for folks. Right? What do you think are the things that might have helped you to make different choices to go down different paths? Even though I recognize the choices you had were limited choices. And there's a whole lot of things that need to change in our communities to give folks more choices and better choices, but what do you think might have helped you to guide you and support you through another path?

CHEYENNE: See, it would have to start at a younger age. Not for myself, but for people that do listen. It's good for children to have both parents in the household. It's good for them if both parents have an education. So their financial state can be right. And they can raise their kids in a proper environment. Schooling is important. The time that you spend with your children is important. Even if you don't think so, it pays off in the end. Kids remember everything. The things you do around your children. The way you carry yourself, your company, and it don't look like it's gonna rub off on them, but it does. The TV, the music, it rubs off in the end. When they get older . . . and they start fabricating these people that they're used to seeing, or the bad language they are used to hearing, or music or just the way people are carrying ourselves around them for a long period of time. They don't know it's gonna rub off on them. It just does. It just becomes their character.

Me, growing up with a single-parent mother, always at work, never really had enough time for me because she always had to pay the bills. Me, having too much free time. Me, always being in the street, out with the wrong people. Our money being limited. Her not being able to give me the things I wanted. Or me, seeing her struggle with the bills and cry and try to do the best she can. It kind of made me want to be like, "Alright, I gotta find a way to help her help me." You know, just to give her some kind of help. I am tired of seeing my mom sad and struggling. Rest in peace. She died while I was gone. And I thank her for all she did, all her struggles. Rest in peace, Mom. But, yeah, your children, you got to pay attention. You got to bring them up right. You got to keep them in a positive environment, because it does rub off when they get older.

BRYONN: This is a little sensitive, so if you want to go in another direction, I'm happy to do that. I want to talk about trauma. And trauma is this thing that we all carry with us when we have really painful experiences from a young age, from our childhood, when we experience near-death situations or experiences that cause us to have a lot of fear or pain. And then we all end up carrying it. We all have different kinds of trauma because we've all had our own experiences. I want to ask you about the experience of losing your moms while you were inside. What were you going through at that time? What do you want her to know? Because I know she's listening and watching and paying attention right now. So what was that experience like for you? And what words do you have for her?

CHEYENNE: It was rough. It was bad. It was real bad. I was like, I had a year and a half left to come home. Even before I left, she was a little sick. She wasn't that sick. And then as time started going on. . . . Every once in a while that hit me, like your mom's doing bad, she's in a nursing home now. Now she's in the hospital. And every time I speak to her, I can hear it in her voice, or her letters will come. Her handwriting is getting worse and worse. And I would tell her, "Mom, just hold on. I'll be there in a minute, man. Do not die on me while I'm not there for you!" And she fought, they said. They said she fought and fought. And she kept on telling them, "I'm fighting until he comes home. I'm trying to fight . . ."

And then one day I was in the gym working out and the pastor from the jail called me. See, I thought, because in the camp when you work out with the weights, you got to make the weights out of bricks and stuff. So we lifting weights, and I see him come to the gym, and I'm thinking like, "Damn, we got caught. He's gonna give me a shot. I'm gonna lose good time." He's calling me, and I'm like, "Damn, he's just calling me by myself?" [*laughs*] There were a bunch of us. So I'm like, "What do you want?" He's like, "I need to talk to you." And I'm like, "Talk to me right here." You know, that's my way to get up the shot. I'm trying to bounce. And he's like, "I got to talk to you in private, Mr. Simpson." So now I go with him, and he brings me to his office. Now I'm like, "This is weird. You can just take my ID and write me a shot." He got me in his office like, "Sit down." I was like, "Sit down for what?" And he was like, "Your mom died." And I just froze, and I was like, "What?" And I didn't believe him at first. He was like, "Your mom just passed away. I have a number for you to call right here." I'm looking at this dude like, "Are you sure, man? Are you sure?" And he's like, "Yeah. I think you should call this number." It wasn't real yet. You know what I'm saying? I didn't believe him, like it wasn't real until I call my girl, L. A. And she picked up the phone and she was like, "I don't know how to tell you this, but she died." And I just lost it. I passed out on the floor. It was crazy.

So then, after that, I go back to the dorm, and I'm trying to deal with it. Now you know I'm in a dorm, with four people to a cube, everybody close, locked up, and I'm trying to hold my manhood together. Like, you know, it's not the place to break down. And definitely you got to deal with it by yourself. I've got no family member there with me or nobody to be like, "It's gonna be okay. . . ." I just got to keep inside and deal with it myself. So I take my work clothes off. I go jump in the shower. And like a real man would do, I broke down in the shower. I started praying to God, talking to her, crying, couldn't believe it, hitting the wall like, "What? *What?*" I've never had life without my mother before. To realize I left her by herself and she died drove me crazy inside me. But I fought through it.

And then I went to my counselor. I was like, "I need to go to my mother's funeral." And then she was like, "Fill out this paperwork. Let me call the funeral hall to see where it's at, what time. . . ." Boom, boom, boom. So I'm thinking I'm going, at least say good-bye for the last time, boom boom boom. The day of the funeral, the morning, I'm about to leave. They call me down and tell me that I'm denied. I'm like, "I'm denied? Why? That's my mother! I'm the only born child. Like, she died. There's a funeral. People are telling you. It's in the paper." They got everything. They were like, "In 2000, you got a charge with attempted murder. You discharged the weapon. So we can't let you go because you have a discharged weapon on your record." So I couldn't go say good-bye to my mom, and to know, like, I messed up. Not just now, leaving her by herself, then too because now that's preventing me from going to say good-bye. So it was a little . . . it was a little rough. But I had to take every bit of me and not say, "Try to forget it," but try to tell myself, "We gonna handle this when we get home." We can't handle it right here in jail because all you will do is go bald, turn gray, lose all kinds of weight. So you have to find a way to fight through this and be a man. Tighten your Timbs up.[9] And let's get through this when we get home. We'll handle it.

And that's what I did. That's what I focused on. I took another class. I worked out instead of twice a day, three times a day. I started running six miles, instead of three miles. I started reading, Michael Matthew's books. Just started working on my body. Just trying to fix my knowledge and my reading. And just trying to be a better person. . . . And I got through it like that.

BRYONN: Is there anything that you wanted to say to her before she passed, even if you didn't get a chance to speak to her while she was still here?

CHEYENNE: I just want her to know I'm thankful for all the sacrifices. And I wish I would have been able to hug her more and to love her more. And I would have realized that at a younger age, what she was really going through, and how hard it was for her to take care of me. And that she was a great mom and did a great job. I never really got to tell her that as a kid; I was always complaining, like, "I can't have this, I can't have that!" Then I'm in the streets trying to get it for myself, and she didn't want me in there. I just didn't understand how, as a young dude, I was just trying to fit in, get what I wanted, and not knowing that I was hurting her that much. I just want to say sorry, you know, and that I love you. Rest in peace.

BRYONN: Do you think that some of the lessons from your relationship with her are going to help you in learning how to be the best father you can be with your kids?

CHEYENNE: Oh, man, definitely! I grew up without a dad, so I always wanted to be a great dad to my kids. Even though my relationship didn't work out with my baby's mother, I was always there for my kids, even if it was every weekend. They spent the night in my house. Friday, Saturday, Sunday, bring them home Monday. During the week, I'm in their house. If there was a problem, she called me. I'm calling [their stepdad] Derek on my phone. I was a hands-on dad. No matter what, try to do the best I can. So when I went to jail it hurt me, but it also hurt them to not to have me there for the school projects, school plays, softball, football. You know? I have my daughter and my son and everything. We're doing everything together like that. So it's like they say: "You do the time, but the family do the time with you."

BRYONN: Just one or two things I want to touch on as we close up here. You talk about your health in terms of your physical, like challenging yourself to run more, lost a lot of weight. How much weight did you lose?

CHEYENNE: Like 120 pounds.

BRYONN: That's amazing! 120 pounds? You look fantastic. You talked about the emotional health of trying to deal with your emotions and letting yourself cry. It's important. So many of us have this really toxic, poisonous way of thinking about what it means to be a man that limits us to not be in touch with our emotions. So it's important that you cry. It's important you actually come to terms with your emotions because, you know . . . locking your emotions down is what cuts down on life expectancy. And we don't want that. You know? So I'm also curious about your *spiritual* health. How do you think about the spiritual side of yourself and that development, that part of you? Did any of the reading or the studying, or the time with the pastor, any of that make you think about your spirit, your soul? You know? Think about the part of you that goes beyond just this physical form? And what does spirituality, not religion so much but, really, spirituality mean to you?

CHEYENNE: In jail, you by yourself, you ripped from everything. So it gets stressful sometimes, and you feel alone and things get rough like that when you feel alone. But if you read the Bible, it tells you . . . we went to church. We were raised in the Seventh Day Adventist Church. So I took religion serious all the time. I really got serious with it because I didn't want to be by myself. And I kept on reading the Bible and Psalms and scriptures, and you'd always seen that God finds you and sticks with you, no matter what you're going through. Even if you run with him for a little bit and then you leave, he's still there for you when you come back.

And it was just like, every Sunday they called church, and I'd go. I started participating in the church. I started feeling like I had somebody with me at all times. I started praying more, not just when I ate, throughout the day and just trying to talk to my mom through Him, or just when I got sad, or things got rough in there. I talked to Him and then it didn't feel like I let it out to somebody. . . . I got my spirit, my faith, got real strong in there. And I think He got me through the roughest time of my life, right? That was the roughest time of my life right there. And then the fact that for me to come home and have all my loved ones and my family, I don't got my mom, but I know she's watching over me. But the people I do have around me, they are not suspect. They're real. They're giving me their hearts as much as I give them my heart. And they're making my path a lot easier in my transition. And I think everybody around me right now is the people that God wants around.

BRYONN: If you could write a letter to yourself five and half years ago . . . go back in time and just get in your own ear, you know? We don't listen to everybody who talks to us, but if you had to speak to yourself, like five or six years ago, before the raid happened . . . before going inside, what do you think you would say to yourself that would get through to you, that is important for you to think about, that points your life in a new direction? I know you're already working on starting a business, starting your own entrepreneurship and everything, but what do you think you could have said to yourself that would have communicated in an urgent way that you needed to make some changes in your life? Because there might be somebody else who's at that point right now who hears your words.

CHEYENNE: See, right now, knowing what I know already, what I went through, all the hurt and pain, all the time away from my family, lost my mom, what my children had to go through . . . the money does not equal out to it. There is no amount of money that you can make selling drugs, stealing, doing drugs that is going to pay for what you're going to go through in the future if you stay on that path. I wish I could go back and go to the college that my mom was gonna send me to, do my culinary college degree, and went off to be a chef. I wish I would have not followed the people that I was following. I should have had better self-esteem.

I should have like . . . just found myself, not wanting to be in the crowd. I should have paid more attention in school. I should have not thought the nerds were nerds and the cool people were cool people. I should have just looked at everybody in one way, so I could see, like, "Alright, dumb people going down the wrong path. These people going down the right path, no matter if they're cool or not." The path is *righteous,* and it's gonna pay off in the long run. I was always looking for *right now.* I wanted it fast. "I want to do it right now, and I want it to be big." You got to have patience with life. It takes time, and you got to put the work in and you can't be lazy. That's what I wish I would have told myself.

BRYONN: That's so powerful and so beautiful to say, "Choose the *righteous* path instead of the *right now* path." Truly profound. Last thing I want to ask you about is the future. What do you envision in the future? Let's say you have a magic wand, a crystal ball, and you can make the future whatever you want it to be from this moment forward. What do you see in your future from this day forward?

CHEYENNE: See, I learned a lot through all these rough times I went through. And in my future, I mean it's good to be financially stable, but I don't want to build my life around money no more. I want to have a little business that makes enough money to keep a roof over my head. Have fun with my children. Be happy in life. I don't want to be stressed looking over my shoulder. So I'm gonna work to open up a little tree business. And just make an honest dollar. You know what I'm saying? And be happy. Money's not everything. Time with your family. Just to be happy. That's what everybody should really focus on—family time and happiness. Because all that other stuff—it'll kill you, Man.

BRYONN: Wise words spoken. I've got to say, thank you, Chey. I'm so happy you're home! You are one of the most genuine and most generous people that I know in the world. And I'm just glad you're here and so happy you've had this opportunity to actually take life in another direction, because this is the beginning of the rest of your life, Brother. Welcome home!

CHEYENNE: Thank you. We good?

BRYONN: Yeah. We good.

LINER NOTES

Track #10's interview took place on July 19, 2020, in New York. Published courtesy of Cheyenne Michael Simpson and developed in collaboration with the Narratives of Freedom (NOF) Collective, a participatory oral history initiative examining the effects of racialized hyperincarceration on families. Special thanks to graduate researcher Annalea Forrest.

1. Wendy Sawyer and Peter Wagner, "Mass Incarceration: The Whole Pie 2018," Prison Policy Initiative, March 14, 2018, www.prisonpolicy.org/reports/pie2018 .html.

2. Halfway houses are residential reentry centers that help transition people back into their communities after being released from prison. Since the late 1970s, nearly 60 percent of the halfway houses in the US were reportedly privately owned. By the mid-1980s, 65 percent of the clients in halfway house programs were considered "successful" and 35 percent were "unsuccessful." This is slightly higher than the average success rate of 61 percent found in another survey. Patrick G. Donnelly and Brian E. Forschner, "Client Success or Failure in a Halfway House," *Sociology, Anthropology, and Social Work Faculty Publications* 39 (1984), https://ecommons.udayton.edu/soc_fac_pub/39.

3. SHU stands for Security Housing Unit, also referred to as solitary confinement, an isolation ward located separately from the main cell blocks. The SHU is "one of the most miserable and mentally damaging experiences that the Federal Bureau of Prisons offers. While some prisoners lose touch with reality, others are less so harmed, but do tend to become angry, aggressive, and/or severely depressed. The best way for family and friends to help alleviate such suffering is to visit as much as possible and to order their loved ones books, magazines, and newspapers—anything to occupy their time and mind while in the hole. Letters are also essential. These lifelines help to ground the SHU-confined prisoner in reality and provide a light in the darkness." Christopher Zoukis, "Prison Life in America: Special Housing Units (SHUs)," Zoukis Consulting Group, April 7, 2016, www .prisonerresource.com/prison-life/special-housing-units-shus.

4. Brooklyn Metropolitan Detention Center has received reports of unsafe and inhumane prison conditions. Recent cases include a thirty-five-year-old man incarcerated there who died after being pepper-sprayed by a correctional officer, a power outage in December 2019 that led to more than 1,600 incarcerated men in below-zero temperatures for a week, and its 2020 mishandling of a coronavirus outbreak in the detention center. Jessica Parks, "Detainees Report Inhumane Conditions . . .," *Brooklyn Paper*, June 17, 2020, www.brooklynpaper.com/detainees-report-inhumane-conditions-at-brooklyns-metropolitan-detention-center.

5. The "kingpin statute" is the Continuing Criminal Enterprise Statute, or the CCE Statute. It denotes the crime of large-scale drug trafficking for long-term drug conspiracies. "Unlike the RICO Act, which covers a wide range of 'organized crime' enterprises, the CCE statute covers only major narcotic organizations. CCE is codified as Chapter 13 of Title 21 of the United States Code, 21 USC § 848. The statute makes it a federal crime to commit of conspire to commit a continuing series of felony violations of the Comprehensive Drug Abuse Prevention and Control Act of 1970 when such acts are taken in concert with five or more other persons. For conviction under this statute, the offender must have been an organizer, manager, or supervisor of the continuing operation and have obtained substantial income or resources from the drug violations." K. Carlson, *Prosecuting Criminal Enterprises*, National Criminal Justice Reference Series, US Bureau of Justice Statistics Special Report 12, 1993.

6. The BOP is the Federal Bureau of Prisons, which incarcerates 153,248 federal prisoners across thirty-seven states as of December 17, 2020. These inmates are held in 127 stand-alone federal prisons, 68 satellite prison camps, and 12 private prisons. In fiscal year 2019, 76,656 criminal defendants were sentenced in federal courts. This constitutes a 10.2 percent increase in federal criminal sentencing over fiscal year 2018. This is the single largest percentage increase in federal criminal sentencing in the past fifteen years. The majority of those incarcerated in federal prisons are housed in low-security federal prisons (36.5 percent) and medium-security federal prisons (31.6 percent). Minimum-security

prisons, or federal prison camps, house 15.9 percent of those incarcerated in federal correctional facilities, while high-security federal prisons hosue 12.5 percent. Christopher Zoukis, "Federal Bureau of Prisons," Zoukis Consulting Group, accessed August 26, 2021, www.prisonerresource.com/federal-prisons.

7. RDAP, the Residential Drug Abuse Program, is an intensive treatment program provided by the Federal Bureau of Prisons. "Substance Abuse Treatment," Federal Bureau of Prisons, accessed August 26, 2021, www.bop.gov/inmates /custody_and_care/substance_abuse_treatment.jsp.

8. CDL refers to the Commercial Driver's License Program at the BOP. The Commercial Motor Vehicle Safety Act of 1986 established minimum requirements for a state to issue a CDL. In certain states, it may be required to drive a recreational vehicle or agricultural vehicle. However, at the federal level, such vehicles are exempt from the CDL requirement. "Commercial Driver's License Program," Federal Motor Carrier Safety Administration, updated September 15, 2021, archived from the original on March 13, 2009, accessed August 26, 2021, www.fmcsa.dot.gov/registration/commercial-drivers-license.

9. "Timbs" is a nickname for Timberland boots, a fashion mainstay in New York City, urban cities throughout the northeastern US, and anywhere influenced by 1980s–'90s hip hop fashion. Dictionary.com, accessed August 26, 2021, https:// www.dictionary.com/e/slang/timbs.

Acknowledgments

Blame my head and not my heart for anyone I fail to recognize. The list of those who have shaped me and this work is endless, but it must begin with the Most High: Veronica Mohamed Bain. Rolly Bain. The one and only K. King David. CMS. Rene. Placid Anissa and the Bone clan. The GOATs: Indigo, Immanuel, and Idries. Lissa and Lindy. Lani Guinier. Soffiyah Elijah. Gina, Pamela, and Harry Belafonte. Rosie Rios. The Reiners. And my dear brother from another mother, Nanon Williams. All my sisters and brothers behind the bars fighting for freedom—we fight with you. You keep teaching me the power and the meaning of resilience. This is for us all.

The dedicated researchers whose genius supported the development of this work: Andre Chapman, Annalea Forrest, Matthew Griffith, Joanna Itzel Navarro, Christina Novakov-Ritchey, Jeremy Peretz, Savannah Ramirez, Brisa Smith-Flores, Armando Tellez, Lena Wang, Nathaniel Whitfield, Anthony Williams, Diana Williams. My infinite gratitude for the invaluable support and insightful guidance of Kathy Boudin, Eddie Bruce-Jones, Sandro Duranti, Lolita Files, Katryce Lassle, Miguel Martinez-Saenz, Pedro Noguera, Raina Polivka, Ananya Roy, Todd Rubenstein, Madison Wetzell and the University of California Press team, Teresa Barnet and the Center for Oral History Research, Kimiyo Bone and Mastermind Graphics, and the rising star among stars, Blaze Bautista.

The organizations that have nurtured, supported, and facilitated my work include the Actors' Gang/Prison Theater Project, A New Way of Life Reentry Project, the Anti-Recidivism Coalition, Beyond the Bars, Black Lives Matter LA, the Blackout Arts Collective, the Center for Constitutional Rights, the Center for NuLeadership on Human Justice and Healing, Community Capacity Development, Critical Resistance, Decolonizing Sociology (Cambridge), Dignity and Power Now, Drug Policy Alliance, the Ella Baker Center for Human Rights, For Freedoms, the Gathering for Justice, the Guild of Future Architects, Harm Reduction Coalition, Hudson Link, InsideOut Writers, the Malcolm X Grassroots Movement, the Movement for Black Lives, the National Black Theatre, the Prison Education Project (Cal Poly Pomona), Prison Moratorium Project, Project Rebound, Ruskin School of the Arts (Oxford), Sankofa.org, Underground Scholars Initiative, the Wide Awakes, and Youth Justice Coalition.

Recognition and credit is due to those who blessed each of this mixtape's ten tracks. Specifically . . .

Track #1: The movement leaders and elders whose conversation with me was the spark that inspired this work, the legendary Dolores Huerta and my arts/activism mentor Harry Belafonte. It was our July 17, 2013, convening by the Ford Foundation (www.fordfoundation.org) that produced the original source of our dialogue; the foundation made it accessible for the revised and annotated excerpt included in the *National Black Law Journal* article revised here as per Ford's Creative Commons policy, Attribution 4.0 International.

Track #2: "Angola 3" activist Albert Woodfox and LA's iconic, independent, and Black-owned Eso Won Books, which hosted our dialogue in support of the release of his memoir, *Solitary.*

Track #3: Susan Burton, A New Way of Life Reentry Project, and the *Harvard BlackLetter Law Journal*, which published an earlier version of this track in spring 2019.

Track #4: My critical race studies mentor and inspiration Lani Guinier, as well as the organizers of the We Rise Conference, from Gina Belafonte, Cristina Pacheco, and Yosi Sergant of TaskForce to the Los Angeles County Department of Mental Health, which made that dialogue possible, and the movement leaders who joined me and dropped transformative jewels—Melina Abdullah, Joel Martinez, Topeka Sam, and Shaka Senghor.

Track #5: Jennifer Claypool, Wendy Staggs, and all of the women in the CIW Think Tank and Creative Writing Workshop where we first collaborated together, and the UCLA *Women's Law Journal*, which released the original version of this track.

Tracks #6–7: Chuck D, Gaye Theresa Johnson, Aloe Blacc, Maya Jupiter, Rosie Rios, Alicia Virani, and the radical visionary organizers of the Connecting Art and Law for Liberation (CALL) Festival, whose work made these collaborations we all imagined a reality.

Track #8: Executive producer James Champion, TRT (Turkish Radio and Television) World, and the production team behind *Route 66*, as well as the divinely inspired Pastor Michael Fisher of Greater Zion Church Family (formerly

Little Zion Missionary Baptist Church) in Compton, Daniel Yi of MedMen, legalization advocate and entrepreneur Virgil Grant of the California Minority Alliance, and drug war survivor Will Robinson.

Track #9: Michael Capra at Sing Sing who allowed the interview here as well as our two TED talks and my Hip Hop and Spoken Word intensive course—which led to the questions I asked on behalf of the brothers who participated and taught me so much, from Chris, Dennis, Ivan, Jermaine, J.J., Jonadrian, Kenyatta, Laron, Lawrence, Markey, Sedwick, Sundiata, and Tyrone to the entire Hudson Link family, including photo guru Babita and the dynamic duo Lori and Sean.

Track #10: My generous brother, Cheyenne Michael Simpson, who shared so much of his story just after completing a five-year bid and starting his transition back home, and my youngest brother, David, who filmed that interview to make this track possible.

Special thanks and praise to Taij Kumarie Moteelall, Rafiq Kalam Id-Din, and all my Blackout Arts Collective family; Tania Cuevas-Martinez; Tongo Eisen-Martin and the Lyrical Minded crew; Cava Menzies; Priya Parmar; Francisca Sanchez; Mei Ann Teo; Mona Webb; and a major shout-out for the guidance of H. Samy Alim; Tabia Shawel and the Hip Hop Studies Work Group; Robin D. G. Kelley and Cheryl Harris; the Ralph Bunche Center for African American Studies and the departments of African American Studies and World Arts and Cultures/Dance for supporting the development and impact of the Prison Education Program at UCLA; and my collaborator-in-chief Claudia Linnette Peña, for her divine patience in combing through countless drafts of these pages and offering uncompromising critical and constructive feedback. And to Assata Shakur, for teaching me it is our duty to fight for freedom—and it is our duty to win.

We are and so I am.

Index